Operating Systems: Design and Implementation

Operating Systems: Design and Implementation

Mary Holmes

MURPHY & MOORE
www.murphy-moorepublishing.com

Operating Systems: Design and Implementation
Mary Holmes
ISBN: 978-1-63987-409-5 (Hardback)

MURPHY & MOORE

Published by Murphy & Moore Publishing,
1 Rockefeller Plaza,
New York City, NY 10020, USA

Cataloging-in-Publication Data

Operating systems : design and implementation / Mary Holmes.
    p. cm.
Includes bibliographical references and index.
ISBN 978-1-63987-409-5
1. Operating systems (Computers). 2. Operating systems (Computers)--Design and construction.
3. System design. I. Holmes, Mary.
QA76.77 .O64 2022
005.43--dc23

For more information regarding Murphy & Moore Publishing and its products, please visit the publisher's website www.murphy-moorepublishing.com

Table of Contents

Preface

An operating system is a system software that allows a user to interact with the system hardware. It acts as a bridge between the two and is responsible for hardware functions such as input, output, memory allocation and system security. Operating systems are categorized into batch systems, real-time systems, multi-user systems, time-sharing systems and single-user systems. This classification is based upon the accessibility of the system by the user and sequence of job execution. Every successful operating system design fulfils the user goal of being reliable, safe, and fast. It also fulfils the system goal of being easy to implement and maintain. Designing an operating system is a rigorous task which requires intricate knowledge of various fields such as networking, hardware, machine language, etc. Most of the operating systems today are designed using high level languages such as C++ and Java. They offer certain benefits since the code can be written faster and is easier to understand, making it easier to debug. Also, the code can be moved easily from one hardware to another. This book provides comprehensive insights into the field of operating systems. It is compiled in such a manner, that it will provide in-depth knowledge about the theories related to operating system design. This textbook will provide comprehensive knowledge to the readers.

A detailed account of the significant topics covered in this book is provided below:

Chapter 1- The collection of software which performs the basic tasks in a computer is known as the operating system. Memory management, file management, handling output and input, process management, and controlling peripheral devices are a few of the tasks performed by operating system. This is an introductory chapter which will briefly introduce all these significant aspects of operating systems.

Chapter 2- There are different categories of operating systems such as batch operating system, distributed operating system, embedded operating system, real time operating system, single user operating system and multi-user operating system. All these categories of operating systems are explained in detail in this chapter.

Chapter 3- All the related activities in a system that work together to make it function are known as processes. Some of the topics studied under system processes are process concepts, inter process communication, system calls, CPU scheduling, process synchronization, etc. The topics elaborated in this chapter will help in gaining a better perspective about the system processes.

Chapter 4- The application which is used to store, arrange and access the files which are stored on a disk or any other storage location is termed as a file management system. The process of controlling and coordinating computer memory, and assigning blocks of memory to various running programs in order to optimize the overall performance of the system is called memory management. This chapter discusses in detail the different aspects of file system management and memory management.

Chapter 5- There are various components which make up operating systems such as kernel, process, memory management, virtual memory, preemption, device driver, etc. The computer program that is the core of operating systems and controls everything in the system is known as the kernel. The chapter closely examines these key aspects of operating systems to provide an extensive understanding of the subject.

I would like to make a special mention of my publisher who considered me worthy of this opportunity and also supported me throughout the process. I would also like to thank the editing team at the back-end who extended their help whenever required.

Mary Holmes

Operating Systems: An Introduction

The collection of software which performs the basic tasks in a computer is known as the operating system. Memory management, file management, handling output and input, process management, and controlling peripheral devices are a few of the tasks performed by operating system. This is an introductory chapter which will briefly introduce all these significant aspects of operating systems.

An operating system is a program that acts as an intermediary between a user of a computer and the computer hardware. It is a software. It acts as an interface between the user who is using the computer and the hardware that is present in the computer. So for users to easily use the computer, the operating system plays a role. Users may not know what's happening inside a computer and how the hardware is actually working. So we have the operating system that sits between the user and hardware and does the interfacing work.

An operating system manages a computer's resources for users and applications. There are a number of resources in the computer like the CPU, I/O devices, memory etc. These resources have to be utilized properly by the different applications of different/same users/user that are running in the computer. There can be many applications running in the computer and each application may have to use different resources of the computer. Hence the resources have to be managed properly by allocating them properly to different applications. An operating system acts like a control program that controls the execution of user programs and operations of I/O devices. An operating system is one program that is running at all times in the computer.

Goals of an Operating System

- Execute user programs and make solving user problems easier.
- Convenience.
- Efficiency.

One of the goals of an operating system is to execute the users' programs in an easier way. Convenience is another criterion that has been looked at for the design of the operating system. For example, the Windows operating system was designed in a way that it is easier for the users to use. But in the earlier UNIX systems, efficiency was the main concern while designing the operating system. But these days, UNIX systems have a user interface which is easier and convenient for people to use. So, depending on the kind of application for which the system is used for, convenience or efficiency can be taken as the criterion during the design of the operating system.

Evolution of Operating Systems

Different operating systems have evolved over time. Right from when operating systems came into existence, different functionalities have been gradually added to operating systems.

Mainframe Systems

Initially, computers were mainframe systems. The computers were very large, sometimes occupying one full floor in a building. The computers were very expensive and could be used only by a single person. Users had to take their programs in cards and handover to the person who is incharge of the computer. The users could then collect the results the next day. So, users had to wait one after the other to submit the input and wait till the next day to collect the results.

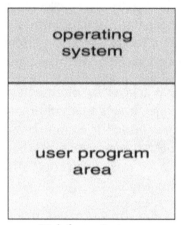

Mainframe Systems

Hence the operating system in this case had to just transfer control from one job to another in a sequential manner. This sequential execution causes unnecessary time consumption. The operating system can reduce set up time by matching similar jobs together. It is seen that the operating system in this type of systems has very limited functionalities. As seen in Figure there is a resident monitor/operating system that resides in the system. Initially the control will be with the monitor. Then the control is transferred to a job. After completion of the job, control is transferred to the monitor. So, there is a possibility for the CPU to remain idle for a lot of time.

When disk technology was introduced, jobs could be put into a disk and could be read from the disk rather than being read from the input card reader. Hence, it was possible to place multiple jobs into the disk at the same. Thus, the multi-programmed batch systems came into existence.

Multi-programmed Batch Systems

In a multi-programmed batch system, multiple programs can be brought into the main memory from the disk simultaneously at a particular time as shown in Figure. One of the jobs in the main memory will be given the CPU. The operating system now has additional functionalities of selecting jobs from the disk to be brought into the main memory and selecting one of the jobs in the main memory to be given to the CPU. If there are 10 jobs in the disk and there is space in the main memory for only 3, 3 out of the 10 jobs must be chosen to be brought into the main memory. This is done by the job scheduler. As only one job can be given to the CPU at a particular time, choosing one of the different jobs present in the main memory to be given to the CPU is done by the CPU scheduler. When the 3 jobs are placed in the main memory, decision has to be made as to where to place the jobs in the main memory. Hence memory management was added as a functionality of the operating system. I/O devices also have to be allocated to processes. Hence I/O management was included as functionality to the operating system.

In these systems, multiple programs can be kept in the memory. But a one-to-one interaction between the user and computer was missing. Hence, a new system was developed called the time-sharing systems. These time-sharing systems are basically an extension of multiprogramming systems and are called multitasking systems.

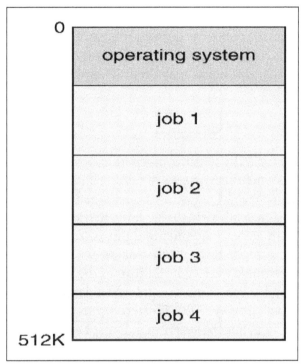

Multi-programmed batch systems.

Time Sharing/Multitasking Systems

The operating systems like Windows, MacOS and Linux that we see today are all time sharing systems. A time sharing system is a logical extension of multiprogramming systems. In these systems, the CPU is multiplexed among several jobs that are kept in memory and on disk and hence job scheduling and CPU scheduling are included in the functions of the operating system. Here, a direct communication between the user and the system is provided. It is possible for many users to use the system at a particular time. Since the speed of users is much less than the speed of the CPU, CPU time can be shared among the different users' programs. Since many jobs can be brought into the main memory, memory management is needed.

It may be necessary for some process to wait for I/O to happen (say read an input from the user). Then this process may be moved/swapped from the main memory to the disk. Another partially executed process which was moved to the disk earlier can be brought into the main memory. Thus partially executed jobs can be moved in and out of memory to the disk. Hence the concept of virtual memory is introduced. Virtual memory also allows programs to be larger than the physical memory.

Since many users are using the computer, each user will have his/her own files and these files have to be placed in the secondary storage device / disks. When there are many files, the files have to be arranged in a logical manner. Hence, file systems were included as a part of operating systems. Since files are present in disks, disk management was also needed.

It is possible to have many processes of a particular user or different users to run concurrently. At a particular time, only one process can use the CPU. When one process is waiting for I/O, another process may use the CPU and vice versa. This may not be felt by the users using the computer. Thus concurrent execution of processes is possible.

When many processes execute concurrently, they may have to communicate among themselves or may have to share common variables or data structures. Hence job synchronization and communication are needed. Similarly, when processes execute concurrently and share resources of the computer, it is possible that deadlocks may occur. Hence the operating system must have the capability to handle deadlocks.

Desktop Systems

Initially, the CPUs in PCs lacked the features needed to protect an operating system from user programs. PC operating systems therefore were neither multiuser nor multitasking. The goals of these operating systems have changed with time; instead of maximizing CPU and peripheral utilization, the systems opt for maximizing user convenience and responsiveness. Initially, file protection was not needed in a personal machine. But since computers are connected to other networks these days, other computers and other users can access the files on a PC and hence file protection again has become a necessary feature of the operating system. The lack of such protection has made it easy for malicious programs to destroy data on systems such as MS-DOS and the Macintosh operating system. These programs may be self-replicating, and may spread rapidly via worm or virus mechanisms and disrupt entire companies or even worldwide networks.

Multiprocessor Systems/Parallel Systems

But multiprocessor systems have more than one processor in close communication, sharing the computer bus, the clock, and sometimes memory and peripheral devices. These systems are also called as tightly coupled systems.

The advantages of multiprocessor systems are increased throughput, economy of scale and increased reliability. When there are more number of processors, more work is done in less time. Multiprocessor systems can save more money than multiple single-processor systems, because they can share peripherals, storage and power supplies. If several programs operate on the same set of data, it is cheaper to store those data on one disk and to have all the processors share them, than to have many computers with local disks and many copies of the data. If functions can be distributed properly among several processors, then the failure of one processor will not halt the system, only slow it down. Hence the system becomes more reliable.

There are two types of multiprocessing systems: symmetric and asymmetric multiprocessing. In symmetric multiprocessing (SMP), each processor runs an identical copy of the operating system, and these copies communicate with one another as needed. In asymmetric multiprocessing, each processor is assigned a specific task. Each processor can have different capabilities as well. A master processor controls the system; the other processors either look to the master for instructions or have predefined tasks. This scheme defines a master-slave relationship. The master processor schedules and allocates work to the slave processors.

Distributed Systems

Distributed systems depend on networking for their functionality. Distributed systems communicate among themselves using high–speed communication lines. Hence they are able to share computational tasks and provide a lot of features for the users. These systems do not share memory or a clock. Instead, each processor has its own local memory. Hence these systems are usually referred to as loosely coupled systems (or distributed systems).

Client-server Systems

Earlier, terminals which were connected to a centralized system provided the user interface for the user. Now, personal computers (PCs) have replaced the terminals. In client-server systems, multiple clients connect to a server and the server provides the necessary service for the clients. Client-server systems can be either compute-server systems or file-server systems. In compute-server systems, the server provides computational services to the user. In file-server systems, a file-system interface is provided where clients can create, update, read, and delete files.

Peer-to-peer Systems

In this type of systems, all computers are peers. Each computer can communicate with the other computers using communication lines or a network. Different processes on different computers can exchange messages. A network operating system which is an operating system that provides features such as file sharing across the network and communication, can help in this kind of communication. A computer running a network operating system acts autonomously from all other computers on the network, although it is aware of the network and is able to communicate with other networked computers. The different operating systems present in different computers communicate closely enough to provide the illusion that only a single operating system controls the network.

Real-time operating systems

A real-time system is used when rigid time requirements have been placed on the operation of a processor or the flow of data; thus, it is often used as a control device in a dedicated application. A real-time system has well-defined, fixed time constraints. Processing must be done within the defined constraints, or the system will fail. For instance, it would not do for a robot arm to be instructed to halt after it had smashed into the car it was building. A real-time system functions correctly only if it returns the correct result within its time constraints. There are two types of real-time systems: hard real-time systems and soft real-time systems.

In hard real-time systems, the time constraint is very rigid. All delays in the system must be bounded, from the retrieval of stored data to the time that it takes the operating system to finish any request made of it. Because of this, facilities that are available in hard real-time systems are less. Secondary storage of any sort is usually limited or missing, with data instead being stored in short-term memory or in read-only memory (ROM). Most advanced operating-system features are also absent, since they tend to separate the user from the hardware, and that separation results in uncertainty about the amount of time an operation will take. For instance, virtual memory is almost never found on real-time systems.

In soft real-time systems, the restrictions are less. A real-time process gets a higher priority over the other processes. Hence, other non-critical processes can also run in the computer. The real-time processes are not made to wait for a long amount of time. These systems need advanced operating-system features that cannot be supported by hard real-time systems.

Handheld Systems

Handheld systems include PDAs, cellular phones etc. The main issues with these systems are that they have a small size, small amount of memory, include slow processors, and feature small display screens. Examples of handheld operating systems are android, iOS, Symbian etc.

As the size of memory is small, the operating system and applications must manage memory efficiently. This includes returning all allocated memory back to the memory manager once the memory is no longer being used.

Processors for most handheld devices often run at a fraction of the speed of a processor in a PC. Faster processors require more power. To include a faster processor in a handheld device would require a larger battery that would have to be replaced (or recharged) more frequently. To minimize the size of most handheld devices, smaller, slower processors which consume less power are typically used. Therefore, the operating system and applications must be designed not to tax the processor.

As the size of the display is small, familiar tasks, such as reading e-mail or browsing web pages, must be condensed onto smaller displays. One approach for displaying the content in web pages is web clipping, where only a small subset of a web page is delivered and displayed on the handheld device. Since it is possible to access the internet using handheld devices, security is also an issue that has to be considered by the operating systems of handheld devices.

Embedded Systems

A number of machines are being used these days like the microwave oven, washing machine, set-top boxes, cars, medical devices etc. These machines need customized operating systems developed specifically for those particular machines. These operating systems must be developed very cautiously such that they do not lead to failure of the task-specific application that is running, because software errors can have devastating effects.

Future of Operating Systems

The future of operating systems also depends of the future of hardware. In the future, there will be very large scale data centers coordinating thousands of computers to support some essential service, very large scale multicore systems – many processors per machine, ubiquitous portable devices, heterogeneous systems and supercomputers to refrigerators to light switches. Operating systems may have to be designed looking into all these developments.

Goals of the Operating System

There are two types of goals of an Operating System i.e. Primary Goals and Secondary Goal:

- Primary Goal: The primary goal of an Operating System is to provide a user-friendly and convenient environment. We know that it is not compulsory to use the Operating System, but things become harder when the user has to perform all the process scheduling and converting the user code into machine code is also very difficult. So, we make the use of an Operating System to act as an intermediate between us and the hardware. All you need to do is give commands to the Operating System and the Operating System will do the rest for you. So, the Operating System should be convenient to use.

- Secondary Goal: The secondary goal of an Operating System is efficiency. The Operating System should perform all the management of resources in such a way that the resources are fully utilised and no resource should be held idle if some request to that resource is there at that instant of time.

Functions of Operating System

The Operating System provides certain services to the users which can be listed in the following manner:

- Program Execution: The Operating System is responsible for execution of all types of programs whether it be user programs or system programs. The Operating System utilises various resources available for the efficient running of all types of functionalities.

- Handling Input/Output Operations: The Operating System is responsible for handling all sort of inputs i.e. from keyboard, mouse, desktop, etc. The Operating System does all interfacing in the most appropriate manner regarding all kind of Inputs and Outputs. For example, there is difference in nature of all types of peripheral devices such as mouse or keyboard then Operating System is responsible for handling data between them.

- Manipulation of File System: The Operating System is responsible for making of decisions regarding the storage of all types of data or files, i.e. floppy disk/hard disk/pen drive, etc. The Operating System decides as how the data should be manipulated and stored.

- Error Detection and Handling: The Operating System is responsible for detection of any types of error or bugs that can occur while any task. The well secured OS sometimes also acts as countermeasure for preventing any sort of breach to the Computer System from any external source and probably handling them.

- Resource Allocation: The Operating System ensures the proper use of all the resources available by deciding which resource to be used by whom for how much time. All the decisions are taken by the Operating System.

- Accounting: The Operating System tracks an account of all the functionalities taking place in the computer system at a time. All the details such as the types of errors occurred are recorded by the Operating System.

- Information and Resource Protection: The Operating System is responsible for using all the information and resources available on the machine in the most protected way. The Operating System must foil an attempt from any external resource to hamper any sort of data or information.

Components of OS

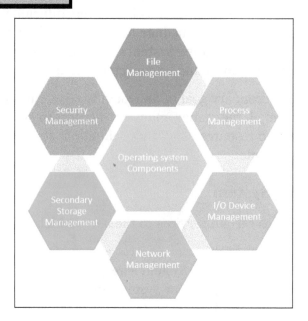

An operating system provides the environment within which programs are executed. To construct such an environment, the system is partitioned into small modules with a well-defined interface. The design of a new operating system is a major task. It is very important that the goals of the system be will defined before the design begins. The type of system desired is the foundation for choices between various algorithms and strategies that will be necessary.

A system as large and complex as an operating system can only be created by partitioning it into smaller pieces. Each of these pieces should be a well-defined portion of the system with carefully defined inputs, outputs, and function. Obviously, not all systems have the same structure.

Process Management

The CPU executes a large number of programs. While its main concern is the execution of user programs, the CPU is also needed for other system activities. These activities are called processes. A process is a program in execution. Typically, a batch job is a process. A timeshared user program is a process. A system task, such as spooling, is also a process. For now, a process may be considered as a job or a time-shared program, but the concept is actually more general.

In general, a process will need certain resources such as CPU time, memory, files, I/O devices, etc., to accomplish its task. These resources are given to the process when it is created. In addition to the various physical and logical resources that a process obtains when it is created, some initialization data (input) may be passed along. For example, a process whose function is to display on the screen of a terminal the status of a file, say F1, will get as an input the name of the file F1 and execute the appropriate program to obtain the desired information.

We emphasize that a program by itself is not a process; a program is a passive entity, while a process is an active entity. It is known that two processes may be associated with the same program, they are nevertheless considered two separate execution sequences.

A process is the unit of work in a system. Such a system consists of a collection of processes, some of which are operating system processes, those that execute system code, and the rest being user processes, those that execute user code. All of those processes can potentially execute concurrently. The operating system is responsible for the following activities in connection with processes managed:

- The creation and deletion of both user and system processes.

- The suspensions are resumption of processes.

- The provision of mechanisms for process synchronization.

- The provision of mechanisms for deadlock handling.

Memory Management

Memory is central to the operation of a modern computer system. Memory is a large array of words or bytes, each with its own address. Interaction is achieved through a sequence of reads or writes of specific memory address. The CPU fetches from and stores in memory.

In order for a program to be executed it must be mapped to absolute addresses and loaded in to memory. As the program executes, it accesses program instructions and data from memory by generating these absolute is declared available, and the next program may be loaded and executed.

In order to improve both the utilization of CPU and the speed of the computer's response to its users, several processes must be kept in memory. There are many different algorithms depends on the particular situation. Selection of a memory management scheme for a specific system depends upon many factor, but especially upon the hardware design of the system. Each algorithm requires its own hardware support. The operating system is responsible for the following activities in connection with memory management:

- Keep track of which parts of memory are currently being used and by whom.

- Decide which processes are to be loaded into memory when memory space becomes available.

- Allocate and de-allocate memory space as needed.

Secondary Storage Management

The main purpose of a computer system is to execute programs. These programs, together with the data they access, must be in main memory during execution. Since the main memory is too small to permanently accommodate all data and program, the computer system must provide secondary storage to backup main memory. Most modem computer systems use disks as the primary on-line storage of information, of both programs and data. Most programs, like compilers, assemblers, sort routines, editors, formatters, and so on, are stored on the disk until loaded into memory, and then use the disk as both the source and destination of their processing. Hence the proper management of disk storage is of central importance to a computer system.

There are few alternatives. Magnetic tape systems are generally too slow. In addition, they are limited to sequential access. Thus tapes are more suited for storing infrequently used files, where speed is not a primary concern. The operating system is responsible for the following activities in connection with disk management:

- Free space management.
- Storage allocation.
- Disk scheduling.

I/O System

One of the purposes of an operating system is to hide the peculiarities of specific hardware devices from the user. For example, in Unix the peculiarities of I/O devices are hidden from the bulk of the operating system itself by the I/O system. The I/O system consists of:

- A buffer caching system.
- A general device driver code.
- Drivers for specific hardware devices.

Only the device driver knows the peculiarities of a specific device.

File Management

File management is one of the most visible services of an operating system. Computers can store information in several different physical forms; magnetic tape, disk, and drum are the most common forms. Each of these devices has it own characteristics and physical organization.

For convenient use of the computer system, the operating system provides a uniform logical view of information storage. The operating system abstracts from the physical properties of its storage devices to define a logical storage unit, the file. Files are mapped, by the operating system, onto physical devices.

A file is a collection of related information defined by its creator. Commonly, files represent programs (both source and object forms) and data. Data files may be numeric, alphabetic or alphanumeric. Files may be free-form, such as text files, or may be rigidly formatted. In general a file is a sequence of bits, bytes, lines or records whose meaning is defined by its creator and user. It is a very general concept.

The operating system implements the abstract concept of the file by managing mass storage device, such as types and disks. Also files are normally organized into directories to ease their use. Finally, when multiple users have access to files, it may be desirable to control by whom and in what ways files may be accessed. The operating system is responsible for the following activities in connection with file management:

- The creation and deletion of files.
- The creation and deletion of directory.
- The support of primitives for manipulating files and directories.

- The mapping of files onto disk storage.

- Backup of files on stable (non-volatile) storage.

Protection System

The various processes in an operating system must be protected from each other's activities. For that purpose, various mechanisms which can be used to ensure that the files, memory segment, cpu and other resources can be operated on only by those processes that have gained proper authorization from the operating system.

For example, memory addressing hardware ensures that a process can only execute within its own address space. The timer ensures that no process can gain control of the CPU without relinquishing it. Finally, no process is allowed to do its own I/O, to protect the integrity of the various peripheral devices.

Protection refers to a mechanism for controlling the access of programs, processes, or users to the resources defined by a computer controls to be imposed, together with some means of enforcement.

Protection can improve reliability by detecting latent errors at the interfaces between component subsystems. Early detection of interface errors can often prevent contamination of a healthy subsystem by a subsystem that is malfunctioning. An unprotected resource cannot defend against use (or misuse) by an unauthorized or incompetent user.

Networking

A distributed system is a collection of processors that do not share memory or a clock. Instead, each processor has its own local memory, and the processors communicate with each other through various communication lines, such as high speed buses or telephone lines. Distributed systems vary in size and function. They may involve microprocessors, workstations, minicomputers, and large general purpose computer systems.

The processors in the system are connected through a communication network, which can be configured in the number of different ways. The network may be fully or partially connected. The communication network design must consider routing and connection strategies, and the problems of connection and security. A distributed system provides the user with access to the various resources the system maintains. Access to a shared resource allows computation speed-up, data availability, and reliability.

Command Interpreter System

One of the most important components of an operating system is its command interpreter. The command interpreter is the primary interface between the user and the rest of the system. Many commands are given to the operating system by control statements. When a new job is started in a batch system or when a user logs-in to a time-shared system, a program which reads and interprets control statements is automatically executed. This program is variously called:

- The control card interpreter,

- The command line interpreter,

- The shell (in Unix), and so on. Its function is quite simple: get the next command statement, and execute it.

The command statement themselves deal with process management, I/O handling, secondary storage management, main memory management, file system access, protection and networking.

Classification of Operating System

There are different categories of operating systems such as batch operating system, distributed operating system, embedded operating system, real time operating system, single user operating system and multi-user operating system. All these categories of operating systems are explained in detail in this chapter.

Batch Operating System

Batch Operating system is one of the important types of operating system. The users who is using a batch operating system do not interact with the computer directly. Each user prepares its job on an off-line device like punch cards and submits it to the computer operator. To speed up the processing, jobs with similar needs are batched together and run as a group. The programmers exit their programs with the operator and the operator then sorts the programs with similar requirements into batches.

There are two types of batched system:

- Simple batched system
- Multiprogrammed batched system

Simple Batched System

In simple batch operating system user did not directly interact with computer system for job execution rather, the user required to prepare a job which entailed of the program the control information and data about the nature of job the control cards. Then this job was submitted to the computer operator which were usually in the form of punch card. Output appeared after some time it may took minutes, hours or days. The output of the program was consisted of results as well as registers and dumps of memory in case of program errors.

Its main task was to transfer the control from one job to the next in automatic manners. To enhance the processing speed jobs with similar needs were bathed together and were run as a group through the processor. The programmers used the operators in programs to make the batches with similar requirements. Computer run the batches one by one when it became available. This system usually reads a stream of separate jobs and each has its own control cads with predefined job's task.

The delay in turnaround time may result from the amount of computing needed or from delays before the operating system starts to process a job. In this case of execution environment, the CPU is often idle. spooling process were used to pint the output from the line printer in which card reader was used to take the input and disk is use copy the command into system buffer and written to the disk CPU read command from dick execute it and send back to disk then ultimately output is printed at line printer.

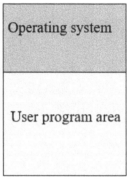

Memory layout for simple batch system.

Multiprogrammed Batched System

Spooling deals with several jobs that have already been read waiting on disk ready to run. Disk which contains a pool of jobs allows operating system to select job to run next for sack of CPU's proper utilization. When jobs come in direct manner on magnetic tape or cards jobs cannot run in a different order. Jobs execute on the bases of first come, first serve so they must run in sequential fashion. Jobs scheduling become possible when several jobs are on a direct access device such as disk. The main characteristic of job scheduling is the ability to multiprogram. Spooling and offline operations for overlapped I/O have their limitations. In general, a single user cannot keep the I/O devices and CPU buys at all time.

In this case jobs are organized in such a way that CPU execute one job at a time to increase the CPU utilization. Several jobs are kept by operating system in memory at a time. Operating system pick the one job and begin to execute it in the memory. Ultimately the job has to wait for some task such as a tape to be mounted on an I/O operation to complete. In case of multiprogramming system do not sit idle because operating system switches to another job. Whenever on job is on wait condition and current job finished then it gets the CPU back.

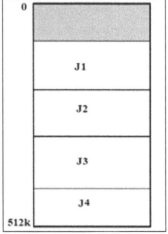

Memory layout for multiprogramming system.

Multiprogramming operating system is very sophisticated because it must make decisions for the user.

Need for Batch Systems

But there was another problem too. Suppose one job is in C language and other one is in Java. We know that both the jobs now require entirely different environments for their execution. So, the I/O magnetic tapes needed to be loaded and unloaded again and again. As the number of users increased, so did the number of jobs and it was really a time-consuming process. Most of the time was wasted in this I/O work only and CPU remained idle for too long.

Then a solution to this problem was devised that jobs requiring similar environmental conditions will be submitted altogether within a batch. Since similar jobs were put together in a batch, this system was termed as a batch system.

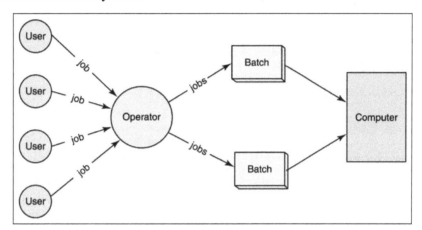

How Users uses Batch Operating System

Batch operating system users do not interact with the computer directly. Each job is prepared by each user on an off-line device like punch cards and submits it to the computer operator. To increase the processing speed, jobs with similar needs are batched together and run as a group. After completing the coding for the programs the programmers hand over their programs to the operator and the operator then analyisis the programs having similar requirements and then devide them into batches.

Why BOS are Used?

Batch operating systems load very less stress on cpu and involve lesser user interaction so that's why we can use batch system in now a days also. Another advantage of batch operating systems is that the large repeated jobs can done without interacting with computer to tell the system that you have to do that job after finishing that job. Old batch operating systems were not interactive i.e. the user interaction was not involved when the program is running. Now in modern batch operating systems we have interactions also. For example we can schedule the job and when the specific time comes then computer acknowledge the processor that time is over. This helps us tin avoiding too many errors and makes debuging easier.

Role of a Batch Operating System

The main role of a batch operating system is to automatically executing the jobs in a batch. This is the primary task of a batch processing system i.e. performed by the 'Batch Monitor' resides in the low end of main memory. This technique was feasible due to the invention of hard-disk drives and card readers. Now the jobs can be saved on the disk to make the pool of jobs for its execution as a batch. Firstly the extracted jobs are read and executed by the batch monitor, and then these jobs are grouped, placing the similar jobs (jobs with the similar needs) in the same batch, So, in the batch operating system, the batched jobs were executed automatically one after the other saving its time by performing the tasks (like loading of compiler) only for once. It resulted in better system utilization due to reduced turn-around time.

Advantages of Batch Processing System

- A lot of manual work is reduced.

- Execution becomes fast and well managed.

- CPU's idle time is reduced.

- Repetitive use of Punched cards and magnetic tapes is reduced.

Disadvantages of Batch Processing System

- Sequential execution: This is one of the major disadvantages of Batch Systems. Jobs in a batch are always executed sequentially. For example, if there are 4 jobs in one batch, then they are always executed one by one and the output is obtained only once all 4 jobs are completed. Difficult to provide the desired priority.

- Starvation: Different jobs in a single batch might take different amounts of time in execution. This might lead to starvation of some jobs. Suppose there are 4 jobs in a batch and the first job takes too long to execute then the other three jobs in the same batch will have to wait for long until the first one is completed.

- No interaction between job and user: Once a batch is submitted to the computer the user is no longer able to interact with any of the jobs. Suppose there is a job which requires the user to give the input data during runtime. Now, He must wait until all the jobs in that batch are completed. So, the overall execution time is increased a lot.

Distributed Operating System

A distributed operating system (DOS), is a recent advancement in the technological world of computers, furthermore, they are being accepted/utilised all over the world, as one of the main advantageous characteristics of these systems are that they provide great pace.

A DOS is a system which contains multiple components located on different machines, which coordinate and communicate actions in order to appear as a single coherent working system to the user. A distributed operating system (DOS) are systems which model where distributed applications are running on multiple computers, linked by communications. Processors in a DOS communicate with each other through various communication lines like high-speed buses.

High-Speed Buses

A mechanism that transfers data between components inside a computer. A DOS involves a collection of autonomous computer systems, which are able to communicate with each other through LAN/WAN. This system will provide a virtual machine abstraction to its users and wide sharing of resources like computational capacity and input/output etc.

This system incorporates various autonomous interconnected computers that communicate with each other using a shared communication network, furthermore they are independent systems that possess their own memory unit and CPU.

Another term which is used along side-distributed operating systems is a loosely coupled system. The processors in these systems may differ in size and function. The fundamental implementations of primitive distributed operating systems data back to the 1950's. Some of these concepts were not focused directly on DOS, and at the time many not have had realised their important impact. These pioneering efforts had laid down the fundamentals and inspired more research. However it was only when the acceleration of multi-processor/multi-core processor system ignited, that it led to the resurgence of DOS.

One of the big advantages of working with DOS is that it is always possible that one user can access the files or software, which they require, and utilise them, however in reality these files are present on another system network (so think of it similar to remote working).

Distributed systems can be considered to be more reliable than a central system because if the system has only one instance of a critical peripheral/component, like the CPU, network interface, disk, and so if that one instance fails, the system will go down completely.

However when there are multiple instances in the system, like in a distributed operating system, then if a component fails, the system may be able to continue to function despite the failure. Distributed systems also allow software failures to be dealt with, rather than stopping the whole system.

Architecture of a Distributed Operating System

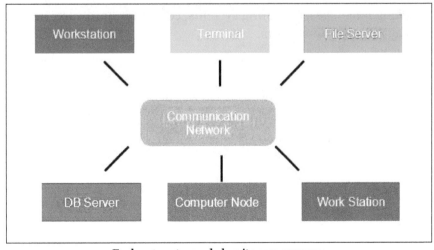

Each computer node has its own memory.

In a DOS the following occurs:

- All software and hardware compounds are located remotely. In order for them to communicate with each other, they pass messages.

- One of the most important aspects of a distributed system is resource sharing. Resources are managed by servers and clients use these resources.

A DOS runs on a number of independent sites which are connected through a communication network. However it is portrayed to the user that they run their own operating system.

Distributed Systems Design Considerations

Types of Distributed Systems: There are four main types of distributed systems:

- Client-server: This type of system requires the client to request a resource, and then the server provides that resource which was requested. When a client is in contact with one server, the server itself may serve multiple clients at the same time. Both the server and the client will communicate over a computer network, which is part of a distributed system.

- Three-tier: The information about the client is stored in the middle tier, instead of storing it in the client, this is done to simplify development. This architecture is most common in web applications.

- n-tier: n-tier systems are used when the server or application needs to forward requests to additional enterprise services on the network.

- Peer-to-peer: This type of system contains nodes that are equal participants in data sharing, furthermore, all the tasks are equally divided between all the nodes. These nodes will interact with each other as required as "share resources". To accomplish this, a network is needed.

What are the Characteristics of a Distributed Operating System?

Common characteristics, which DOS have are:

- Heterogeneity: In distributed systems, the components can have differences and variety in programming languages, operating systems, computer hardware, networks, and implementations by different developers.

- Resource sharing: (Every resource has its own management policies and methods, furthermore every resource is managed by a module, commonly known as a resource manager). Resource sharing is the ability to use hardware, software, or data anywhere in the system. The resource manager controls access, moreover, it also provides naming scheme and controls concurrency in the DOS. The hardware resources are shared for convenience and reductions in cost, in contrast, the data is shared for consistency and exchange of information.

- Openness: With DOS, the "openness" is related to the extensions and improvements of disturbed systems.

  ○ A well-defined and detailed interface of the components must be published.

- The new component, which is to be added, must be easily integrated with existing components.

- Concurrency: This characteristic of the system enables multiple activities in the system to be executed in the same time. In the distributed system, the simultaneous execution of tasks happens in different components running on multiple machines, furthermore, these tasks could execute interactions between each other.

The benefit of concurrency is increases the efficiency while reducing the latency in the system. In the DOS, the components access and update shared resources (device drivers, variables, databases), moreover, if concurrent updates are not coordinated it may result in inconsistent analysis.

- Scalability: In a DOS, the scalability of a system refers to how it handles the growth as number of users on the system platform increases. Scaling best occurs by adding more systems to the network. These components must be designed in a way that allows them to be scalable too.

- Fault tolerance: The system is designed in a way that it is still available to the user despite a failure in the hardware, software, or the network. Fault tolerance is achieved by recovery and redundancy.

- Security: In a DOS, the clients send requests to access data managed by servers and resources in the networks. In a DOS security is acquired for the following:

  - Concealing the contents of messages.

  - Authentication.

- No global clock: In a DOS, computers are connected through a network, and each computer has its own clock (so a system can have many clocks). Nodes communicate between each other through message passing furthermore, their coordination is dependent on time, as every client/computer has a different time span.

- Even if the clocks were in sync, the individual clocks on each component may run at a different rate, leading them to be out of sync after one local clock cycle. Though accurate time synchronisation is impossible in a DOS because it doesn't provide a global clock.

- Flexibility: Flexibility in a DOS is enhanced through modular characteristics, and by providing a more enhanced set of high level services. The quality and completeness of the kernel/microkernel simplifies implementation of such services.

- Synchronisation: Systems, which are cooperating concurrent process, have an inherent need for synchronisation. This ensures that changes happen in a correct and predictable manner. The three basic circumstances, which define the scope of synchronisation, are:

  - Synchronisation between one or more processes must happen at a single point in order for one or more other processes to continue.

  - One or more processes have to wait for an asynchronous (not existing or occurring at the same time) condition in order to continue.

  - A process must get exclusive access to a shared resource.

If synchronisation is not done properly it may lead to multiple points of failure modes including loss of consistency, isolation and durability, deadlock, lick, atomicity, and loss of serialisability.

- Transparency: DOS are perceived by programmers and users as a whole system, rather than a collection of cooperating components. Thus meaning the communication between components is hidden. Transparency directly affects the decision making in every aspect of design of a DOS, it can imply certain requirements and/or restrictions on other design considerations.

Main Types of Transparency linked with DOS

- Access Transparency: This allows local and remote information objects to be accessed using identical operations. (i.e. SQL Queries).

- Location Transparency: Allows information objects to be accessed without knowledge of their location. (i.e. File system operation in a network file system).

- Migration Transparency: The system solely controls resources and activities, which migrate from one element to another. The system controls them without user/application knowledge or intervention.

- Concurrency Transparency: Allows several processes to work simultaneously while using a shared information objects without interference between them. (i.e. Database management system).

- Replication Transparency: This allows multiple instances of information objects to be used to increase reliability and performance without the knowledge of the replicas by users or application programs. (i.e. Distributed DMBS).

- Failure Transparency: This type of transparency enables the faults to be hidden, therefore allowing users and applications alike to complete their tasks despite failure of other components. (i.e. Database managements system).

- Mobility Transparency: This allows the movement of information objects within the system without having an affect to the application program or users. (i.e. Web pages).

- Performance Transparency: System can be reconfigured to improve performance as loads vary.

- Scaling Transparency: Allows the system and application to expand in scale without having to change the application architecture or the system architecture.

- Revision Transparency: System is responsible for revisions, upgrades, and changes that are made to the system infrastructure without the user knowledge or action.

- Control Transparency: System is responsible to provide all the system constants, properties, information, and configuration settings etc. The system must be able to do this in connotation and denotation to all users and application in a consistent appearance.

- Data Transparency: System provides data to applications without the user knowledge/action as to where the system stores it.

- Parallelism Transparency: System exploits any ability to parallelise task execution without the need for user action or knowledge. This is probably the most difficult aspect of transparency.

Advantages of a Distributed Operating System

- Scalability: As computing occurs on each node independently, it is simple and inexpensive to add more nodes and functionality as required.

- Reliability: Most distributed systems are made from many nodes that work together which ultimately make them fault tolerant. The system doesn't experience any disruptions if a single machine fails.

- Performance: These systems are regarded to be very efficient as the work load can be broken up and sent to multiple machines, therefore reducing data processing.

- Data sharing: Nodes can easily share data with other nodes as they are connected with each other.

- No domino effect in case of a node failure: The failure of one node in a DOS does not have a domino effect and enables all other nodes fail. Other nodes can still communicate with each other despite the failure.

- Shareable: Resources, for instance like printers, can be shared with multiple nodes rather than just being constrained to just one node.

Disadvantages of a Distributed Operating System

- Scheduling: The system has to decide which jobs need to be executed, when they should be executed, and where they should be executed. A scheduler will have limitations this may lead to under-utilised hardware and unpredictable runtimes.

- Latency: The more widely distributed a system is the more latency can be experienced with communications. This therefore results in teams/developers to make tradeoffs between availability, consistency and latency.

- Observability: It can be a real challenge to gather, process, present, and monitor hardware usage metrics for large clusters.

- Security: It is difficult to place adequate security in DOS, as the nodes and the connections need to be secured.

- Data loss: Some data/messages may be lost in the network while moving from one node to another.

- Complicated database: In comparison to a single user system, the database connected to a DOS is relatively complicated and difficult to handle.

- Overloading: If multiple nodes in DOS send data all at once, then the system network may become overloaded.

- Expensive: These systems are not readily available, as they are regarded to be very expensive.

- Complex software: Underlying software is highly complex and is not understood very well compared to other systems.

Applications of Distributed Operating Systems

- Telecommunication Networks: DOS are useful in phone network and cellular networks. Networks such as the Internet, Wireless sensor networks, routing algorithms are also examples of a DOS.

- Network Applications: Many network applications utilise DOS, such as Web, P2P networks, multiplayer web based games and virtual communities. (P2P (peer to peer network) network are computer systems which connect to each other via the Internet. Files of these systems can be shared directly without requiring a central server, ultimately meaning that each computer on a P2P network becomes a file server and a client). An example of such systems includes: banking systems, and airline reservation booking systems.

- Real Time Process Control: Real time process control system that operates with a deadline, such examples include aircraft control systems.

- Parallel Computation: Systematic computer, which includes cluster computing and grid computing as well as varied volunteer computing projects are based on DOS.

Examples of Distributed Operating System

- LOCUS: In LOCUS operating system, can be accessed local and remote file in simultaneously without any location hindrance.

- MICROS: MICROS operating system maintains the balance load of data while allotting the jobs to all nodes of entire system.

- IRIX: IRIX operating system is used in the UNIX system V and LINUX.

- DYNIX: DYNIX operating system is developed for the Symmetry multiprocessor computers.

- AIX: AIX operating system is designed for IBM.

- Solaris: Solaris operating system designed for SUN multiprocessor workstations.

- Mach: Mach operating system allows the multithreading and multitasking features.

- OSF/1: OSF/1 operating system is compatible with UNIX, and it is designed by Open Foundation Software Company.

Other Important Examples of Distributed Operating System

- Windows server 2003
- Windows server 2008
- Windows server 2012
- Ubuntu
- Eden
- Galaxy
- MDX
- MICROS

- Linux (Apache Server)
- AEGIS
- AMOEBA
- Arachne
- Charlotte
- CHOICES
- Clouds
- CMDS
- CONDOR
- Cronus
- DEMOS/MP
- DISTOS
- DISTRIX

- MOS
- MOSIX
- Newark
- NSMOS
- Plan9
- REPOS
- RIG
- Roscoe
- Saguaro
- SODA
- SODS/OS
- Spring
- Uniflex

Embedded Operating System

An embedded operating system is an operating system for embedded computer systems. These operating systems are designed to be compact, efficient at resource usage, and reliable, forsaking many functions that standard desktop operating systems provide, and which may not be used by the specialised applications they run. The hardware running an embedded operating system is usually very limited in resources. Systems made for embedded hardware tend to be very specific, which means that due to the available resources (low if compared to non-embedded systems) these systems are created to cover specific tasks.

Embedded means something that is attached to another thing. An embedded system can be thought of as a computer hardware system having software embedded in it. An embedded system can be an independent system or it can be a part of a large system. An embedded system is a microcontroller or microprocessor based system which is designed to perform a specific task. For example, a fire alarm is an embedded system; it will sense only smoke.

An embedded system has three components:

- It has hardware.

- It has application software.

- It has Real Time Operating system (RTOS) that supervises the application software and provide mechanism to let the processor run a process as per scheduling by following a plan to control the latencies. RTOS defines the way the system works. It sets the rules during the execution of application program. A small scale embedded system may not have RTOS.

So we can define an embedded system as a Microcontroller based, software driven, reliable, real-time control system.

Characteristics of an Embedded System

- Single-functioned: An embedded system usually performs a specialized operation and does the same repeatedly. For example: A pager always functions as a pager.

- Tightly constrained: All computing systems have constraints on design metrics, but those on an embedded system can be especially tight. Design metrics is a measure of an implementation's features such as its cost, size, power, and performance. It must be of a size to fit on a single chip, must perform fast enough to process data in real time and consume minimum power to extend battery life.

- Reactive and Real time: Many embedded systems must continually react to changes in the system's environment and must compute certain results in real time without any delay. Consider an example of a car cruise controller; it continually monitors and reacts to speed and brake sensors. It must compute acceleration or de-accelerations repeatedly within a limited time; a delayed computation can result in failure to control of the car.

- Microprocessors based: It must be microprocessor or microcontroller based.

- Memory: It must have a memory, as its software usually embeds in ROM. It does not need any secondary memories in the computer.

- Connected: It must have connected peripherals to connect input and output devices.

- HW-SW systems: Software is used for more features and flexibility. Hardware is used for performance and security.

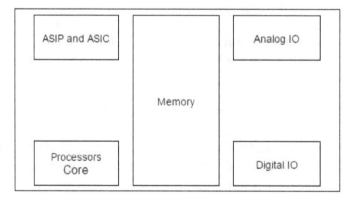

- Advantages:
  ◦ Easily Customizable.
  ◦ Low power consumption.
  ◦ Low cost.
  ◦ Enhanced performance.

- Disadvantages:
  ◦ High development effort.
  ◦ Larger time to market.

Basic Structure of an Embedded System

The following illustration shows the basic structure of an embedded system:

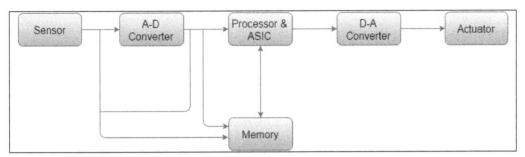

- Sensor: It measures the physical quantity and converts it to an electrical signal which can be read by an observer or by any electronic instrument like an A2D converter. A sensor stores the measured quantity to the memory.

- A-D Converter: An analog-to-digital converter converts the analog signal sent by the sensor into a digital signal.

- Processor and ASICs: Processors process the data to measure the output and store it to the memory.

- D-A Converter: A digital-to-analog converter converts the digital data fed by the processor to analog data.

- Actuator: An actuator compares the output given by the D-A Converter to the actual (expected) output stored in it and stores the approved output.

Types of Embedded Operating Systems

Single System Control Loop

Single system control loop is the simplest type of embedded operating system. It is so like operating system but it is designed to run the only single task. It still under debate that this system should be classified as a type of operating system or not.

Multi-tasking Operating System

As the name suggests that this operating system can perform multiple tasks. In multi-tasking operating system there are several tasks and processes that execute simultaneously. More than one function can be performed if the system has more than one core or processor.

The operating system is switched between tasks. Some tasks wait for events while other receive events and become ready to run. If one is using a multitasking operating system, then software development is simplified because different components of software can be made independent to each other.

Rate Monotonic Operating System

It is a type of operating system that ensures that task runs in a system can run for a specific interval of time and for a specific period of time. When it is not ensured, there comes a notification of failure to system software to take suitable action. This time limit cannot be ensured if the system is oversubscribed, at this point another event may occur during run time and the failure notification comes.

Preemptive Operating System

A preemptive operating system is a type of multitasking operating system that interprets the preemptive predominance for tasks. A higher priority is task is always defined and run before a lower priority task. Such multi-tasking operating systems are efficient in increasing system response to events and also simplify the development of software making the system more reliable. The designer of the system may be able to calculate the time required for the service interprets in a system and also the time is taken by the scheduler for switching tasks. Such systems may fail to meet the deadline of a system and the software is unaware of the missed deadline. CPU loading in a preemptive operating system can be measured naturally by defining a lower priority task that only increments counter and do nothing else.

Embedded Operating System vs. Desktop Operating System

The difference between embedded OS and desktop OS are shown in the below table:

Embedded Operating System	Desktop Operating System
The first embedded OS is Apollo guidance computer in 1965.	The first desktop OS is NLC (On-Line system) developed in 1960.
It is designed to run only a single task.	It is designed to run many tasks simultaneously.
Boot time is faster compared to desktop OS.	Boot time is slower in desktop OS.
Performance of the web browser takes less time to load the websites.	Performance of the web browser takes a long time to load the websites.
It takes less time to run the applications.	It takes a longer time to run the applications.
It uses only flash drives for storage.	It uses hard drives and flash drives for storage.
Embedded OS cost is less.	Cost is expensive.
It requires less storage compared to desktop OS.	It requires more storage.
It has fewer application features.	It has more application features.

Real-time Operating System

Real-time operating system (RTOS) is an operating system intended to serve real time application that process data as it comes in, mostly without buffer delay. The full form of RTOS is Real time operating system.

In a RTOS, Processing time requirement is calculated in tenths of seconds increments of time. It is time-bound system that can be defined as fixed time constraints. In this type of system, processing must be done inside the specified constraints. Otherwise, the system will fail.

Importance of RTOS

Here are important reasons for using RTOS:

- It offers priority-based scheduling, which allows you to separate analytical processing from non-critical processing.

- The Real time OS provides API functions that allow cleaner and smaller application code.

- Abstracting timing dependencies and the task-based design results in fewer interdependencies between modules.

- RTOS offers modular task-based development, which allows modular task-based testing.

- The task-based API encourages modular development as a task, will typically have a clearly defined role. It allows designers/teams to work independently on their parts of the project.

- An RTOS is event-driven with no time wastage on processing time for the event which is not occur.

Components of RTOS

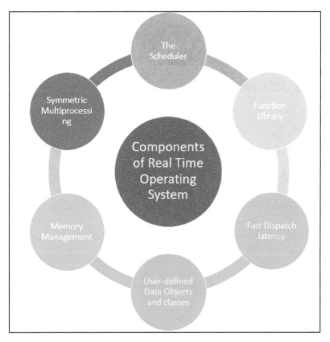

Important Component of RTOS

- The Scheduler: This component of RTOS tells that in which order, the tasks can be executed which is generally based on the priority.

- Symmetric Multiprocessing (SMP): It is a number of multiple different tasks that can be handled by the RTOS so that parallel processing can be done.

- Function Library: It is an important element of RTOS that acts as an interface that helps you to connect kernel and application code. This application allows you to send the requests to the Kernel using a function library so that the application can give the desired results.

- Memory Management: This element is needed in the system to allocate memory to every program, which is the most important element of the RTOS.

- Fast dispatch latency: It is an interval between the termination of the task that can be identified by the OS and the actual time taken by the thread, which is in the ready queue, that has started processing.

- User-defined data objects and classes: RTOS system makes use of programming languages like C or C++, which should be organized according to their operation.

Types of RTOS

Three types of RTOS systems are:

- Hard Real Time: In Hard RTOS, the deadline is handled very strictly which means that given task must start executing on specified scheduled time, and must be completed within the assigned time duration. Example: Medical critical care system, Aircraft systems, etc.

- Firm Real time: These type of RTOS also need to follow the deadlines. However, missing a deadline may not have big impact but could cause undesired affects, like a huge reduction in quality of a product. Example: Various types of Multimedia applications.

- Soft Real Time: Soft Real time RTOS, accepts some delays by the Operating system. In this type of RTOS, there is a deadline assigned for a specific job, but a delay for a small amount of time is acceptable. So, deadlines are handled softly by this type of RTOS. Example: Online Transaction system and Livestock price quotation System.

Terms Used in RTOS

Here, are essential terms used in RTOS:

- Task: A set of related tasks that is jointly able to provide some system functionality.

- Job: A job is a small piece of work that can be assigned to a processor, and that may or may not require resources.

- Release time of a job: It's a time of a job at which job becomes ready for execution.

- Execution time of a job: It is time taken by job to finish its execution.

- Deadline of a job: It's time by which a job should finish its execution.

- Processors: They are also known as active resources. They are important for the execution of a job.

- Maximum it is the allowable response time of a job is called its relative deadline.

- Response time of a job: It is a length of time from the release time of a job when the instant finishes.

- Absolute deadline: This is the relative deadline, which also includes its release time.

Features of RTOS

Here are important features of RTOS:

- Occupy very less memory.
- Consume fewer resources.
- Response times are highly predictable.
- Unpredictable environment.
- The Kernel saves the state of the interrupted task ad then determines which task it should run next.
- The Kernel restores the state of the task and passes control of the CPU for that task.

Factors for Selecting an RTOS

Here, are essential factors that you need to consider for selecting RTOS:

- Performance: Performance is the most important factor required to be considered while selecting for a RTOS.
- Middleware: if there is no middleware support in Real time operating system, then the issue of time-taken integration of processes occurs.
- Error-free: RTOS systems are error-free. Therefore, there is no chance of getting an error while performing the task.
- Embedded system usage: Programs of RTOS are of small size. So we widely use RTOS for embedded systems.
- Maximum Consumption: we can achieve maximum Consumption with the help of RTOS.
- Task shifting: Shifting time of the tasks is very less.
- Unique features: A good RTS should be capable, and it has some extra features like how it operates to execute a command, efficient protection of the memory of the system, etc.
- 24/7 performance: RTOS is ideal for those applications which require to run 24/7.

Difference between GPOS and RTOS

Here are important differences between GPOS and RTOS:

General-Purpose Operating System (GPOS)	Real-Time Operating System (RTOS)
It used for desktop PC and laptop.	It is only applied to the embedded application.
Process-based Scheduling.	Time-based scheduling used like round-robin scheduling.
Interrupt latency is not considered as important as in RTOS.	Interrupt lag is minimal, which is measured in a few micro-seconds.
No priority inversion mechanism is present in the system.	The priority inversion mechanism is current. So it cannot modify by the system.

Kernel's operation may or may not be pre-empted.	Kernel's operation can be pre-empted.
Priority inversion remain unnoticed.	No predictability guarantees.

Applications of Real-time Operating System

Real-time systems are used in:

- Airlines reservation system.

- Air traffic control system.

- Systems that provide immediate updating.

- Used in any system that provides up to date and minute information on stock prices.

- Defense application systems like RADAR.

- Networked Multimedia Systems.

- Command Control Systems.

- Internet Telephony.

- Anti-lock Brake Systems.

- Heart Pacemaker.

Disadvantages of RTOS

Here, are drawbacks/cons of using RTOS system:

- RTOS system can run minimal tasks together, and it concentrates only on those applications which contain an error so that it can avoid them.

- RTOS is the system that concentrates on a few tasks. Therefore, it is really hard for these systems to do multi-tasking.

- Specific drivers are required for the RTOS so that it can offer fast response time to interrupt signals, which helps to maintain its speed.

- Plenty of resources are used by RTOS, which makes this system expensive.

- The tasks which have a low priority need to wait for a long time as the RTOS maintains the accuracy of the program, which are under execution.

- Minimum switching of tasks is done in Real time operating systems.

- It uses complex algorithms which is difficult to understand.

- RTOS uses lot of resources, which sometimes not suitable for the system.

Microkernel RTOS

A microkernel RTOS is structured with a tiny kernel that provides minimal services. The microkernel works with a team of optional cooperating processes that run outside kernel space (in the user space), which provides higher-level OS functionality. The microkernel itself lacks file systems and many other services normally expected of an OS. A microkernel RTOS embodies a fundamental innovation in the approach to delivering OS functionality: modularity is the key, and the small size is a side effect.

In a microkernel, only the core RTOS kernel is granted access to the entire system, which improves reliability and security. The microkernel protects and allocates memory for other processes and provides task switching. All other components, including drivers and system-level components, are each contained within their own isolated process space.

Isolation prevents errors in a component from affecting other parts of the system – the only thing that a component can crash is itself. Such crashes can be easily detected, and the faulty component can be re-started hot – while the system is still running – so quickly that the restart has no effect on performance.

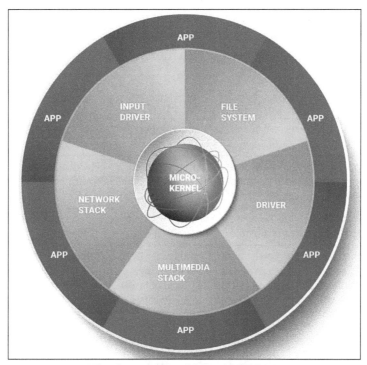

Microkernel OS architecture diagram.

In a microkernel RTOS, isolation prevents errors in a component from affecting the rest of the system – the only thing a component can crash is itself. During code development, the isolation of all processes has two significant benefits:

- Bugs are found earlier in development and are easily traced to a line of code in the faulty process. In comparison, latent bugs can remain from driver development for a monolithic OS, even after deployment, because stray pointers or other bugs do not cause an easily identified process crash.

- Drivers are treated like application processes, making them far easier to write and debug. You don't need to be a device driver specialist or a kernel debugger to write a driver for a microkernel.

Advantages and Disadvantages of a Microkernel RTOS

Microkernel RTOS	
Advantages	Disadvantages
Fault isolation and recovery for high availability.	Requires more context switching, which can increase overhead.
Restart a failed system service dynamically without impacts to the kernel (no system reboot).	
Easy expansion – develop device drivers and OS extensions without a kernel guru and without recompiling.	
Easier to debug.	
Small footprint.	
Less code running in kernel space reduces attack surface and increases security.	

Monolithic Kernel vs. Microkernel

Three big differences stand out when comparing a monolithic kernel versus microkernel OS architecture:

Category	Microkernel	Monolithic
Performance	Slightly slower performance due to higher number of context switches.	Better performance due to smaller number of context switches.
System Updates	New drivers and OS services updates can be performed with no changes to the kernel and thus do not require an OS reboot.	New drivers and OS services updates will require an OS rebuild and reboot.
Power Fail Recovery	Can restart any service individually, without interrupting the kernel.	Recovery of a failed service requires an OS reboot.
Qualification and Certification	Easier and less costly to qualify and certify the kernel. Most system updates do not require a full qualification and certification cycle but rather are limited to the updated service or driver.	Difficult and more costly to qualify and certify. System updates require a full qualification and certification cycle as the OS is generally rebuilt.
Maintenance	Easier and less time consuming to maintain and troubleshoot deployed systems. Users can update, troubleshoot and reboot a service without requiring an entire OS reboot.	Challenging and more time consuming to maintain and troubleshoot. Users require an OS reboot when performing most system updates, troubleshooting steps or a service reboot.

Single User Operating System

Single user operating system is also known as "Single Tasking Operating System", and single user operating system is designed especially for using on the home computers. Single user operating system allows the permission for accessing your personal computer at a time by single user, but some time it can support multiple profile. Single user operating system is used in the officially work and other environment as well. So, this operating system is not required for supporting the memory protection, file protection, and system security as well.

Types of Single User Operating System

Single user operating system can be classified into two parts like as:

- Single-User Single-Tasking operating system.
- Single-User Multi-Tasking operating system.

Single User Single-Tasking OS

In the Single-User Single-Tasking operating system, only one user in permitted for performing single task at a time. This operating system is designed especially for wireless phone as well as two way messaging devices. Some functions such as print a document, downloading images and video are performed one given frame time. Examples O/S are – MS-DOS, Palm OS, etc.

Advantages are:

- Use less area in memory.
- It is Cost Effective.

Disadvantages are:

- It is able to execute only one task at a time duration.
- It is less optimized.

Single-User Multi-Tasking OS

Single-User Multi-Tasking operating system is developed specially for one user, but this single user is able to perform to multiple tasks run at a same time frame. Some examples such as you can write any text, while surfing internet and downloading images with watching movies, etc. Example O/S are – Windows, Linux, Mac O/S.

Advantages:

- Time saving.
- High productivity in less time frame.
- Less memory is used for performing multiple tasks.

Disadvantages:

- Require more space.
- It has more complexity.

Features of Single User Operating System

- It has no security.
- It does not use MMU.

- It does not use scheduling process for I/O.

- It uses less scheduling for the users.

- It is only dedicated to single use.

- It is not intended for several tasks as same given time.

Advantages of Single User Operating System

There are various benefits of single user operating system such as:

- Single operating system permits such interface, in which only one user work at a time, and other user cannot create interruption in the processing. So this operating system does not need to bear the overloading the multiple users' requests.

- Multiple resources are not used in the single operating system, so they have less complexity. Due to that reasons, this O/S is needed only simple maintenance and debug as well.

- Due to less overload of sending requests by user, to hardware and software at once. So they have no more probability to damage them.

- Due to single user interface, this operating system allows only task execute at a given time. So user focuses only one task instead of multiple tasks.

Disadvantages of Single User Operating System

There are some limitation of single user operating system. Describe each one below:

- Single user operating system is not capable to run multiple tasks at same frame time, so CPU waits to execution, until one task complete.

- This system is not able to optimize of CPU, memory and disk I/O at the optimal level, due to high CPU's waiting pool request.

- It is slow nature.

- It has high response time.

- It uses high idle time.

Examples of Single User Operating System

- Windows 1.0

- Windows 2.0

- Windows 3.0

- Windows 3.1x

- Windows 95

- Windows 97

- Windows 98

- Windows ME

- MS – DOS

- Symbian OS

Multi-User Operating System

A multi-user operating system is an operating system that allows multiple users to connect and operate a single operating system. The users interact with it through terminals or computers that gave them access to the system through a network or machines such as printers. The operating system should have to meet the requirements of all its users in a balanced way, so that if any problem would arise with one user, it does not affect any other user in the chain.

Examples of Multi-User Operating System

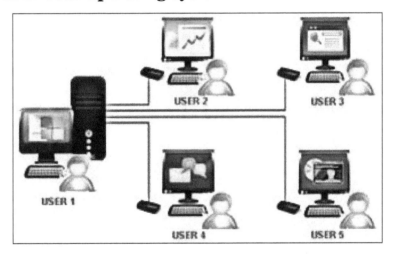

- Multiple Virtual Storage: An operating system from IBM that runs on the Mainframe. It is widely used in Enterprise computing which involves high intensity I/O. Example: Banking, Insurance, and Aviation business.

- Unix: An open system Architecture that is highly reliable for small and medium scale business computing solutions. Since, it's based on Open system Architecture, Tech giants have their version of Unix such as Solaris, AIX, even Mac OS. Example: Hospitality industry, Healthcare.

Types of Multi-User Operating System

- Distributed System

- Time – sliced System

- Multi-processor system

Distributed Operating System

- Distributed Operating system also known as distributed computing is a collection of multiple components located on different computers that interact, co-ordinates, and emulates as a single coherent system to the end-user. End-user will communicate or operate them with the help of the Network.

- This system divides resources in a way that multiple requests can be handled and in turn each, individual request can be satisfied eventually. Example of the distributed system:

  - Electronic banking and Mobile Apps can be sited as the best example of Applications that can be hosted on Distributed OS. Users can conduct numerous transactions using a single network from the comfort of their place.

Time-Sliced System

- It is the system where each user task is allocated to a short span of CPU time. In other words, each task is assigned to a short period. These time slices appear too small to the eyes of the user. The decision to run the next piece of job is decided by an internal component called the 'Scheduler'. This scheduler identifies and executes the run instruction or task that needs to be executed depending on the priority cycle.

- The users can take turns and thus the Operating System will handle user's requests among the users who are connected. This feature is not available in the Single User Operating System, where the user and the machine come in contact directly. Example of Time sliced system:

  - Mainframe, a practical exam of the time-sliced system, where a user will be allocated a specific time slice to perform a complex task.

Multi-Processor System

- Multi-Processor system is the one, where the system uses more than one processor at the same time. Since all the processors would be working side by side, the work would be completed at a pace that would be much faster than the single-user operating system. Example of Multi-processor system:

  - We can take Windows Operating System as a practical example of a multi-processing system where word processor, spreadsheets, music player etc., everything can be opened at the same time without affecting the efficiency of any application that is being opened.

Features of Multi-User Operating System

The Multi-user operating system can be documented with 4 features:

- Multiple processing:

  - We can execute multiple programs at the same time.

- ○ For instance, students can edit a word document by surfing the internet (maybe Google) and also attach an excel file in the document instantaneously.

- Sharing of resources:

    - ○ It is the feature that can be mapped to time slicing. Multiple peripherals such as printers, hard drives, etc. can be shared or we can even share different files or data.

    - ○ One such example which can be quoted here is the webmail system. In this, thousands of users log on at a time to check their emails, and send messages etc., which proves that the OS supports even millions of users at the same time. Thus, a webmail application requires thousands of computers which can in turn serve thousands of people at a time.

- Processing of data at the back end:

    - ○ This feature allows data to be processed at the back end when they are not allowed to be processed at the front end.

    - ○ This allows other programs to interact with the processor in the front end simultaneously.

- Invisibility:

    - ○ Many functions of the multi-user operating system is invisible to the users. This is because of the aspects such as the OS is instinctive or it happens at the lower end such as formatting of the disk and so on.

Working Mode of Multi-User Operating System

Ideally, the multi-operating system consists of the Master system. This Master system can be used by all users at any place and at any time, the users can also open their own working view of the system. This view is called "Local view". This is the working model of the multi user operating system. The users can add, delete, and update records based on their requirements. This working model will not be visible to the other users of the system unless a user shares it or saves it to the Master system.

Components of Multi-User Operating System

The multi user operating system has three Components:

- Processer: The core of the computer called CPU (Central Processing Unit) is otherwise called the brain of the computer. In large machines, CPU would require more ICS. Whereas on smaller machines, CPU is mapped in a single chip popularly called as Microprocessor.

- Memory: The physical memory that is present inside the computer is where storage happens. It is otherwise called Random Access Memory (RAM). The system can correct data that is present in the main memory therefore every program that is executed must be copied from a physical storage such as hard disk. Main memory is always marked important because, it determines how many programs can be executed at one time and the amount of data that would be available. The types of physical storage can be segregated as:

    - ○ Hard Disks: It can hold large amount of data and how also determines how many programs can be run at a single time.

- Floppy Disks: It is inexpensive but can hold only less data when compared to hard drives. It is also portable.

- Optical Disks: They use Lasers to read and write data. They can hold large data like hard disks but they are not portable like hard drives. CD (Compact Disk) is used to write and read files.

- Tapes: They are inexpensive as well. They hold large memory but data access in random cannot be done.

- Terminals:

  - Dumb Terminal:

    - It is featured with its computer and keyboard.

    - It does not have the processing power.

    - They are used to do remote work on mainframe systems.

    - Smart Terminals: Simple editing and processing can be done using a smart terminal. They are inexpensive but do not have any physical storage devices such as hard drives.

- Input/Output devices:

  - They are used to transfer and receive data. Input devices can be mouse and keyboard.

  - Output devices can be printers and monitors.

Software Components

- Kernel: Kernel is called the low-level component of the computer system. Kernel is written in the low-level programming language and is present in the main component of the computer, that is processor and it can interact with the hardware of the system.

- Device handler: The concept that is behind the device handler is "Queue "where we follow "first in, first out "strategy. It functions on each input and output device. It works continuously and it also discards any blocks on the input/ output device.

- Spooler: Spooler executes all the processes that are running on the computer and it also provides appropriate output. Spooler is mainly used in output devices such as printer.

- User Interface: UI is the point of communication between users and the software/hardware. It creates an easy work platform for all users and thus serves to be an inexplicable component in the multi-user operating system. Let's see one example in detail which is being used across the world in a major way. The Mainframe is one of the systems which works on the concept of a multi-user operating system. It is widely used in banks, to store bank accounts and transaction details.

Mainframe

Most of today's business workloads rely on Mainframe. Web transactions would easily be made possible with the help of mainframe systems, because it's hardware and software components are ideal for accommodating a large number of users and they allow to access data rapidly and simultaneously, without any interference.

Why Mainframe?

- Security: The Mainframe is unique as most of the data gets encrypted at the hardware level which makes it nearly impossible to breakthrough. Enterprises handling critical banking transactions, Government data etc., rely on Mainframe for its robust security system.

- Scalability: By scalability, what we mean today is the system should be able to function normally with a change in the amount of data it handles. The performance should be constant even when processors, memory, etc. would be added or deleted. The ability of an organization to carry on with its work without any hindrance be it with large or small networks and any degree of complexity would define scalability of the network with which it is operating. The Mainframe satisfies one such requirement among users, thus making it a perfect example for a multi-user operating system.

- Reliability: The system's hardware s equipped so well that it can detect and recover its problems on its own. Health checker can be quoted as an example here as it can identify any problem before it could cause any impact.

- Serviceability: Mainframe's serviceability is a trademark feature that it owns. It can detect any failure and on point, it can determine the reason for that particular failure. If we say that a system is serviceable, it means that if any error has occurred that has caused operations to stop, the system should be able to fix it in a relatively short period of time. In that way, we could say that the mainframe is one of the most serviceable multi-user systems.

- Compatibility: Some applications in the mainframe were developed years back and some applications might have been developed recently. Mainframe works on all kinds of system and that determines the ability of mainframe. Records over 100 years are still present on the mainframe system, untouched in the same format.

Now let's talk about how businesses rely on mainframe systems:

- They perform transactions on a large basis (millions of transactions per second).

- They support a large number of users and applications and they are allowed to operate simultaneously.

- Large bandwidth communication is possible with the help of mainframe systems.

Advantages of Multi-User Operating System

- Avoids Disruption: We have already seen that multiple computers operate on the same network. So, if one computer gets disturbed it doesn't affect any other computer present on that network, making it as the primary advantage of the Operating System.

- Distribution of Resources: Users can share their work with the other users, thus marking the exemplary boon of multi user operating system. Say for example, if a user wants to view a pdf version of file which the other user is working on, the user who is working on the file can simply share it so that the required user can access the file.

- Library: It is used in library to record the name and author of books, which is in turn connected to the other computers on the network, so that any librarian can open the system and view the details of a book.

- Used in Airlines: It is used in Airlines, tickets reservation system, where in one user can login and book a ticket, whereas the other can use it to cancel a ticket, it can also be used to check the availability and status of tickets.

- Economy Improvement: Most of the companies are marching towards multi operating system to reduce their expenditure. For large companies, where expenditure plays a major role, investment is required in hardware and software components. In that case, companies would naturally look up to avoid that expenditure by deploying minimum machines for maximum number of users.

- Backing up of Data: With the use of multi user operating system, backing up of data can be done on the machine which the user is using. Therefore, it would be a kind of surprise if data would get lost, thereby saving time and expenses for the company.

- Speed Efficiency: The speed at which data is exchanged is increased by using electronic mailing system. Lakhs of mails can be sent and received at the same time thus making work easier.

- Stability of Servers: Servers are very systematic and stable. The technologies which are emerging go hand in hand with the up- gradation of hardware and software. Access to serves is possible remotely from different countries at different timeframes.

- Real Time Scenario: Time taken for shifting of tasks is comparatively less in real time systems. The occurrence of errors is less when compared to other systems. The size of programs written is smaller thus avoiding hanging up of applications. The allocation of memory is well organized in real time systems. The major boon of multi user operating system is that with the use of it, jobs won't get interlaced and the resulting output would not be baffling. Each user's logs are maintained as to when and what job they did which is the most efficient feature of multi user operating system.

Disadvantages of Multi-User Operating System

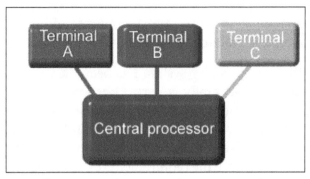

Multiuser operating system share processor time.

- Virus: In the multi-user operating system, since many computers are used on a single network, if the virus affects one computer, the computers on the network would be affected as well, paving the way for viruses attacking all systems.

- Visibility of Data: Information on the computer is shared with the public, so privacy becomes a concern here.

- Multiple Accounts: Creating multiple accounts on a single computer might be dangerous at times. So, it's better to have an individual machine for each user.

Single vs. Multi-User Operating System

A single-user operating system is a system in which only one user can access the computer system at a time. On the other hand, a multi-user operating system allows more than one user to access a computer system at one time.

An operating system is one of the most important programs that run on a computer or server. It is referred to as the underlying software that helps in carrying out basic functions like running programs, managing resources, manipulating files, controlling the keyboard and screen, etc.

A single user operating system provides the facilities to be used on one computer by only one user. In other words, it supports one user at a time. However, it may support more than one profile. Single keyboard and single monitor are used for the purpose of interaction. The most common example of a single user operating system is a system that is found in a typical home computer.

On the other hand, a multi-user operating system has been designed for more than one user to access the computer at one time. Generally, a network is laid down, so that a computer can be remotely used. Mainframes and minicomputers work on multi-user operating systems. These operating systems are complex in comparison to single user operating systems. Each user is provided with a terminal and all these terminals are connected to the main computer. In a multi-user environment, it is very important to balance the requirements of the users, as the resources of the main computer are shared among the users.

Table: Comparison between Single User and Multi-User Operating System.

	Single User	Multi-User
Definition	A single user operating system provides facilities to be used on one computer by only one user.	A multi-user operating system has been designed for more than one user to access the computer at the same or different time.
Types	Single user, single task: A single task is performed by one user at a time. Example- The Palm OS for Palm handheld computers. Single user, multi-task: Several programs are run at the same time by a single user. For example- Microsoft Windows.	Time-sharing systems: These systems are multi-user systems in which CPU time is divided among the users. The division is made on the basis of a schedule. Most batch processing systems for the mainframe computers can also be considered as 'multi-user.'
Attributes	Simple	Complex
Examples	Windows 95, Windows NT Workstation and Windows 2000 professional.	Unix, Linux, and mainframes such as the IBM AS400.

References

- Batch-operating-systems: padakuu.com, Retrieved 17, March 2020

- Distributed-operating-system: teachcomputerscience.com, Retrieved 29, July 2020

- Distributed-operating-system-tutorial-with-their-types-examples: digitalthinkerhelp.com, Retrieved 05, January 2020

- Embedded-operating-system: microcontrollerslab.com, Retrieved 17, June 2020

- What-is-real-time-operating-system: blackberry.qnx.com, Retrieved 02, February 2020

- What-is-single-user-operating-system-full-detail-with-example: digitalthinkerhelp.com, Retrieved 11, July 2020

- Multi-user-operating-system: teachcomputerscience.com, Retrieved 21, April 2020

- Difference-between-single-user-and-multi-user-operating-system: differencebetween.info, Retrieved 23, August 2020

System Processes

All the related activities in a system that work together to make it function are known as processes. Some of the topics studied under system processes are process concepts, inter process communication, system calls, CPU scheduling, process synchronization, etc. The topics elaborated in this chapter will help in gaining a better perspective about the system processes.

Process Concepts

A process is a program in execution. The execution of a process progresses in a sequential fashion. A program is a passive entity while a process is an active entity. A process includes much more than just the program code. A process includes the text section, stack, data section, program counter, register contents and so on. The text section consists of the set of instructions to be executed for the process. The data section contains the values of initialized and uninitialized global variables in the program. The stack is used whenever there is a function call in the program. A layer is pushed into the stack when a function is called. The arguments to the function and the local variables used in the function are put into the layer of the stack. Once the function call returns to the calling program, the layer of the stack is popped. The text, data and stack sections comprise the address space of the process. The program counter has the address of the next instruction to be executed in the process.

It is possible to have two processes associated with the same program. For example, consider an editor program, say Microsoft Word. The program has the same text section. But, the data section will be different for each file that is opened in Microsoft Word, that is, each file has a different data section.

Process States

As a process executes, it changes state. The state of a process refers to what the process currently does. A process can be in one of the following states during its lifetime:

- New: The process is being created.
- Running: Instructions are being executed.
- Waiting: The process is waiting for some event to occur.
- Ready: The process is waiting to be assigned to a processor.
- Terminated: The process has finished execution.

Figure shows the state transition diagram of a process. The process is in the new state when it is being created. Then the process is moved to the ready state, where it waits till it is taken for execution. There can be many such processes in the ready state. One of these processes will be selected and will be given the processor, and the selected process moves to the running state. A process, while running, may have to wait for I/O or wait for any other event to take place. That process is now moved to the waiting state. After the event for which the process was waiting gets completed, the process is moved back to the ready state. Similarly, if the time-slice of a process ends while still running, the process is moved back to the ready state. Once the process completes execution, it moves to the terminated state.

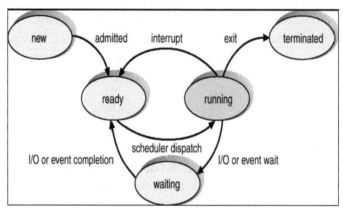

Process state transition diagram.

Process Control Block (PCB)

The information about each process is maintained in the operating system in a process control block, which is also called a task control block. Figure shows a PCB. The PCB contains extensive information about the process. The information present in the PCB includes the following:

- Process state – Current state of the process.

- Program counter – Address of the next instruction to be executed.

- CPU registers: Accumulators, index registers, stack pointer, general purpose registers.

- CPU scheduling information o Process priority sched: Value of base and limit registers.

- Accounting information: Amount of CPU used, time limits, process numbers.

- I/O status information: List of I/O devices allocated to the process, list of open files and so on.

Table: Process control block (PCB).

Pointer	Process state
Process number	
Program counter	
Registers	
Memory limits	
List of open files	

Table shows how the contents of the PCB of a process are used when the CPU switches from one process to another process. Process P_0 is executing first, and there is an interrupt. Process P_0 should now release the CPU and the CPU should be assigned to the next process P_1. Before the CPU is assigned to the next process P_1, the state of the process currently using the CPU, P_0, is saved in its PCB. The state of the next process P_1 is then loaded from the PCB of P_1. When there needs to be a switch from P_1 to P_0, the state of P_1 is saved and the state of P_0 is loaded.

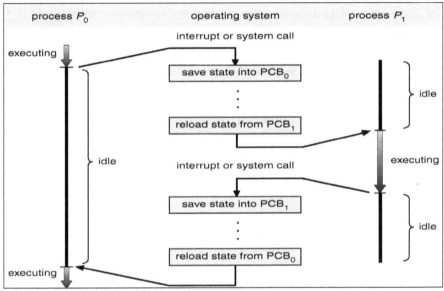

CPU switch from process to process.

Process Scheduling

In multi-programmed systems, some process must run at all times, to increase CPU utilization. In time-sharing systems, processes must be switched to increase interaction between the user and the system. If there are many processes, only one can use the CPU at a particular time and the remaining must wait during that time. When the CPU becomes free, the next process can be scheduled.

Process Scheduling Queues

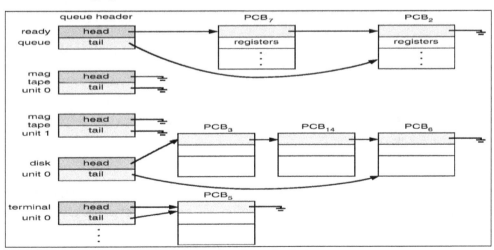

Ready queue and various I/O device queues.

When processes enter the system, they are put into a job queue. This job queue is the set of all processes in the system. The set of all processes residing in main memory, ready and waiting to execute is kept in a ready queue. The ready queue is maintained as a linked list. A ready-queue header contains pointers to the first and final PCBs in the list.

In addition to the ready queue, there are other queues in the system in which a process may be kept during its lifetime. When a process has to wait for I/O, the PCB of the process is removed from the ready queue and is placed in a device queue. The device queue corresponds to the I/O device from/to which the process is waiting for I/O. Hence, there are a number of device queues in the system corresponding to the devices present in the system. Figure below shows the ready queue and the various device queues in the system. Any process during its lifetime will migrate between the various queues.

Figure below shows a common representation of process scheduling using a queuing diagram. The rectangular boxes represent the various queues. The circles denote the resources that serve the queues and the arrows show the flow of processes in the system.

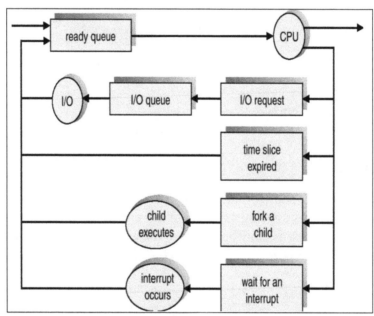

Queuing diagram representation of process scheduling.

A new process is initially placed in the ready queue. When the process is given the CPU and is running one of the following may occur:

- The process may request for I/O and may be placed in an I/O queue. After I/O gets completed, the process is moved back to the ready queue.

- The time slice allotted to the process may get over. The process is now forcibly removed from the CPU and is placed back in the ready queue.

- The process may create (fork) a new process and may wait for the created child process to finish completion. Once the child completes execution, the process moves back to the ready queue.

- While the process executes, an interrupt may occur. The process is now removed from the CPU, the process waits till the interrupt is serviced and is then moved to the ready state.

Schedulers

A process moves between different queues during its lifetime. The OS should select the process that should move to the next queue and the queue to which the selected process should move, in some fashion. This selection is done by schedulers. The different schedulers available are long-term scheduler, short-term scheduler and medium-term scheduler.

In batch systems, more processes are submitted than those that can be executed. These processes are placed in a job pool. The long-term scheduler (or job scheduler) selects those processes that should be brought into the ready queue from the job pool, and brings them from the job pool to main memory. The short-term scheduler (or CPU scheduler), selects the process that be executed next and allocates the CPU.

The main difference between the job scheduler and the CPU scheduler is the frequency of execution. The long-term scheduler controls the degree of multiprogramming (number of processes in memory). It is invoked only when a process leaves the system. The short-term scheduler is invoked whenever the CPU switches from one process to another. Hence, the short-term scheduler is run more frequently than the long-term scheduler.

As the long-term scheduler controls the degree of multiprogramming, it should select a good mix of I/O-bound and CPU-bound processes and bring them into the main memory. An I/O-bound process spends most of its time performing I/O than computation. A CPU-bound process spends most of its time performing computations than I/O. If all processes are I/O-bound, then the CPU will be under-utilized. If all processes are CPU-bound, the I/O devices will not be used fully. Hence, proper selection of jobs by the job scheduler will ensure that the system is stable.

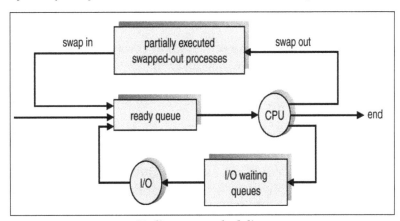

Medium-term scheduling.

Some operating systems, like the time-sharing systems introduce an additional, intermediate level of scheduling, called medium-term scheduling. Any process that is in the running state has to be kept in the main memory. Such a process may not be in the running state throughout its life time till its termination. It may be moving to the waiting state or to the ready queue and then may move back to the running state and so on. Moreover, when one process moves to the waiting state or to the ready queue, another process moves to the running state. The process that is currently in the running state should be kept in the main memory. If there are many processes are in the waiting state or in the ready queue and if all the processes are still kept in the main memory, the main memory may not be enough to accommodate the currently running process. When there is no enough space in the main memory, the medium-term scheduler removes these partially executed processes from the main memory and moves to the swap space in the secondary storage device. Later, when there is space in the main memory, the processes can be brought into the memory and will continue where they left off. This process is also known as swapping. Figure shows how a medium-term scheduler works.

Context of a Process

The context of a process is represented in the PCB of the process. It includes the values in CPU registers, process state, memory management information, open files for the process and so on. When the CPU switches from one process to another process, it is said that a context switch occurs. During a context switch, the system must save the context of the old process and load the saved context for the new process. Context-switch time is overhead, because the system does no useful work while switching.

Context-switch time depends on the memory speed, number of registers to be copied and the existence of special instructions. It is also dependent on hardware support. For example, some processors provide multiple sets of registers. Then, the context for each process can be stored in each set of registers. In this case, context switch will only be moving a pointer from one register set to another.

Operations of Processes

The operating system must provide support for creation and termination of processes.

Process Creation

Any process can create other processes. The process that creates is called the parent process. The parent process creates children processes, which, in turn create other processes, forming a tree of processes. Each process is identified by a process identifier (pid). In UNIX systems, the ps command is used to list all processes in the system along with their pids.

Any process will need resources such as CPU time, memory and other resources to complete its task. When a parent process creates children processes, the children may obtain resources from the system or may share the resources with the parent. Thus, in some operating systems, the parent and children share all resources. In some other operating systems, the children share a subset of the parent's resources and in some others, the parent and child share no resources.

Once a child process is created, the parent and child execute concurrently. In some cases, the parent does not wait for the child to terminate. In some others, the parent waits until some or all the children terminate. There are again two possibilities about the address space (text, data and stack) of the newly created process. The address space of the child process may be the duplicate of that of the parent process. Instead, the child may have another program loaded into it.

Process Creation in UNIX

The fork system call is used to create a new process in UNIX. The address space of the child process is a copy of the address space of the parent process. If the child has to execute some program other than the program that the parent executes, the exec system call is used. The exec system call, when used after a fork, replaces the child process' memory space with a new program. Figure shows the flow of the parent and the child processes after a fork is being called by the parent. The parent after creating the child may even wait for the child to exit using the wait system call. In UNIX, the parent can even choose to exit without waiting for the child to exit.

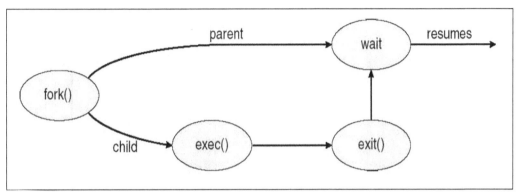

Process creation in UNIX.

Interprocess Communication

Interprocess communication (IPC) refers to the coordination of activities among cooperating processes. A process can be of two types:

- Independent process
- Co-operating process

An independent process is not affected by the execution of other processes while a co-operating process can be affected by other executing processes. Though one can think that those processes, which are running independently, will execute very efficiently, in reality, there are many situations when co-operative nature can be utilised for increasing computational speed, convenience and modularity. Inter process communication (IPC) is a mechanism which allows processes to communicate with each other and synchronize their actions. The communication between these processes can be seen as a method of co-operation between them. Processes can communicate with each other through both:

- Shared Memory
- Message passing

The figure shows a basic structure of communication between processes via the shared memory method and via the message passing method. An operating system can implement both method of communication. First, we will discuss the shared memory methods of communication and then message passing. Communication between processes using shared memory requires processes to share some variable and it completely depends on how programmer will implement it. One way of communication using shared memory can be imagined like this: Suppose process 1 and process 2 are executing simultaneously and they share some resources or use some information from another process. Process 1 generate information about certain computations or resources being used and keeps it as a record in shared memory. When process 2 needs to use the shared information, it will check in the record stored in shared memory and take note of the information generated by process 1 and act accordingly. Processes can use shared memory for extracting information as a record from another process as well as for delivering any specific information to other processes. Let's discuss an example of communication between processes using shared memory method.

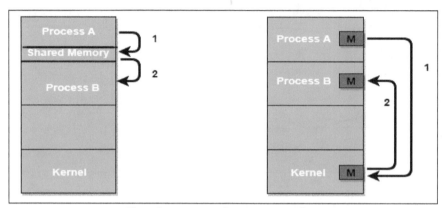

Shared memory and message passing.

Shared Memory Method

Ex: Producer-Consumer Problem

There are two processes: Producer and Consumer. Producer produces some item and Consumer consumes that item. The two processes share a common space or memory location known as a buffer where the item produced by Producer is stored and from which the Consumer consumes the item, if needed. There are two versions of this problem: the first one is known as unbounded buffer problem in which Producer can keep on producing items and there is no limit on the size of the buffer, the second one is known as the bounded buffer problem in which Producer can produce up to a certain number of items before it starts waiting for Consumer to consume it. We will discuss the bounded buffer problem. First, the Producer and the Consumer will share some common memory, then producer will start producing items. If the total produced item is equal to the size of buffer, producer will wait to get it consumed by the Consumer. Similarly, the consumer will first check for the availability of the item. If no item is available, Consumer will wait for Producer to produce it. If there are items available, Consumer will consume it. The pseudo code to demonstrate is provided below:

Shared Data Between the Two Processes

```
#define buff_max 25
#define mod %
struct item{
// different member of the produced data
// or consumed data
---------
}
// An array is needed for holding the items.
// This is the shared place which will be
```

```
// access by both process
// item shared_buff [ buff_max ];
// Two variables which will keep track of
// the indexes of the items produced by producer
// and consumer The free index points to
// the next free index. The full index points to
// the first full index.
int free_index = 0;
int full_index = 0;
```

Producer Process Code

```
item nextProduced;
while(1){
// check if there is no space
// for production.
// if so keep waiting.
while((free_index+1) mod buff_max == full_index);
shared_buff[free_index] = nextProduced;
free_index = (free_index + 1) mod buff_max;
}
```

Consumer Process Code

```
item nextConsumed;
while(1){
// check if there is an available
// item for consumption.
// if not keep on waiting for
// get them produced.
while((free_index == full_index);
nextConsumed = shared_buff[full_index];
full_index = (full_index + 1) mod buff_max;
}
```

In the above code, the Producer will start producing again when the (free_index+1) mod buff max will be free because if it it not free, this implies that there are still items that can be consumed by the Consumer so there is no need to produce more. Similarly, if free index and full index point to the same index, this implies that there are no items to consume.

Messaging Passing Method

Now, we will start discussion of the communication between processes via message passing. In this method, processes communicate with each other without using any kind of shared memory. If two processes p1 and p2 want to communicate with each other, they proceed as follows:

- Establish a communication link (if a link already exists, no need to establish it again).

- Start exchanging messages using basic primitives. We need at least two primitives:

  ○ Send (message, destinaion) or send (message)

  ○ Receive (message, host) or receive (message)

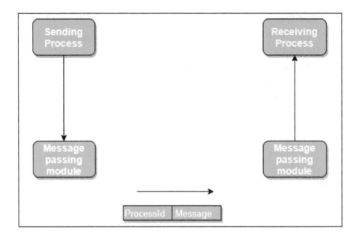

The message size can be of fixed size or of variable size. If it is of fixed size, it is easy for an OS designer but complicated for a programmer and if it is of variable size then it is easy for a programmer but complicated for the OS designer. A standard message can have two parts: header and body. The header part is used for storing message type, destination id, source id, message length, and control information. The control information contains information like what to do if runs out of buffer space, sequence number, priority. Generally, message is sent using FIFO style.

Message Passing through Communication Link

Direct and Indirect Communication Link

Now, We will start our discussion about the methods of implementing communication link. While implementing the link, there are some questions which need to be kept in mind like:

- How are links established?
- Can a link be associated with more than two processes?
- How many links can there be between every pair of communicating processes?
- What is the capacity of a link? Is the size of a message that the link can accommodate fixed or variable?
- Is a link unidirectional or bi-directional?

A link has some capacity that determines the number of messages that can reside in it temporarily for which every link has a queue associated with it which can be of zero capacity, bounded capacity, or unbounded capacity. In zero capacity, the sender waits until the receiver informs the sender that it has received the message. In non-zero capacity cases, a process does not know whether a message has been received or not after the send operation. For this, the sender must communicate with the receiver explicitly. Implementation of the link depends on the situation it can be either a direct communication link or an in-directed communication link. Direct Communication links are implemented when the processes use a specific process identifier for the communication, but it is hard to identify the sender ahead of time. For example: the print server.

In-direct Communication is done via a shared mailbox (port), which consists of a queue of messages. The sender keeps the message in mailbox and the receiver picks them up.

Message Passing through Exchanging the Messages

Synchronous and Asynchronous Message Passing

A process that is blocked is one that is waiting for some event, such as a resource becoming available or the completion of an I/O operation. IPC is possible between the processes on same computer as well as on the processes running on different computer i.e. in networked/distributed system. In both cases, the process may or may not be blocked while sending a message or attempting to receive a message so message passing may be blocking or non-blocking. Blocking is considered synchronous and blocking send means the sender will be blocked until the message is received by receiver. Similarly, blocking receive has the receiver block until a message is available. Non-blocking is considered asynchronous and Non-blocking send has the sender sends the message and continue. Similarly, Non-blocking receive has the receiver receive a valid message or null. After a careful analysis, we can come to a conclusion that for a sender it is more natural to be non-blocking after message passing as there may be a need to send the message to different processes. However, the sender expects acknowledgement from the receiver in case the send fails. Similarly, it is more natural for a receiver to be blocking after issuing the receive as the information from the received message may be used for further execution. At the same time, if the messages send keep on failing, the receiver will have to wait indefinitely. That is why we also consider the other possibility of message passing. There are basically three preferred combinations:

- Blocking send and blocking receive.

- Non-blocking send and Non-blocking receive.

- Non-blocking send and Blocking receive (Mostly used).

In Direct message passing: The processes which want to communicate must explicitly name the recipient or sender of communication. E.g. send (p1, message) means send the message to p1. similarly receive(p2, message) means receive the message from p2. In this method of communication, the communication link gets established automatically, which can be either unidirectional or bidirectional, but one link can be used between one pair of the sender and receiver and one pair of sender and receiver should not possess more than one pair of links. Symmetry and asymmetry between sending and receiving can also be implemented i.e. either both process will name each other for sending and receiving the messages or only the sender will name receiver for sending the message and there is no need for receiver for naming the sender for receiving the message. The problem with this method of communication is that if the name of one process changes, this method will not work.

In Indirect message passing, processes use mailboxes (also referred to as ports) for sending and receiving messages. Each mailbox has a unique id and processes can communicate only if they share a mailbox. Link established only if processes share a common mailbox and a single link can be associated with many processes. Each pair of processes can share several communication links and these links may be unidirectional or bi-directional. Suppose two processes want to communicate though indirect message passing, the required operations are: create a mail box, use this mail box for sending and receiving messages then destroy the mail box. The standard primitives used are: send (A, message) which means send the message to mailbox A. The primitive for the receiving the message also works in the same way e.g. received (A, message). There is a problem in this mailbox implementation. Suppose there are more than two processes sharing the same mailbox and suppose the process p1 sends a message to the mailbox, which process will be the receiver?

This can be solved by either enforcing that only two processes can share a single mailbox or enforcing that only one process is allowed to execute the receive at a given time or select any process randomly and notify the sender about the receiver. A mailbox can be made private to a single sender/receiver pair and can also be shared between multiple sender/receiver pairs. Port is an implementation of such mailbox which can have multiple sender and single receiver. It is used in client/server applications (in this case the server is the receiver). The port is owned by the receiving process and created by OS on the request of the receiver process and can be destroyed either on request of the same receiver process or when the receiver terminates itself. Enforcing that only one process is allowed to execute the receive can be done using the concept of mutual exclusion. Mutex mailbox is create which is shared by n process. Sender is non-blocking and sends the message. The first process which executes the receive will enter in the critical section and all other processes will be blocking and will wait.

Now, let's discuss the Producer-Consumer problem using message passing concept. The producer places items (inside messages) in the mailbox and the consumer can consume an item when at least one message present in the mailbox. The code is given below:

Producer Code

```
void Producer(void){
int item;
Message m;
while(1){
receive(Consumer, &m);
item = produce();
build_message(&m, item ) ;
send(Consumer, &m);
}
}
```

Consumer Code

```
void Consumer(void){
int item;
Message m;
while(1){
receive(Producer, &m);
item = extracted_item();
send(Producer, &m);
consume_item(item);
}
}
```

Examples of IPC systems:

- Posix: Uses shared memory method.

- Mach: Uses message passing.

- Windows XP: Uses message passing using local procedural calls.

Communication in client/server Architecture:

There are various mechanisms:

- Pipe

- Socket

- Remote Procedural calls (RPCs)

System Calls

A system call is a mechanism that provides the interface between a process and the operating system. It is a programmatic method in which a computer program requests a service from the kernel of the OS. System call offers the services of the operating system to the user programs via API (Application Programming Interface). System calls are the only entry points for the kernel system.

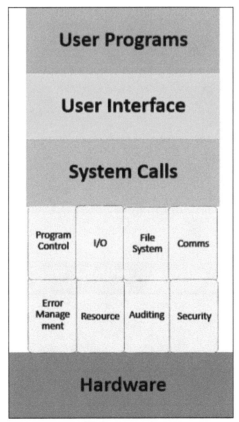

System Calls in Operating System.

Example of System Call

For example if we need to write a program code to read data from one file, copy that data into another file. The first information that the program requires is the name of the two files, the input and output files. In an interactive system, this type of program execution requires some system calls by OS.

- First call is to write a prompting message on the screen.

- Second, to read from the keyboard, the characters which define the two files.

Working of System Call

Here are steps for System Call:

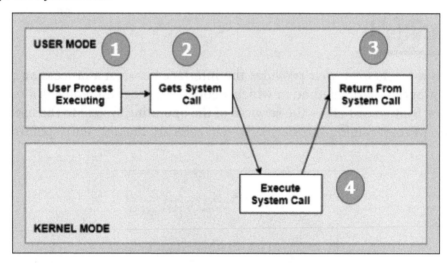

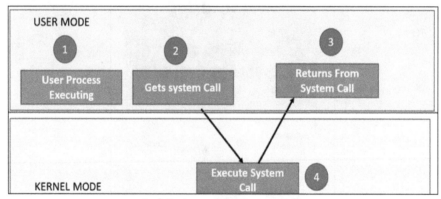

Architecture of the System Call.

Need of System Calls in OS

Following are situations which need system calls in OS:

- Reading and writing from files demand system calls.

- If a file system wants to create or delete files, system calls are required.

- System calls are used for the creation and management of new processes.

- Network connections need system calls for sending and receiving packets.

- Access to hardware devices like scanner, printer, need a system call.

Types of System Calls

Here are the five types of system calls used in OS:

- Process Control,
- File Management,
- Device Management,
- Information Maintenance,
- Communications.

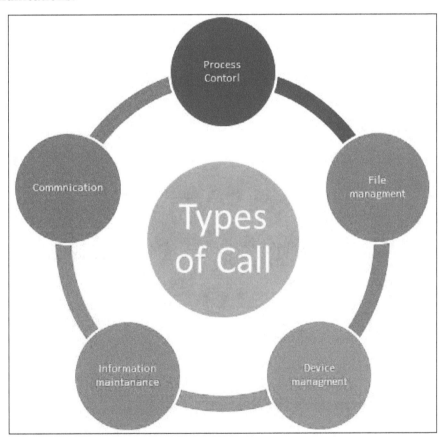

Process Control

This system calls perform the task of process creation, process termination, etc. Functions:

- End and Abort,
- Load and Execute,
- Create Process and Terminate Process,
- Wait and Signed Event,
- Allocate and free memory.

File Management

File management system calls handle file manipulation jobs like creating a file, reading, and writing, etc. Functions:

- Create a file,
- Delete file,
- Open and close file,
- Read, write, and reposition,
- Get and set file attributes.

Device Management

Device management does the job of device manipulation like reading from device buffers, writing into device buffers, etc. Functions:

- Request and release device,
- Logically attach/ detach devices,
- Get and Set device attributes.

Communication

These types of system calls are specially used for interprocess communications. Functions:

- Create, delete communications connections.
- Send, receive message.
- Help OS to transfer status information.
- Attach or detach remote devices.

Rules for Passing Parameters for System Call

Here are general common rules for passing parameters to the System Call:

- Parameters should be pushed on or popped off the stack by the operating system.
- Parameters can be passed in registers.
- When there are more parameters than registers, it should be stored in a block, and the block address should be passed as a parameter to a register.

Important System Calls used in OS

- Wait(): In some systems, a process needs to wait for another process to complete its execution. This type of situation occurs when a parent process creates a child process, and the execution of the parent process remains suspended until its child process executes. The suspension of the parent process automatically occurs with a wait() system call. When the child process ends execution, the control moves back to the parent process.

- Fork(): Processes use this system call to create processes that are a copy of themselves. With the help of this system Call parent process creates a child process, and the execution of the parent process will be suspended till the child process executes.

- Exec(): This system call runs when an executable file in the context of an already running process that replaces the older executable file. However, the original process identifier remains as a new process is not built, but stack, data, head, data, etc. Are replaced by the new process.

- Kill(): The kill() system call is used by OS to send a termination signal to a process that urges the process to exit. However, a kill system call does not necessarily mean killing the process and can have various meanings.

- Exit(): The exit() system call is used to terminate program execution. Specially in the multi-threaded environment, this call defines that the thread execution is complete. The OS reclaims resources that were used by the process after the use of exit() system call.

Categories	Windows	Unix
Process control	CreateProcess() ExitProcess() WaitForSingleObject()	fork() exit() wait()
Device manipulation	SetConsoleMode() ReadConsole() WriteConsole()	loctl() read() write()
File manipulation	CreateFile() ReadFile() WriteFile() CloseHandle()	Open() Read() write() close!)
Information maintanence	GetCurrentProcessID() SetTimer() Sleep()	getpid() alarm() sleep()
Communication	CreatePipe() CreateFileMapping() MapViewOfFile()	Pipe() shm_open() mmap()
Protection	SetFileSecurity() InitlializeSecurityDescriptor() SetSecurityDescriptorGroup ()	Chmod() Umask() Chown()

System Calls in Linux

Here we presents the way to use the most common system calls in order to make input-output operations on files, as well as operations to handle files and directories in the Linux operating system.

File Descriptors

The operating system assigns internally to each opened file a descriptor or an identifier (usually this is a positive integer). When opening or creating a new file the system returns a file descriptor to the process that executed the call. Each application has its own file descriptors. By convention, the first three file descriptors are opened at the beginning of each process. The 0 file descriptor identifies the standard input, 1 identifies the standard output and 2 the standard output for errors. The rest of the descriptors are used by the processes when opening an ordinary, pipe or special file, or directories. There are five system calls that generate file descriptors: *create, open, fcntl, dup and pipe.*

System Calls when Working with Files

System Call OPEN

Opening or creating a file can be done using the system call open. The syntax is:

```
#include <sys/types.h>
#include <sys/stat.h>
#include <fcntl.h>
int open(const char *path,
int flags,... /* mode_t mod */);
```

This function returns the file descriptor or in case of an error -1. The number of arguments that this function can have is two or three. The third argument is used only when creating a new file. When we want to open an existing file only two arguments are used. The function returns the smallest available file descriptor. This can be used in the following system calls: *read, write, lseek* and *close*. The effective UID or the effective GID of the process that executes the call has to have read/write rights, based on the value of the argument *flags*. The file pointer is places on the first byte in the file. The argument *flags* is formed by a bitwise OR operation made on the constants defined in the *fcntl.h* header.

O_RDONLY

Opens the file for reading.

O_WRONLY

Opens the file for writing.

O_RDWR

The file is opened for reading and writing.

O_APPEND

It writes successively to the end of the file.

O_CREAT

The file is created in case it didn\92t already exist.

O_EXCL

If the file exists and O_CREAT is positioned, calling open will fail.

O_NONBLOCK

In the case of pipes and special files, this causes the open system call and any other future I/O operations to never block.

O_TRUNC

If the file exists all of its content will be deleted.

O_SYNC

It forces to write on the disk with function write. Though it slows down all the system, it can be useful in critical situations.

The third argument, mod, is a bitwise OR made between a combination of two from the following list:

```
S_IRUSR, S_IWUSR, S_IXUSR
```

Owner: read, write, execute.

```
S_IRGRP, S_IWGRP, S_IXGRP
```

Group: read, write, execute.

```
S_IROTH, S_IWOTH, S_IXOTH
```

Others: read, write, execute.

The above define the access rights for a file and they are defined in the sys/stat.h header.

System Call Create

A new file can be created by:

```
#include <sys/types.h>
#include <sys/stat.h>
#include <fcntl.h>
int creat(const char *path, mode_t mod);
```

The function returns the file descriptor or in case of an error it returns the value -1. This call is equivalent with:

```
open(path, O_WRONLY | O_CREAT | O_TRUNC, mod);
```

The argument path specifies the name of the file, while mod defines the access rights. If the created file doesn't\92 exist, a new i-node is allocated and a link is made to this file from the directory it was created in. The owner of the process that executes the call - given by the effective UID and the effective GUID - must have writing permission in the directory. The open file will have the access rights that were specified in the second argument. The call returns the smallest file descriptor available. The file is opened for writing and its initial size is 0. The access time and the modification time are updated in the i-node. If the file exists (permission to search the directory is needed), it looses its contents and it will be opened for writing. The ownership and the access permissions won\92t be modified. The second argument is ignored.

System Call Read

When we want to read a certain number of bytes starting from the current position in a file, we use the read call. The syntax is:

```
#include <unistd.h>
ssize_t read(int fd, void* buf, size_t noct);
```

The function returns the number of bytes read, 0 for end of file (EOF) and -1 in case an error occurred. It reads noct bytes from the open file referred by the fd descriptor and it puts it into a buffer buf. The pointer (current position) is incremented automatically after a reading that certain amount of bytes. The process that executes a read operation waits until the system puts the data from the disk into the buffer.

System Call Write

For writing a certain number of bytes into a file starting from the current position we use the write call. Its syntax is:

```
#include <unistd.h>
ssize_t write(int fd, const void* buf, size_t noct);
```

The function returns the number of bytes written and the value -1 in case of an error. It writes noct bytes from the buffer buf into the file that has as its descriptor fd. It is interesting to note that the actual writing onto the disk is delayed. This is done at the initiative of the root, without informing the user when it is done. If the process that did the call or another process reads the data that haven\92t been written on the disk yet, the system reads all this data out from the cache buffers. The delayed writing is faster, but it has three disadvantages:

- A disk error or a system error may cause loosing all the data.

- A process that had the initiative of a write operation cannot be informed in case a writing error occurred.

- The physical order of the write operations cannot be controlled.

To eliminate these disadvantages, in some cases the O_SYNC is used. But as this slows down the system and considering the reliability of today\92s systems it is better to use the mechanism which includes using cache buffers.

System Call Close

For closing a file and thus eliminating the assigned descriptor we use the system call close.

```
#include <unistd.h>
int close(int fd);
```

The function returns 0 in case of success and -1 in case of an error. At the termination of a process an open file is closed anyway.

System Call Lseek

To position a pointer (that points to the current position) in an absolute or relative way can be done by calling the lseek function. Read and write operations are done relative to the current position in the file. The syntax for lseek is:

```
#include <sys/types.h>
#include <unistd.h>
off_t lseek(int fd, off_t offset, int ref);
```

The function returns the displacement of the new current position from the beginning of the file or

-1 in case of an error. There isn\92t done any I/O operation and the function doesn\92t send any commands to the disk controller. It ref is set to SEEK_SET the positioning is done relative to the beginning of the file (the first byte in the file is at position 0). If ref is SEEK_CUR the positioning is done relative to the current position. If ref is SEEK_END then the positioning is done relative to the end of the file. The system calls open, creat, write and read execute an lseek by default. If a file was opened using the symbolic constant O_APPEND then an lseek call is made to the end of the file before a write operation.

System Call Link

To link an existing file to another directory (or to the same directory) link can be used. To make such a link in fact means to set a new name or a path to an existing file. The link system call creates a hard link. Creating symbolic links can be done using symlink system call. The syntax of link is:

```
#include <unistd.h>
int link(const char* oldpath, const char* newpath);
int symlink(const char* oldpath, const char* newpath);
```

The function returns 0 in case of success and -1 in case of an error. The argument oldpath has to be a path to an existing file. Only the root has the right to set a link to a directory.

System Call Unlink

To delete a link (a path) in a directory we can use the unlink system call. Its syntax is:

```
#include <unistd.h>
int unlink(const char* path);
```

The function returns 0 in case of success and -1 otherwise. The function decrements the hard link counter in the i-node and deletes the appropriate directory entry for the file whose link was deleted. If the number of links of a file becomes 0 then the space occupied by the file and its i-node will be freed. Only the root can delete a directory.

System calls Stat, Lstat and Fstat

In order to obtain more details about a file the following system calls can be used: stat, lstat or fstat.

```
#include <sys/types.h>
#include <sys/stat.h>
int stat(const char* path, struct stat* buf);
int lstat(const char* path, struct stat* buf);
int fstat(int df, struct stat* buf);
```

These three functions return 0 in case of success and -1 in case of an error. The first two gets as input parameter a name of a file and completes the structure of the buffer with additional information read from its i-node. The fstat function is similar, but it works for files that were already opened and for which the file descriptor is known. The difference between stat and lstat is that in case of a symbolic link, function stat returns information about the linked file, while lstat returns information about the symbolic link file. The struct stat structure is described in the sys/stat.h header and has the following fields:

```
truct stat {
mode_t st_mode; /* file type & rights */
ino_t st_ino; /* i-node */
dev_t st_dev; /* număr de dispozitiv (SF) */
nlink_t st_nlink; /* nr of links */
uid_t st_uid; /* owner ID */
gid_t st_gid; /* group ID */
off_t st_size; /* ordinary file size */
time_t st_atime; /* last time it was accessed */
time_t st_mtime; /* last time it was modified */
time_t st_ctime; /* last time settings were changed */
dev_t st_rdev; /* nr. dispozitiv */
/* pt. fișiere speciale /
long st_blksize; /* optimal size of the I/O block */
long st_blocks; /* nr of 512 byte blocks allocated */
};
```

The Linux command that the most frequently uses this function is ls. Type declarations for the members of this structure can be found in the sys/stat.h header. The type and access rights for the file are encrypted in the st_mode field and can be determined using the following macros:

Table: Macros for obtaining the type of a file.

Macro	Meaning
S_ISREG(st_mode)	Regular file.
S_ISDIR(st_mode)	Directory file.
S_ISCHR(st_mode)	Special device of type character.
S_ISBLK(st_mode)	Special device of type block.
S_ISFIFO(st_mode)	Pipe file or FIFO.
S_ISLNK(st_mode)	Symbolic link.

Decrypting the information contained in the st_mode field can be done by testing the result of a bitwise AND made between the st_mode field and one of the constants (bit mask): S_IFIFO, S_IFCHR, S_IFBLK, S_IFDIR, S_IFREG, S_IFLNK, S_ISUID (suid bit set), S_ISGID (sgid bit set), S_ISVTX (sticky bit set), S_IRUSR (read right for the owner), S_IWUSR (write right for the owner), S_IWUSR (execution right for the owner), etc.

System Call Access

When opening a file with system call open the root verifies the access rights in function of the UID and the effective GID. There are some cases though when a process verifies these rights based upon the real UID and GID. A situation when this can be useful is when a process is executed with other access right using the suid or sgid bit. Even though a process may have root rights during execution, sometimes it is necessary to test whether the real user can or cannot access the file. For this we can use access which allows verifying the access rights of a file based on the real UID or GID. The syntax for this system call is:

```
#include <unistd.h>
int access(const char* path, int mod);
```

The function returns 0 if the access right exists and -1 otherwise. The argument mod is a bitwise AND between R_OK (permission to read), W_OK (permission to write), X_OK (execution right), F_OK (the file exists).

System Call Umask

To enhance the security in case of operations regarding the creation of files, the Linux operating system offers a default mask to reset some access rights. Encrypting this mask is made in a similar way to the encrypting of the access rights in the i-node of a file. When creating a file those bits that are set to 1 in the mask invalidate the corresponding bits in the argument that specify the access rights. The mask doesn't affect the system call chmod, so the processes can explicitly set their access rights independently form the umask mask. The syntax for the call is:

```
#include <sys/types.h>
#include <sys/stat.h>
mode_t umask(mode_t mask);
```

The function returns the value of the previous mask. The effect of the call is shown below:

```
main() /* test umask */
{
int fd;
umask(022);
if ((fd=creat(„temp", 0666))==-1)
perror(„creat");
system(„ls -l temp");
}
```

The result will be of the following form:

```
-rw-r--r-- temp
```

Note that the write permission for the group and other users beside the owner was automatically reset.

System Call Chmod

To modify the access rights for an existing file we use:

```
#include <sys/types.h>
#include <sys/stat.h>
int chmod(const char* path, mode_t mod);
```

The function returns 0 in case of a success and -1 otherwise. The chmod call modifies the access rights of the file specified by the path depending on the access rights specified by the mod argument. To be able to modify the access rights the effective UID of the process has to be identical to the owner of the file or the process must have root rights. The mod argument can be specified by one of the symbolic constants defined in the sys/stat.h header. Their effect can be obtained by making a bitwise OR operation on them:

Table: Bit masks for testing the access rights of a file.

Mode	Description
S_ISUID	Sets the suid bit.
S_ISGID	Sets the sgid bit.
S_ISVTX	Sets the sticky bit.
S_IRWXU	Read, write, execute rights for the owner obtained from: S_IRUSR | S_IWUSR | S_IXUSR
S_IRWXG	Read, write, execute rights for the group obtained from: S_IRGRP | S_IWGRP | S_IXGRP
S_IRWXO	Read, write, execute rights for others obtained from: S_IROTH | S_IWOTH | S_IXOTH

System Call Chown

This system call is used to modify the owner (UID) and the group (GID) that a certain file belongs to. The syntax of the function is:

```
#include <sys/types.h>
#include <unistd.h>
int chown(const char* path, uid_t owner, gid_t grp);
```

The function returns 0 in case of success and -1 in case of an error. Calling this function will change the owner and the group of the file specified by the argument path to the values specified by the arguments owner and grp. None of the users can change the owner of any file (even of his/her own files), except the root user, but they can change the GID for their own files to that of any group they belong to.

System Call Utime

There are three members of the structure stat that refer to time. They are presented in the following table:

Table: Timing information associated with a file.

Field	Description	Operation
st_atime	Last time the data in the file was accessed	Read
st_mtime	Last time the data in the file was modified	Write
st_ctime	Changing the settings for the i-node	chmod, chown

The difference between the time the file was last modified and the change in the setting of the i-node is that the first one refers to the time when the contents of the file were modified while the second one refers to the time when the information in the i-node was last modified. This is due to the fact that the information in the i-node is kept separately from the contents of the file. System calls that change the i-node are those ones which modify the access rights of a file, change the UID, change the number of links, etc. The system does not keep the time when the i-node was last accessed. This is why neither of the system calls access or stat do not change these times. The access time and last modification time of any kind of files can be changed by calling one of the system call presented below:

```
#include <sys/time.h>
int utimes(const char* path,
const struct timeval* times);
int lutimes(const char* path,
const struct timeval* times);
int futimes(int fd, const struct timeval* times);
```

The functions return 0 in case of success and -1 otherwise. Only the owner of a file or the root can change the times associated with a file. The parameter times represents the address (pointer) of a list of two timeval structures, corresponding to the access and modification time. The fields of the timeval structure are:

```
struct timeval {
long tv_sec; /* seconds passed since 1.01.1970 */
suseconds_t tv_usec; /* microseconds */
}
```

To obtain the current time in the form it is required by the timeval structure, we can use the get time of day function. For different conversions between the normal format of a data and hour and the format specific to the timeval structure the function ctime can be used or any other functions belonging to the same family.

Functions for Working with Directories

A directory can be read as a file by anyone whoever has reading permissions for it. Writing a directory as a file can only be done by the kernel. The structure of the directory appears to the user as a succession of structures named directory entries. A directory entry contains, among other information, the name of the file and the i-node of this. For reading the directory entries one after the other we can use the following functions:

```
#include <sys/types.h>
#include <dirent.h>
DIR* opendir(const char* pathname);
struct dirent* readdir(DIR* dp);
void rewinddir(DIR* dp);
int closedir(DIR* dp);
```

- The opendir function opens a directory. It returns a valid pointer if the opening was successful and NULL otherwise.

- The readdir function, at every call, reads another directory entry from the current directory. The first readdir will read the first directory entry; the second call will read the next entry and so on. In case of a successful reading the function will return a valid pointer to a structure of type dirent and NULL otherwise (in case it reached the end of the directory, for example).

- The rewinddir function repositions the file pointer to the first directory entry (the beginning of the directory).

- The closedir function closes a previously opened directory. In case of an error it returns the value -1.

- The structure dirent is defined in the dirent.h file. It contains at least two elements:

```
struct dirent {
ino_t d_fileno; // i-node nr.
char d_name[MAXNAMLEN + 1]; // file name
}
```

Windows System Calls

System calls in Windows are used for file system control, process control, interprocess communication, main memory management, I/O device handling, security etc. The programs interact with the Windows operating system using the system calls. Since system calls are the only way to access the kernel, all the programs requiring resources must use system calls.

Details about some of the important system calls in Windows are given as follows:

System Call	Description
CreateProcess()	A new process is created using this command.
ExitProcess()	This system call is used to exit a process.
CreateFile()	A file is created or opened using this system call.
ReadFile()	Data is read from the file using this system call.
WriteFile()	Data is written into the file using this system call.
CloseHandle()	This system call closes the file currently in use.
SetTimer()	This system call sets the alarm or the timer of a process.
CreatePipe()	A pipe is created using this system call.
SetFileSecurity()	This system call sets the security for a particular process.
SetConsoleMode()	This sets the input mode or output mode of the console's input buffer or output screen buffer respectively.
ReadConsole()	This reads the characters from the console input buffer.
WriteConsole()	This writes the characters into the console output buffer.

Process Synchronization

Process Synchronization is the task of coordinating the execution of processes in a way that no two processes can have access to the same shared data and resources. It is specially needed in a multi-process system when multiple processes are running together, and more than one processes try to gain access to the same shared resource or data at the same time.

This can lead to the inconsistency of shared data. So the change made by one process not necessarily reflected when other processes accessed the same shared data. To avoid this type of inconsistency of data, the processes need to be synchronized with each other.

Working of Process Synchronization

For Example, process a changing the data in a memory location while another process B is trying to read the data from the same memory location. There is a high probability that data read by the second process will be erroneous.

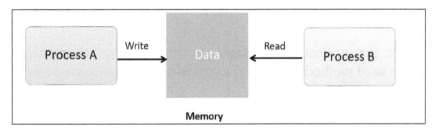

Sections of a Program

Here, are four essential elements of the critical section:

- Entry Section: It is part of the process which decides the entry of a particular process.

- Critical Section: This part allows one process to enter and modify the shared variable.

- Exit Section: Exit section allows the other processes that are waiting in the Entry Section, to enter into the Critical Sections. It also checks that a process that finished its execution should be removed through this Section.

- Remainder Section: All other parts of the Code, which is not in Critical, Entry, and Exit Section, are known as the Remainder Section.

Critical Section Problem

A critical section is a segment of code which can be accessed by a signal process at a specific point of time. The section consists of shared data resources that required to be accessed by other processes.

- The entry to the critical section is handled by the wait() function, and it is represented as P().

- The exit from a critical section is controlled by the signal() function, represented as V().

In the critical section, only a single process can be executed. Other processes, waiting to execute their critical section, need to wait until the current process completes its execution.

Rules for Critical Section

The critical section need to must enforce all three rules:

- Mutual Exclusion: Mutual Exclusion is a special type of binary semaphore which is used for controlling access to the shared resource. It includes a priority inheritance mechanism to avoid extended priority inversion problems. Not more than one process can execute in its critical section at one time.

- Progress: This solution is used when no one is in the critical section, and someone wants in. Then those processes not in their reminder section should decide who should go in, in a finite time.

- Bound Waiting: When a process makes a request for getting into critical section, there is a specific limit about number of processes can get into their critical section. So, when the limit is reached, the system must allow request to the process to get into its critical section.

Solutions to the Critical Section

In Process Synchronization, critical section plays the main role so that the problem must be solved. Here are some widely used methods to solve the critical section problem.

Peterson Solution

Peterson's solution is widely used solution to critical section problems. This algorithm was developed by a computer scientist Peterson that's why it is named as a Peterson's solution. In this solution, when a process is executing in a critical state, then the other process only executes the rest of the code, and the opposite can happen. This method also helps to make sure that only a single process runs in the critical section at a specific time.

Example

```
PROCESS Pi
FLAG[i] = true
while( (turn != i) AND (CS is !free) ){ wait;
}
CRITICAL SECTION FLAG[i] = false
turn = j; //choose another process to go to CS
```

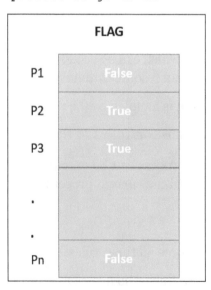

- Assume there are N processes (P1, P2,... PN) and every process at some point of time requires to enter the Critical Section.

- A FLAG[] array of size N is maintained which is by default false. So, whenever a process requires to enter the critical section, it has to set its flag as true. For example, If Pi wants to enter it will set FLAG[i]=TRUE.

- Another variable called TURN indicates the process number which is currently wating to enter into the CS.

- The process which enters into the critical section while exiting would change the TURN to another number from the list of ready processes.

- Example: turn is 2 then P2 enters the Critical section and while exiting turn=3 and therefore P3 breaks out of wait loop.

Synchronization Hardware

Sometimes the problems of the Critical Section are also resolved by hardware. Some operating system offers a lock functionality where a Process acquires a lock when entering the Critical section and releases the lock after leaving it. So when another process is trying to enter the critical section, it will not be able to enter as it is locked. It can only do so if it is free by acquiring the lock itself.

Mutex Locks

Synchronization hardware not simple method to implement for everyone, so strict software method known as Mutex Locks was also introduced. In this approach, in the entry section of code, a LOCK is obtained over the critical resources used inside the critical section. In the exit section that lock is released.

Semaphore Solution

Semaphore is simply a variable that is non-negative and shared between threads. It is another algorithm or solution to the critical section problem. It is a signaling mechanism and a thread that is waiting on a semaphore, which can be signaled by another thread. It uses two atomic operations:

- Wait,

- Signal for the process synchronization.

Example

```
WAIT ( S ):
while ( S <= 0 );
S = S - 1;
SIGNAL ( S ):
S = S + 1;
```

Semaphore

A semaphore is a synchronization tool that does not require busy waiting. The semaphore is an integer variable. The semaphore, being an integer variable, is assigned an initial value. The initial value denotes the number of processes that can simultaneously access the shared resource guarded by the semaphore. For example, if the shared resource can be accessed by only one process, then the initial value is set to 1. The semaphore can be accessed only via two atomic operations, namely, wait (P operation) and signal (V operation).

The definition of the wait operation is given below:

```
wait (S):

  while S≤ 0 do no-op;

  S--;
```

Here S is the semaphore. Any process that wants to enter its critical section should first perform the wait operation on the semaphore. The wait operation works as follows: If the value of the semaphore is less than or equal to zero, the process waits in the while loop. If the value of the semaphore is greater than zero, then the process comes out of the while loop and the value of the semaphore is decremented. Any process that comes out of its critical section should perform the signal operation on the semaphore.

The definition of the signal operation is given below:

```
signal (S):

        S++;
```

In the signal operation, the value of the semaphore is incremented. The wait and signal operations are atomic or indivisible. Indivisibility of the wait and signal operations is ensured by the programming language or the operating system that implements it. It ensures that race conditions cannot arise over a semaphore. We can use semaphores to deal with the n-process critical-section problem. Here we explain how a semaphore can be used to solve the critical-section problem.

Critical Section of n Processes

```
semaphore mutex; //initially mutex = 1
The algorithm for process Pi is given below:
do {
    wait (mutex);
          critical section
    signal (mutex);
          remainder section
    } while (1);
```

A semaphore called 'mutex' is used here for guarding a shared resource. The initial value of 'mutex' is set to one. This means that only one process can use the shared resource at a particular time. Process Pi, before entering its critical section, waits on the semaphore mutex. Process Pi, after coming out of its critical section, signals the semaphore 'mutex'. Let us now see a sequence of execution of two processes P_0 and P_1 wanting to enter their respective critical sections.

P_0	mutex	P_1
	1	
wait operation	0	
Process enters critical		wait operation
section		
signal operation	1	Process waits
	0	Process enters critical section signal operation
	1	

Initially, process P_0 wants to enter its critical section. P_0 executes the wait operation on the semaphore mutex. Since the value of mutex is 1, the wait operation decrements the value of mutex. The value of mutex becomes 0. P_0 enters its critical section. In the meantime, if process P_1 wants to enter its critical section, it executes the wait operation. Since the value of mutex is 0, process P_1 continues to wait in the while loop while $S \leq 0$ do no-op. When process P_0 comes out of its critical section, it executes the signal operation on the semaphore mutex. This signal operation increments the value of mutex. The value of mutex now becomes 1. Process P_1, which is checking the value of mutex in the while loop, now comes out of the while loop, decrements the value of mutex to 0 and enters its critical section.

The implementation of the wait and signal operations on a semaphore that we have seen now has a disadvantage – busy waiting. That is, when one process is in its critical section, any other process trying to enter its critical section, continuously checks the value of semaphore in the wait operation. Whenever the process waiting to enter its critical section gets the CPU, it executes while $S \leq 0$ do no-op. That is, the process just keeps on checking if $S \leq 0$. The value of S is not going to change until this process relinquishes the CPU and some other process changes it. This busy waiting wastes CPU cycles in multi-programmed systems with single CPU. Such a semaphore is called a spinlock.

Let us look at an example to understand spinlock. Let the initial value of semaphore S be 1. Assume that one process acquired a resource after executing a wait on the semaphore S and is continuing to use the resource. Let there be 2 other processes waiting to access the shared resource. Let round robin scheduling be the CPU scheduling algorithm. When the second process gets its CPU time slice, it will execute the while loop continuously in wait till its CPU time slice gets over. During this CPU time slice, the CPU time is used without doing any useful work. After this time slice, the third process gets its time slice. The third process also uses its entire time slice by just checking in the while loop of wait. The CPU's time is not used for any useful work. Thus it is seen that spinlock wastes CPU time.

Spinlock is useful in multiprocessor systems. The advantage of spinlock is that no context switch is required when a process must wait on a lock. This is useful when locks are for short times. To overcome this busy waiting, the definitions of the wait and signal operations of the semaphore are modified. The semaphore is implemented as a structure or a record, rather than as just a variable. The structure has two members, an integer value and a list of processes associated with the semaphore.

The semaphore is defined as follows:

```
typedef struct {
      int value;
      struct process *L;
} semaphore;
```

Two operations are defined on processes associated with the semaphore, the block and the wakeup operations. The block operation suspends the process that invokes it. The wakeup(P) operation resumes the execution of a blocked process P. The wait and signal operations on a semaphore are now defined as:

```
wait(S):
      S.value--;
      if (S.value < 0)
      {
            add this process to S.L;
            block;
      }
```

Here S is the semaphore structure. It has an integer value (S.value) and a list of processes (S.L) associated with it. In the wait operation, the value of the semaphore is first decremented (S.value--;). Then the value of the semaphore is checked. If the value of the semaphore is less than zero, it means that the resource is not available. Therefore, the process that is executing wait is added to the list associated with the semaphore and is blocked (i.e., put to the waiting state). Here the process does not keep on checking the value of the semaphore. Once the resource becomes available, this process is moved out of the waiting state and the process accesses the shared resource.

```
signal(S):
      S.value++;
      if (S.value <= 0)
      {
            remove a process P from S.L;
            wakeup(P);
      }
```

In the signal operation, the value of the semaphore is incremented. This means that one more process can access the resource. Then the value of the semaphore is checked. If the value of the semaphore is less than or equal to zero, one of the waiting processes is woken up. The process that is woken up is moved to the ready state and can access the resource.

The value of the semaphore is less than or equal to zero only if there are other processes waiting in the list associated with this semaphore. (The value had become less than zero when other processes had decremented the value of the semaphore earlier while executing wait).

Semaphore as a General Synchronization Tool

Here we see how the semaphore can be used as a synchronization tool. There are two processes P_i

and P_j that want to access a common resource. Let flag be the semaphore that guards the shared resource. The shared resource can be used by only one process at a time. Therefore, the value of the semaphore flag is initialized to 1.

P_i	Semaphore	P_j
wait(flag) access resource	flag=1 flag = 0	wait(flag)
signal(flag)	flag = -1 flag = 0	access resource signal(flag)
	flag = 1	

Process Pi executes the wait operation on the semaphore. The wait operation decrements the value of the semaphore flag, flag becomes zero. Since the value of flag is not less than zero, Pi can access the resource. In the meantime, if Pj wants to access the resource, Pj executes the wait operation on the semaphore flag, flag is decremented and becomes -1. Since the value of flag is < 0, Pj is added to the list associated with the semaphore and is put to the waiting state.

When process Pi completes the usage of the resource, it executes the signal operation on flag. The value of flag is incremented and becomes 0. Process Pj is woken up from the sleeping state. Process Pj now can access the resource. After Pj completes using the resource, Pj executes the signal operation and the value of flag is incremented back to 1. In this way, a semaphore can be used for safeguarding resources.

Deadlock and Starvation

When semaphores are used for synchronization, it is possible to have deadlocks and starvation. Deadlock is a situation where two or more processes are waiting indefinitely for an event that can be caused by only one of the waiting processes. For example, when two or more processes are waiting for the release of some resource that is held by another waiting process, it is a deadlock. Every process in a set of processes will be waiting for an event caused by one of the processes in the set. Starvation means indefinite blocking. A process may never be removed from the semaphore queue in which it is suspended and it starves.

Let us now see how deadlocks and starvation can happen with semaphores. Let S and Q be two semaphores initialized to 1. That is, semaphore S is safeguarding a resource that can be accessed by only one process at a time. Similarly, semaphore Q is also safeguarding another resource that can be accessed by only one process at a time.

P_0	P_1
wait(S);	wait(Q);
wait(Q);	wait(S);
⋮ ⋮	
signal(S);	signal(Q);
signal(Q)	signal(S);

Consider two processes P_0 and P_1. Po executes wait(S) and at the same time, P_1 executes wait(Q).

The values of the semaphores S and Q become 0. P_0 then executes wait(Q) and waits till semaphore Q is signaled. P_1 then executes wait(S) and waits till the semaphore S is signaled. Here, we see that process P_0 is waiting for a resource held by P_1 and process P_1 is held by a resource held by P_0. Each of the two processes is waiting for a resource held by the other process. Therefore, both are unable to proceed. Both the processes wait indefinitely. Both the processes are caught in a deadlock and are starving.

Therefore, the order in which wait and signal are used in processes should be selected carefully. Else, it may result in deadlocks and starvation also. Starvation is indefinite blocking. Starvation can also happen when processes that are added to the semaphore queue are removed in a last in first out manner. That is, whenever processes wait for a resource guarded by a semaphore, the processes are added to the queue associated with the semaphore. When more processes wait for the same resource, all these processes are also added to the end of the semaphore's queue. While removing processes from the queue, if the processes are removed from the end, the processes that were added first will starve.

Types of Semaphores

There are two types of semaphores—counting semaphores and binary semaphores. A counting semaphore takes an integer value that can range over an unrestricted domain. The semaphores that we discussed are counting semaphores. They are called counting semaphores because the value of the semaphores can be any integer value. A binary semaphore takes an integer value that can range only between 0 and 1. Hence, a binary semaphore can be simpler to implement than counting semaphores. If we have the implementation of binary semaphores, we can implement counting semaphores using the implementation of binary semaphores.

We now see how a counting semaphore S can be implemented using binary semaphores. S1 and S2 are the binary semaphores using which the counting semaphore S is implemented. C is an ordinary variable and the initial value of C is set to the initial value of the counting semaphore S. The initial value of the counting semaphore S indicates the number of processes that can access the resource guarded by the semaphore S at the same time.

Data structures:

```
binary-semaphore S1, S2;

int C;
```

S1 and S2 are two binary semaphores and C is an integer variable.

Initialization:

```
S1 = 1

S2 = 0

C = initial value of semaphore S
```

C is assigned the initial value of the counting semaphore S. The initial values of S1 and S2 are assigned 1 and 0 respectively.

Wait and signal operations for binary semaphore: If S1 is a binary semaphore then the wait operation on the binary semaphore is given below:

```
wait(S1)
{
        while(S1==0);
        S1--;
}
```

If the value of the binary semaphore is zero, the process that executes the wait operation, waits in the while loop. If the value is not equal to zero, the process comes out of the while loop and decrements the value of the semaphore.

```
signal(S1)
{
        S1++;
}
```

In the signal operation, the value of the binary semaphore is incremented. The wait and signal operations of the counting semaphore are given below:

Wait operation: The wait operation on the counting semaphore can be implemented using wait and signal operations on the binary semaphore as given below:

```
wait(S1);
C--;
if (C < 0) {
        signal(S1);
        wait(S2);
}
signal(S1);
```

The initial value of S1 is 1. Therefore the wait operation on S1 finds that the value of S1 is not zero and decrements the value of S1. Next, the value of C is decremented. The initial value of C is equal to the value of the counting semaphore S. If the value of C becomes less than zero, then the process executing wait cannot proceed to execute its critical section. It has to wait. Therefore, the process signals S1 semaphore; the value of S1 becomes 1. Then, it waits on semaphore S2. Since the initial value of S2 is 0, the process waits on S2. If the value of C is not less than 0, it means that the process can enter its critical section. In this case, the process signals S1 and proceeds to enter its critical section. Here, we can see that the semaphore S1 guards the decrement of the variable C. The process waits on S1 before decrementing C and signals S1 after decrementing C. Semaphore S2 guards the shared resource.

Signal operation: The signal operation on S is also implemented using wait and signal operations on S1 and S2. The implementation of signal(S) is given below:

```
wait(S1);
C ++;
if (C <= 0)
        signal(S2);
else
        signal(S1);
```

The executing process first waits on S1. If no other process is currently incrementing or decrementing C, the value of S1 will be 1. wait(S1) decrements the value of S1 to 0. Then, C is incremented. If the value of C becomes less than or equal to zero, then it means that there is(are) other process(es) waiting to use the shared resource. In that case, signal(S2) is executed. S2 is the semaphore that guards the shared resource. When signal(S2) is executed, another process waiting on S2 will come out of waiting, signal S1 (this is the signal(S1) in the wait operation) and proceed to use the shared resource. If C > 0, signal(S1) (in the signal operation) is executed.

Let us see with an example, how a counting semaphore is implemented using binary semaphores. Let C = 2 (initial value of semaphore S). Since the value of semaphore S is 2, two processes can use the shared resource at the same time. Let us see what happens when three processes want to use the shared resource at the same time.

When wait(S) is executed by the first process, say P_0.

wait(S) by P_0:

S1	C	S2
1		0
0		
	0	
1		

Initially, S1 is 0, C is 2 and S2 is 0. wait (S1) decrements the value of S1 to 0.Then C is decremented from 2 to 1. signal (S1) increments the value of S1 back to 1. P_0 gets access to the shared resource. In the meantime, suppose process P_1 wants to access the shared resource. The sequence is shown below:

wait(S) by P_1:

S1	C	S2
1	0	0
0		
	-1	
1		Process P_2 waits on S2

wait(S1) decrements the value of S1 from 1 to 0.Then C is decremented from 0 to -1. Since the value of C goes below 0, process P_2 executes wait(S2). P_2 does not get access to the shared resource. Since the initial value of the semaphore S was 2, only two processes are able to access the shared resource. The other processes wait.

Let P_0 complete the usage of the shared resource. P_0 executes signal(S). The changes in the semaphores' values are shown below:

When signal(S) is executed by P_0:

S1	C	S2
1	-1	0
0	0	1
Released process P2 signals S1 1		Process P_2 waiting on S2 is released

wait(S1) in the signal operation decrements the value of S1 from 1 to 0.Then C is incremented from −1 to 0. Since the value of C becomes 0, signal(S2) is executed. Process P_2 waiting on S2 is released. Process P_2 signals S1 (signal(S1) in the wait operation) and gains access to the shared resource.

When signal(S) is executed by P_1:

S1	C	S2
1	0	
0	1	
1		

wait(S1) in the signal operation decrements the value of S1 from 1 to 0. Then C is incremented from 0 to 1. Since the value of C becomes greater than 0, signal(S1) is executed. The value of S1 is changed from 0 to 1. Thus, we see that a counting semaphore can be implemented using binary semaphores.

Deadlock

Any system has many processes and a number of different resources. In such a system, processes request for resources, use them and then release them. If a process requests for resources and the resources are not available, the process waits. If the requested resources are held by other waiting processes, the requesting process continues to wait forever. This situation is called a deadlock.

Bridge Crossing Example

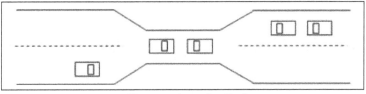

Bridge crossing - deadlock

Vehicles can cross the bridge only in one direction at a particular time. If two vehicles that are moving in opposite directions try to cross the bridge at the same time, both get into a deadlocked situation. The deadlock can be resolved only if one vehicle backs up. To back up one vehicle, several other vehicles may also have to be backed up if a deadlock occurs.

Deadlock Problem in a System

A situation similar to that of crossing a bridge can happen in a system as well. Suppose there is a set of blocked processes, each holding a resource and waiting to acquire a resource held by another process in the set. All the processes will be waiting for each other to release resources. Then, the system will be in a deadlocked state.

Consider the following example: A system has 2 tape drives. There are two processes P_1 and P_2. Each process holds one tape drive and needs another one. Since there are only two tape drives in the system, each of the two processes is waiting for the tape drive held by the other waiting process. Now, both the processes are unable to proceed and are deadlocked.

Let us see another example. There are two semaphores, A and B, initialized to 1. Since the initial value is 1, each of the semaphores A and B is guarding resources that can be accessed only by one process at a time. Let P_0 and P_1 be two processes that are executing the following sequence of statements respectively.

P_0	P_1
wait (A);	wait(B);
wait (B);	wait(A);

Suppose P_0 executes wait(A) first. This operation decrements the value of semaphore A from 1 to 0. Suppose there is a context switch and P_1 executes wait(B). This will decrement the value of semaphore B from 1 to 0. Next, P_1 continues to execute wait(A). Since the value of semaphore A is 0, process P_1 waits. There is a context switch now and process P_0 executes wait(B). Since the value of semaphore B is 0, process P_0 waits. Here, we see that process P_0 is waiting for semaphore B held by process P_1 and process P_1 is waiting for semaphore A held by process P_0. Thus, both the processes are in a deadlocked state.

System Model

Any system has a finite number of resources, distributed among a number of competing processes. The resources are categorized into several resource types R_1, R_2,..., R_m. The resource types in a system may be CPU cycles, memory space, I/O devices and so on. Each resource type Ri has Wi instances. For example, if there are 5 printers, then there are 5 instances of the resource type printer.

Each process utilizes resources as follows: Each process requests for resources, uses the resources and releases the resources after using the resources. A process may request as many resources as it requires carrying out its designated task. The number of resources requested by the process cannot exceed the total number of resources available in the system. That is, if there are five printers, the process cannot request for six.

There are system calls available for the request and release of resources like the request and release device, open and close file, allocate and free memory. Request and release of resources can be accomplished through the wait and the signal operations on semaphores.

A table is maintained in the system that records whether each resource is free or allocated. If a resource is allocated, information is maintained as to which process the resource is allocated. If a process requests a resource currently allocated to another process, the process is added to a queue of processes waiting for that resource.

Deadlock Characterization

In a deadlocked system, processes never finish executing and system resources are tied up, preventing other jobs from starting. We shall now understand the features that characterize deadlocks.

Dead-lock Conditions

The following are the four important deadlock conditions to occur if all the conditions occur simultaneously there are certain chances for the deadlock to occur.

Mutual Exclusion

It means whatever resource we are using it must be used in a mutually exclusive way. Where only one processes use one resource at a time only. For example, the printing process is going on and all sudden another process tries to interrupt the printing process. So here in mutual exclusion situation, only after the printing task is completed then only the next task is processed. Mutual exclusion can be eliminated by sharing resources simultaneously, which is not possible practically.

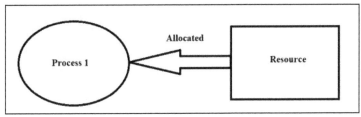

Mutual-exclusion

No Pre-emption

According to pre-emptive based algorithms, if there is a priority task trying to interrupt the current task. The pre-emptive algorithm it holds the current task and firstly executes priority task and get backs to its first task. A situation explained as per the above example where a process holds the resource as long as it gets executed, that is P_1 can release R_1 only after executing, similarly P_2 release R_2 only after execution. If there is no pre-emption the deadlock may occur.

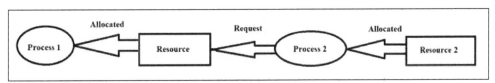

No-reemption-example

Hold and Wait

A process is holding some resources and is waiting for additional resources but those resources are acquired by some other process. From the above example, P_1 is holding R_1 and waiting for R_2, where R_2 is acquired by P_2, and P_2 is holding R_2 and waiting for R_1, where R_1 is acquired by P_1 is a hold and wait situation deadlock may occur in the system.

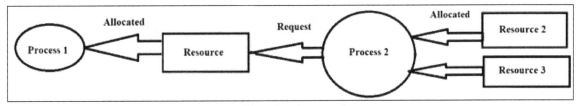

Hold-and-wait-example.

Circular Wait

A set of processes are said to be in deadlock if one process is waiting for a resource that is allocated to another process and that process is waiting for a resource, it is similar to the above-explained example where it is in loop form. Where P_1 is waiting for R_2 and R_2 is allocated for P_2 and P_2 is waiting for R_1 and R_1 allocated for P_1 which is a circular wait form if this condition satisfies deadlock occurs.

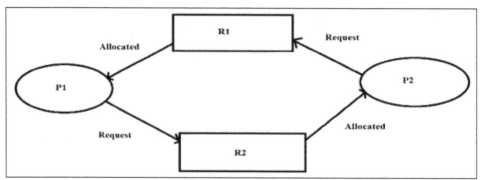

Circular-wait-example.

Resource-allocation Graph

Any system can be described by means of a directed graph called a system resource-allocation graph. The graph consists of a set of vertices V and a set of edges E. The set of vertices V is partitioned into two types, $P = \{P_1, P_2, ..., P_n\}$, the set consisting of all the processes in the system and $R = \{R_1, R_2, ..., R_m\}$, the set consisting of all the resource types in the system. A directed edge from P_i to R_j is denoted as $P_i \rightarrow R_j$ and is called a request edge. A directed edge from R_j to Pi is denoted as $R_j \rightarrow P_i$ and is called an assignment edge.

Pictorially, a process is denoted using a circle as shown below:

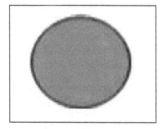

A resource type is denoted using a square. The instances of a resource type are shown using dots inside the square. A resource type with 4 instances is denoted pictorially as shown below:

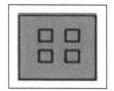

When P_i requests an instance of R_j, it is denoted as an edge from P_i to R_j in the resource-allocation graph.

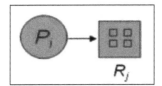

When P_i is holding an instance of R_j it is shown as an edge from a dot in Rj to Pi in the resource-allocation graph.

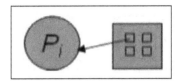

Figure shows an example of a resource-allocation graph. P_1, P_2 and P_3 are the three processes in the system. There are four resource types, R_1, R_2, R_3 and R_4. There is one instance of R_1, two instances of R_2, one instance of R_3 and three instances of R_4. P_1 is holding one instance of R_2 and is requesting for one instance of R_1. P_2 is holding one instance of R_1 and one instance of R_2 and is requesting for one instance of R_3. P_3 is holding one instance of R_3. P_3 is holding one instance of R_3.

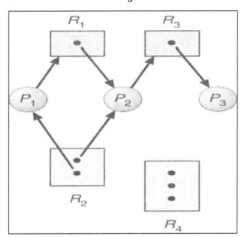

Resource-allocation graph.

Deadlocks can be detected from a resource-allocation graph. If the resource-allocation graph contains no cycles, no process is deadlocked. If the resource-allocation graph contains cycles, deadlocks may exist. If there is only one instance of each resource type and there is a cycle in the graph, there is a deadlock in the system.

Resource-allocation Graph with a Deadlock

Figure shows a resource-allocation graph with a deadlock. In this figure, process P_1 is waiting for an instance of resource type R_1. There is only one instance of R_1 which is held by process P_2. P_2 is waiting for an instance of resource R_3. There is only one instance of R_3, which is held by process P_3. Process P_3 is waiting for an instance of R_2. There are two instances of R_2, each of which is held by P_1 and P_2 respectively. Thus, P_1, P_2 and P_3 are waiting for resources held by other waiting processes.

It is seen that there is a cycle $P_1 \rightarrow R_1 \rightarrow P_2 \rightarrow R_3 \rightarrow P_3 \rightarrow R_2 \rightarrow P_1$. All the processes that are part of the cycle are waiting and there is no free instance of resource. Therefore, all the processes in the cycle are deadlocked. None of the processes is able to proceed further.

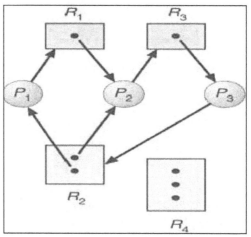

Resource-allocation graph with a deadlock.

Resource-allocation Graph with a Cycle but No Deadlock

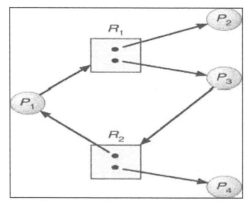

Resource allocation graph with a cycle but no deadlock.

It is always not necessary to have a deadlock if there is a cycle. We now look at an example scenario where there is a cycle in the resource-allocation graph, but there is no deadlock. Figure shows a resource-allocation graph with a cycle $P_1 \rightarrow R_1 \rightarrow P_3 \rightarrow R_2 \rightarrow P_1$. But, in this scenario, an instance of R_1 is held by process P_2, which is not a waiting process. Once P_2 finishes using the resource, it will release the resource. R_1 will now be available for process P_3. Similarly, an instance of R_2 is held by process P_4 and P_4 is not waiting for any other resource. Therefore, P_4 releases the resource R_2 after using the resource. Now, R_2 is available for process P_1.

Thus, from the examples given above, it is seen that:

- If a resource-allocation graph contains no cycles $\Rightarrow$ no deadlock.

- If a resource-allocation graph contains a cycle $\Rightarrow$ if there is only one instance per resource type, then there is deadlock.

- If there are several instances per resource type and there is a cycle in the resource-allocation graph, there is a possibility of deadlock.

Methods for Handling Deadlock

We can deal with the deadlock problem in one of three ways:

- We can use a protocol to prevent or avoid deadlocks, ensuring that the system will never enter a deadlock state.

- We can allow the system to enter a deadlock state, detect it, and recover.

- We can ignore the problem altogether, and pretend that deadlocks never occur in the system.

To ensure that deadlocks never occur in a system, deadlock prevention or deadlock avoidance scheme can be used. Deadlock prevention is a set of methods for ensuring that at least one of the necessary conditions (Mutual exclusion, Hold and wait, No preemption, Circular wait) does not hold. These methods prevent deadlocks by constraining how requests for resources can be made.

Deadlock avoidance requires that the operating system should be given additional information about which resources a process will request and use during its life time. With this information, whenever a request for a resource comes from a process, the system can decide whether the request can be granted immediately or not. The system simulates and finds out if the system will go to a deadlocked state if the request is granted. Based on that, the system decides if the request can be granted or not.

If there is no mechanism employed in the system for deadlock prevention and avoidance, then deadlocks can occur. In this case, the system must employ algorithms for deadlock detection and recovery.

If the system does not employ algorithms even for deadlock detection and recovery, that is, if the problem is ignored altogether, then the system may be in a deadlock state and may not recognize what has happened. In this case, the system performance deteriorates and the system should be restarted manually. Although this method does not seem to be a viable approach, it is used in some operating systems.

Deadlock Prevention and Avoidance

Deadlocks can be prevented by preventing at least one of the four required conditions:

- Mutual Exclusion: Shared resources such as read-only files do not lead to deadlocks. Unfortunately some resources, such as printers and tape drives, require exclusive access by a single process.

- Hold and Wait: To prevent this condition processes must be prevented from holding one or more resources while simultaneously waiting for one or more others. There are several possibilities for this:

  - Require that all processes request all resources at one time. This can be wasteful of system resources if a process needs one resource early in its execution and doesn't need some other resource until much later.

  - Require that processes holding resources must release them before requesting new resources, and then re-acquire the released resources along with the new ones in a single new request. This can be a problem if a process has partially completed an operation using a resource and then fails to get it re-allocated after releasing it.

- ◦ Either of the methods can lead to starvation if a process requires one or more popular resources.

- No Preemption: Preemption of process resource allocations can prevent this condition of deadlocks, when it is possible.

  - ◦ One approach is that if a process is forced to wait when requesting a new resource, then all other resources previously held by this process are implicitly released, (pre-empted), forcing this process to re-acquire the old resources along with the new resources in a single request.

  - ◦ Another approach is that when a resource is requested and not available, then the system looks to see what other processes currently have those resources and are themselves blocked waiting for some other resource. If such a process is found, then some of their resources may get pre-empted and added to the list of resources for which the process is waiting.

  - ◦ Either of these approaches may be applicable for resources whose states are easily saved and restored, such as registers and memory, but are generally not applicable to other devices such as printers and tape drives.

- Circular Wait: One way to avoid circular wait is to number all resources, and to require that processes request resources only in strictly increasing (or decreasing) order. In other words, in order to request resource Rj, a process must first release all Ri such that i >= j. One big challenge in this scheme is determining the relative ordering of the different resources

Deadlock Avoidance

- The general idea behind deadlock avoidance is to prevent deadlocks from ever happening, by preventing at least one of the aforementioned conditions.

- This requires more information about each process, AND tends to lead to low device utilization. I.e. it is a conservative approach.

- In some algorithms the scheduler only needs to know the maximum number of each resource that a process might potentially use. In more complex algorithms the scheduler can also take advantage of the schedule of exactly what resources may be needed in what order.

- When a scheduler sees that starting a process or granting resource requests may lead to future deadlocks, then that process is just not started or the request is not granted.

- A resource allocation state is defined by the number of available and allocated resources, and the maximum requirements of all processes in the system.

Safe State

- A state is safe if the system can allocate all resources requested by all processes up to their stated maximums without entering a deadlock state.

- More formally, a state is safe if there exists a safe sequence of processes { P_0, P_1, P_2,..., P_N } such that all of the resource requests for P_i can be granted using the resources currently allocated to P_i and all processes P_j where j < i. I.e. if all the processes prior to P_i finish and free up their resources, then P_i will be able to finish also, using the resources that they have freed up.

- If a safe sequence does not exist, then the system is in an unsafe state, which MAY lead to deadlock. All safe states are deadlock free, but not all unsafe states lead to deadlocks.

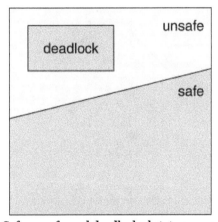

Safe, unsafe, and deadlocked state spaces.

- For example, consider a system with 12 tape drives, allocated as follows. Is this a safe state? What is the safe sequence?

	Maximum Needs	Current Allocation
P_0	10	5
P_1	4	2
P_2	9	2

- What happens if process P_2 requests and is granted one more tape drive?

- Key to the safe state approach is that when a request is made for resources, the request is granted only if the resulting allocation state is a safe one.

Resource-allocation Graph Algorithm

- If resource categories have only single instances of their resources, then deadlock states can be detected by cycles in the resource-allocation graphs.

- In this case, unsafe states can be recognized and avoided by augmenting the resource-allocation graph with claim edges, noted by dashed lines, which point from a process to a resource that it may request in the future.

- In order for this technique to work, all claim edges must be added to the graph for any particular process before that process is allowed to request any resources. Alternatively, processes may only make requests for resources for which they have already established claim edges, and claim edges cannot be added to any process that is currently holding resources.

- When a process makes a request, the claim edge P_i->R_j is converted to a request edge. Similarly when a resource is released, the assignment reverts back to a claim edge.

- This approach works by denying requests that would produce cycles in the resource-allocation graph, taking claim edges into effect.

- Consider for example what happens when process P_2 requests resource R_2:

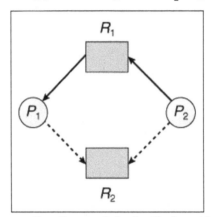

Resource allocation graph for deadlock avoidance.

- The resulting resource-allocation graph would have a cycle in it, and so the request cannot be granted.

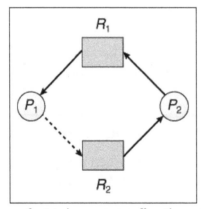

An unsafe state in a resource allocation graph.

Banker's Algorithm

- For resource categories that contain more than one instance the resource-allocation graph method does not work, and more complex and less efficient methods must be chosen.

- The Banker's Algorithm gets its name because it is a method that bankers could use to assure that when they lend out resources they will still be able to satisfy all their clients. A banker won't loan out a little money to start building a house unless they are assured that they will later be able to loan out the rest of the money to finish the house.

- When a process starts up, it must state in advance the maximum allocation of resources it may request, up to the amount available on the system.

- When a request is made, the scheduler determines whether granting the request would leave the system in a safe state. If not, then the process must wait until the request can be granted safely.

- The banker's algorithm relies on several key data structures: where n is the number of processes and m is the number of resource categories.

   ○ Available[m] indicates how many resources are currently available of each type.

   ○ Max[n][m] indicates the maximum demand of each process of each resource.

   ○ Allocation[n] m] indicates the number of each resource category allocated to each process.

   ○ Need[n] [m] indicate the remaining resources needed of each type for each process. (Note that Need[i][j] = Max[i][j] - Allocation[i][j] for all i, j.)

- For simplification of discussions, we make the following notations / observations:

   ○ One row of the Need vector, Need[i], can be treated as a vector corresponding to the needs of process i, and similarly for Allocation and Max.

   ○ A vector X is considered to be <= a vector Y if X[i] <= Y[i] for all i.

Resource-request Algorithm (The Bankers Algorithm)

- Now that we have a tool for determining if a particular state is safe or not, we are now ready to look at the Banker's algorithm itself.

- This algorithm determines if a new request is safe, and grants it only if it is safe to do so.

- When a request is made that does not exceed currently available resources pretend it has been granted, and then see if the resulting state is a safe one. If so, grant the request, and if not, deny the request, as follows:

   ○ Let Request[n][m] indicate the number of resources of each type currently requested by processes. If Request[i] > Need[i] for any process i, raise an error condition.

   ○ If Request[i] > Available for any process i, then that process must wait for resources to become available. Otherwise the process can continue to step 3.

   ○ Check to see if the request can be granted safely, by pretending it has been granted and then seeing if the resulting state is safe. If so, grant the request, and if not, then the process must wait until its request can be granted safely. The procedure for granting a request or pretending to for testing purposes is:

      ▪ Available = Available - Request

      ▪ Allocation = Allocation + Request

      ▪ Need = Need - Request

An Illustrative Example

- Consider the following situation:

	Allocation A B C	Max A B C	Available A B C	Need A B C
P_0	0 1 0	7 5 3	3 3 2	7 4 3
P_1	2 0 0	3 2 2		1 2 2
P_2	3 0 2	9 0 2		6 0 0
P_3	2 1 1	2 2 2		0 1 1
P_4	0 0 2	4 3 3		4 3 1

- If process P_1 requests 1 instance of A and 2 instances of C. (Request[1] = (1, 0, 2)):

	Allocation A B C	Need A B C	Available A B C
P_0	0 1 0	7 4 3	2 3 0
P_1	3 0 2	0 2 0	
P_2	3 0 2	6 0 0	
P_3	2 1 1	0 1 1	
P_4	0 0 2	4 3 1	

Deadlock Detection

If there is no deadlock prevention or deadlock avoidance algorithm running in the system, dead-lock situation may occur. In this case, it is necessary to detect deadlocks and recover from them. Two methods are explained to detect deadlocks. The first method detects deadlocks when there is only one instance of each resource type. This method uses a variant of the resource-allocation graph. The second method detects deadlocks even when there are multiple instances of each resource type. The second method uses a variant of the banker's algorithm.

Deadlock Detection – Single Instance of Each Resource Type

The system maintains a wait-for graph for detecting deadlocks. The wait-for graph is a variant of the resource-allocation graph. In the wait-for graph, the nodes are processes. If there is an edge $P_i \rightarrow P_j$, then it means that process Pi is waiting for process P_j. The corresponding resource-allocation graph would have had edges $P_i \rightarrow R_q$ and $R_q \rightarrow P_j$ which means that P_i is waiting for resource R_q and R_q is held by resource P_j. In the wait-for graph, the resource node is removed and there is an edge from Pi → P_j. Figure shows a resource-allocation graph and the corresponding wait-for graph.

To detect deadlocks from the wait-for graph, it is required to periodically invoke an algorithm that searches for a cycle in the wait-for graph. If there is a cycle in the wait-for graph, then it means that there is a deadlock in the system. If there are no cycles, then it means that there is no deadlock in the system. In the wait-for graph shown in Figure there is a cycle $P_1 \rightarrow P_2 \rightarrow P_3 \rightarrow P_4 \rightarrow P_1$. Hence, the system is in a deadlocked state. An algorithm to detect a cycle in a graph requires an order of n^2 operations, where n is the number of vertices in the graph.

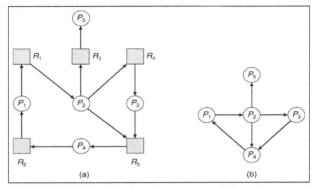

Resource-Allocation Graph and Corresponding wait-for graph.

The disadvantage of this method is that it is not suitable for a resource-allocation system with multiple instances of each resource type.

Deadlock Detection – Several Instances of a Resource Type

Here we learn a deadlock detection algorithm that will detect deadlocks when there are multiple instances of each resource type. Let n denote the number of processes and m denote the number of resource types present in the system.

Data Structures used in the Algorithm:

- Available: A vector of length m indicates the number of available resources of each type.

A	B	C
2	3	0

In the example shown above, there are three resource types A, B and C. The number of available instances of resource types A, B and C are 2, 3 and 0 respectively.

- Allocation: An n x m matrix defines the number of resources of each type currently allocated to each process. The n rows correspond to n processes and the m columns correspond to the m resource types.

	A	B	C
P_0	0	1	0
P_1	2	0	0
P_2	3	0	2
P_3	2	1	1

In the example shown above, there are three resource types A, B and C and four processes P_0, P_1, P_2 and P_3. The number of instances of each resource type currently allocated to each process is shown. Process P_0 is currently allocated 0 instances of resource type A, 1 instance of resource type B and 0 instances of resource type C. Similarly, the current allocation of the other processes P_1, P_2 and P_3 are also shown.

- Request: An n x m matrix indicates the current request of each process. If Request [i,j] = k, then process P_i is requesting k more instances of resource type R_j.

	A	B	C
P_0	7	5	3
P_1	3	2	2
P_2	9	0	2
P_3	2	2	2

In the example shown above, there are three resource types A, B and C and four processes P_0, P_1, P_2 and P_3. The number of instances of each resource type requested by each process is shown. Process P_0 is requesting 7 instances of resource type A, 5 instances of resource type B and 3 instances of resource type C. Similarly, the request of the other processes P_1, P_2 and P_3 are also shown.

Notations Used

If X and Y are vectors of length n,

- $X \leq Y$ iff $X[i] \leq Y[i]$ for all i = 1,2,...,n

That is, the Ith element of vector X is less than or equal to the Ith element of vector Y, for all i.

Consider the following vectors X and Y:

$X = (1,7,3,2), Y = (0,3,2,1)$

In the above example, $Y \leq X$ because each element of vector Y is less than or equal to the corresponding element of vector X. That is, the first element of Y is less than or equal to the first element of X and so on. Also, note that, $Y < X$, if $Y \leq X$ and $Y \neq X$ Each row in the matrices Allocation and Request are treated as vectors and referred to as $Allocation_i$ and $Request_i$ respectively.

Detection Algorithm

- Let Work and Finish be vectors of length m and n, respectively. Initialize:
  - Work = Available
  - For i = 1,2, ..., n, if $Allocation_i \neq 0$, then Finish[i] = false; otherwise,

    Finish[i] = true
- Find an index i such that both:
  - Finish[i] = false
  - $Request_i \leq Work$

    If no such i exists, go to step 4.
- Work = Work + $Allocation_i$
  - Finish[i] = true

go to step 2.

- If Finish[i] == false, for some i, $1 \le i \le n$, then the system is in deadlock state. Moreover, if Finish[i] == false, then P_i is deadlocked.

This algorithm requires an order of $O(m \times n^2)$ operations to detect whether the system is in deadlocked state. The working of this algorithm can be understood by an example.

Example of Detection Algorithm

Consider 5 processes P_0 through P_4; 3 resource types A, B and C. There are 7 instances of A, 2 instances of B and 6 instances of C.

The snapshot at time T_0 is given below:

	Allocation			Request			Available		
	A	B	C	A	B	C	A	B	C
P_0	0	1	0	0	0	0	0	0	0
P_1	2	0	0	2	0	2			
P_2	3	0	3	0	0	0			
P_3	2	1	1	1	0	0			
P_4	0	0	2	0	0	2			

We now simulate the algorithm for the above example.

Initially, Available = (0,0,0); Finish[i] = false for i = 0,1,2,3,4

i = 0

We check if Request$_0$ ≤ Available? Yes

Therefore, Work = Work + Allocation$_0$ = (0,0,0) + (0,1,0) = (0,1,0)

Finish[0] = true, P_0 added to safe sequence < P_0 >

	Allocation			Request			Available		
	A	B	C	A	B	C	A	B	C
P_0	0	1	0	0	0	0	0	0	0
P_1	2	0	0	2	0	2			
P_2	3	0	3	0	0	0			
P_3	2	1	1	1	0	0			
P_4	0	0	2	0	0	2			

Work = (0,1,0);

Is Request$_1$ ≤ Available? No

Since Request$_1$ is not less than Available, check the next process.

	Allocation			Request			Available		
	A	B	C	A	B	C	A	B	C
P_0	0	1	0	0	0	0	0	0	0
P_1	2	0	0	2	0	2			
P_2	3	0	3	0	0	0			
P_3	2	1	1	1	0	0			
P_4	0	0	2	0	0	2			

Work = (0,1,0);

Is $Request_2 \leq$ Available? Yes

Work = Work + $Allocation_2$ =(0,1,0) + (3,0,3) = (3,1,3)

Finish[2] = true, P_2 added to safe sequence < P_0, P_2>

	Allocation			Request			Available		
	A	B	C	A	B	C	A	B	C
P_0	0	1	0	0	0	0	0	0	0
P_1	2	0	0	2	0	2			
P_2	3	0	3	0	0	0			
P_3	2	1	1	1	0	0			
P_4	0	0	2	0	0	2			

Work = (3,1,3);

Is $Request_3 \leq$ Available? Yes

Work = Work + $Allocation_3$ =(3,1,3) + (2,1,1) = (5,2,4)

Finish[3] = true,

P_3 added to safe sequence and the safe sequence is now < P_0, P_2, P_3 >

	Allocation			Request			Available		
	A	B	C	A	B	C	A	B	C
P_0	0	1	0	0	0	0	0	0	0
P_1	2	0	0	2	0	2			
P_2	3	0	3	0	0	0			
P_3	2	1	1	1	0	0			
P_4	0	0	2	0	0	2			

Work = (5,2,4);

Is $Request_4 \leq$ Available? Yes

Work = Work + $Allocation_4$ =(5,2,4) + (0,0,2) = (5,2,6)

Finish[4] = true,

P_4 added to safe sequence and the safe sequence is $< P_0, P_2, P_3, P_4 >$

Now, we check again from the beginning all the other processes that were not added to the safe sequence.

	Allocation			Request			Available		
	A	B	C	A	B	C	A	B	C
P_0	0	1	0	0	0	0	0	0	0
P_1	2	0	0	2	0	2			
P_2	3	0	3	0	0	0			
P_3	2	1	1	1	0	0			
P_4	0	0	2	0	0	2			

Work = (5,2,6);

Is Request$_1$ ≤ Available? Yes

Work = Work + Allocation$_1$ =(5,2,6) + (2,0,0) = (7,2,6)

Finish[1] = true,

P_1 added to safe sequence and the safe sequence now is $< P_0, P_2, P_3, P_4, P_1 >$

	Allocation			Request			Available		
	A	B	C	A	B	C	A	B	C
P_0	0	1	0	0	0	0	0	0	0
P_1	2	0	0	2	0	2			
P_2	3	0	3	0	0	0			
P_3	2	1	1	1	0	0			
P_4	0	0	2	0	0	2			

Sequence $<P_0, P_2, P_3, P_4, P_1>$ now results in Finish[i] = true for all i.

There can be more than one safe sequence, that is there can be correct safe sequences other than$<P_0, P_2, P_3, P_4, P_1>$. We have found one safe sequence. Since there is at least one safe sequence, the system is in a safe state. There is no deadlock in the system.

Let process P_2 now make an additional request for an instance of resource type C. The Request matrix is changed as shown below, after including the request of an instance of resource type C by process P_2.

	Request		
	A	B	C
P_0	0	0	0
P_1	2	0	2
P_2	0	0	1
P_3	1	0	0
P_4	0	0	2

Now, let us check if the system will be in a safe state. The deadlock detection algorithm is run again.

	Allocation			Request			Available		
	A	B	C	A	B	C	A	B	C
P_0	0	1	0	0	0	0	0	0	0
P_1	2	0	0	2	0	2			
P_2	3	0	3	0	0	0			
P_3	2	1	1	1	0	0			
P_4	0	0	2	0	0	2			

Initially, Work = Available = (0,0,0); Finish[i] = false for i = 0,1,2,3,4

When i = 0,

Check if $Request_0$ ≤ Available? Yes

Work = Work + $Allocation_0$ =(0,0,0) + (0,1,0) = (0,1,0)

Finish[0] = true, P_0 is added to safe sequence < P_0>

	Allocation			Request			Available		
	A	B	C	A	B	C	A	B	C
P_0	0	1	0	0	0	0	0	0	0
P_1	2	0	0	2	0	2			
P_2	3	0	3	0	0	0			
P_3	2	1	1	1	0	0			
P_4	0	0	2	0	0	2			

Work is now (0,1,0);

Is $Request_1$ ≤ Available? No

Is $Request_2$ ≤ Available? No

Is $Request_3$ ≤ Available? No

Is $Request_4$ ≤ Available? No

Since the request of all the processes cannot be allocated, the system is not in a safe state. Though it possible to reclaim the resources held by process P_0, there are insufficient resources to fulfil other processes' requests. Thus, a deadlock exists, consisting of processes P_1, P_2, P_3, and P_4.

Deadlock Detection Algorithm Usage

When should we invoke the detection algorithm?

This depends on the answers to the following questions:

- How often is a deadlock likely to occur?
- How many processes will be affected by the deadlock when it happens? If deadlocks occur

frequently, then it is necessary to invoke the detection algorithm frequently. If detection is not done, the resources allocated to deadlocked processes will be idle. The number of processes involved in the deadlock cycle may also grow.

Deadlocks occur when a process makes a request that cannot be granted immediately. Therefore, the detection algorithm can be invoked every time a request for allocation cannot be granted immediately. During the detection process, not only the set of processes that are deadlocked are identified, but also the specific process that caused the deadlock is identified. If the cycle is completed by the most recent request, the process that requested the most recent request is identified as responsible for the deadlock. But invoking the deadlock detection algorithm each and every time a request is made results in considerable overhead in computation time.

Therefore, the other possibility is to invoke the detection algorithm at less frequent intervals. The detection algorithm may be invoked once per hour or when the CPU utilization falls below 40 percent. In this case there may be many cycles in the graph and it may not be possible to tell which process caused the deadlock.

Recovery from Deadlocks

Once deadlocks are detected, it is necessary to recover from deadlocks. There are different ways in which the system can recover from deadlocks. One method is to inform the operator that a deadlock has occurred. The operator deals with the deadlock manually. The second method is to let the system recover from the deadlock automatically. The third method is to break the deadlock. To break the deadlock, there are two ways. One is to abort one or more processes to break the circular wait (process termination). The second is to preempt some resources from one or more of the deadlocked processes (resource preemption).

Process Termination

Termination of processes can be done in two ways. One is to abort all the deadlocked processes. This method will break the deadlock, but the results of all partial computations done by the aborted processes must be discarded and recomputed later. The second way is to abort one process at a time until the deadlock cycle is eliminated. This method involves a lot of overhead, because, after each process is aborted, deadlock-detection algorithm must be invoked to check if the deadlock still exists.

When there are many processes involved in the deadlock, it is necessary to choose a process to terminate first. In which order should we choose a process to abort? There are many factors based on which the process to be aborted can be chosen:

- Priority of the process (process with the least priority is chosen).

- How long process has computed, and how much longer to completion (the process that has done the least computations is chosen).

- Resources the process has used (the process that has used less number of resources is chosen).

- Resources process needs to complete (the process that needs many resources is chosen).

- How many processes will need to be terminated.

- Is process interactive or batch? (batch processes are chosen to be terminated earlier than interactive processes).

Resource Preemption

To recover from deadlocks, resources can be preempted from the deadlocked processes. When resources are preempted, it is necessary to consider certain issues. The issues are discussed below:

- Selecting a victim: It is necessary to select the victim process from which the resources are to be preempted. The victim process has to be selected such that the cost is minimized. Cost factors may include the number of resources a deadlock process is holding and the amount of time a deadlocked process has thus far consumed during its execution.

- Rollback: If a resource is preempted from a process, what to do with the process? The process cannot continue, because it is missing some needed resource. Therefore, the process must be rolled back to some safe state and the process must be restarted from that state. But, the problem is that it is difficult to determine a safe state. Therefore a total rollback might have to be done or the process must be aborted and restarted again.

- Starvation: While selecting a process for preempting resources, the same process may always be picked as victim. In that case, that process may be starved of resources and may not be able to complete its work. To reduce starvation, the number of rollbacks may also be included in the cost factor.

Difference between Starvation and Deadlock

Here, are some important differences between Deadlock and starvation:

Deadlock	Starvation
The deadlock situation occurs when one of the processes got blocked.	Starvation is a situation where all the low priority processes got blocked, and the high priority processes execute.
Deadlock is an infinite process.	Starvation is a long waiting but not an infinite process.
Every Deadlock always has starvation.	Every starvation doesn't necessarily have a deadlock.
Deadlock happens then Mutual exclusion, hold and wait. Here, preemption and circular wait do not occur simultaneously.	It happens due to uncontrolled priority and resource management.

Advantages of Deadlock

Here, are pros/benefits of using Deadlock method:

- This situation works well for processes which perform a single burst of activity.

- No preemption needed for Deadlock.

- Convenient method when applied to resources whose state can be saved and restored easily.

- Feasible to enforce via compile-time checks.
- Needs no run-time computation since the problem is solved in system design.

Disadvantages of Deadlock Method

Here, are cons/ drawback of using deadlock method:

- Delays process initiation.
- Processes must know future resource need.
- Pre-empts more often than necessary.
- Dis-allows incremental resource requests.
- Inherent preemption losses.

References

- Inter-process-communication-ipc: geeksforgeeks.org, Retrieved 27, April 2020
- System-call-operating-system: guru99.com, Retrieved 15, July 2020
- System-calls-in-unix-and-windows: tutorialspoint.com, Retrieved 22, January 2020
- Deadlock-in-operating-system: elprocus.com, Retrieved 17, August 2020
- Deadlocks, operating-systems: cs.uic.edu, Retrieved 05, March 2020
- Deadlock-in-operating-system: guru99.com, Retrieved 12, May 2020

4

Operating Systems: File System and Memory Management

The application which is used to store, arrange and access the files which are stored on a disk or any other storage location is termed as a file management system. The process of controlling and coordinating computer memory, and assigning blocks of memory to various running programs in order to optimize the overall performance of the system is called memory management. This chapter discusses in detail the different aspects of file system management and memory management.

File

What Are Files?

Suppose we are developing an application program. A program, which we prepare, is a file. Later we may compile this program file and get an object code or an executable. The executable is also a file. In other words, the output from a compiler may be an object code file or an executable file. When we store images from a web page we get an image file. If we store some music in digital format it is an audio file. So, in almost every situation we are engaged in using a file. Files are central to our view of communication with IO devices. So let us now ask again: What is a file?

Irrespective of the content any organized information is a file.

So be it a telephone numbers list or a program or an executable code or a web image or a data logged from an instrument we think of it always as a file. This formlessness and disassociation from content was emphasized first in Unix. The formlessness essentially means that files are arbitrary bit (or byte) streams. Formlessness in Unix follows from the basic design principle: keep it simple. The main advantage to a user is flexibility in organizing files. In addition, it also makes it easy to design a file system. A file system is that software which allows users and applications to organize their files. The organization of information may involve access, updates and movement of information between devices. We shall examine the user view of organizing files and the system view of managing the files of users and applications. We shall first look at the user view of files.

User's view of files: The very first need of a user is to be able to access some file he has stored in a non-volatile memory for an on-line access. Also, the file system should be able to locate the file sought by the user. This is achieved by associating an identification for a file i.e. a file must have a name. The name helps the user to identify the file. The file name also helps the file system to locate the file being sought by the user.

Let us consider the organization of my files for the Compilers course and the Operating Systems course on the web. Clearly, all files in compilers course have a set of pages that are related. Also, the pages of the OS system course are related. It is, therefore, natural to think of organizing the files of individual courses together. In other words, we would like to see that a file system supports grouping of related files. In addition, we would like that all such groups be put together under some general category.

This is essentially like making one file folder for the compilers course pages and other one for the OS course pages. Both these folders could be placed within another folder, say COURSES. This is precisely how MAC OS defines its folders. In Unix, each such group, with related files in it, is called a directory. So the COURSES directory may have subdirectories OS and COMPILERS to get a hierarchical file organization. All modern OSs support such a hierarchical file organization. In Figure we show a hierarchy of files. It must be noted that within a directory each file must have a distinct name. For instance, I tend to have ReadMe file in directories to give me the information on what is in each directory. At most there can be only one file with the name "ReadMe" in a directory. However, every subdirectory under this directory may also have its own ReadMe file. Unix emphasizes disassociation with content and form. So file names can be assigned any way.

Some systems, however, require specific name extensions to identify file type. MSDOS identifies executable files with a .COM or .EXE file name extension. Software systems like C or Pascal compilers expect file name extensions of .c or .p (or .pas) respectively. We see some common considerations in associating a file name extension to define a file type.

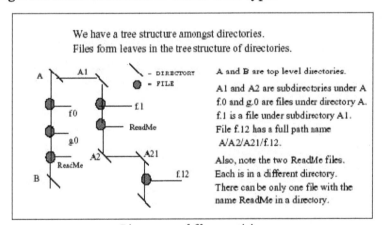

Directory and file orgenision.

File Types and Operations

Many OSs, particularly those used in personal computers, tend to use a file type information within a name. Even Unix software support systems use standard file extension names, even though Unix as an OS does not require this. Most PC-based OSs associate file types with specific applications that generate them. For instance, a database generating program will leave explicit information with a file descriptor that it has been generated by a certain database program. A file descriptor is kept within the file structure and is often used by the file system software to help OS provide file management services. MAC OS usually stores this information in its resource fork which is a part of its file descriptors.

This is done to let OS display the icons of the application environment in which this file was created. These icons are important for PC users. The icons offer the operational clues as well. In Windows, for instance, if a file has been created using *notepad* or *word* or has been stored from the browser, a corresponding give away icon appears. In fact, the OS assigns it a file type. If the icon has an Adobe sign on it and we double click on it the acrobat reader opens it right away. Of course, if we choose to open any of the files differently, the OS provides us that as a choice (often using the right button).

For a user the extension in the name of a file helps to identify the file type. When a user has a very large number of files, it is very helpful to know the type of a file from its name extensions. In Table, we have many commonly used file name extensions. PDP-11 machines, on which Unix was originally designed, used an octal 0407 as a magic number to identify its executable files. This number actually was a machine executable jump instruction which would simply set the program counter to fetch the first executable instruction in the file. Modern systems use many magic numbers to identify which application created or will execute a certain file.

Usage	File extension used	Associated Functionality
An ASCII text file	.txt, .doc	A simple text file
A Word processing file	.wp, .tex	Usually for structured documents
Program files	.c, .p, .f77, .asm	C, Pascal, Fortran, or assembly code
Print of view	.ps, .gif, .dvi	Printing and viewing images, documents
Scripting	.pl, .BAT, .sh	For shell scripts or Web CGI
Program library	.lib	Library routines in packages
Archive generation	.arc, .zip, .tar	Compression and long-term storage
Files that execute	.exe, .out, .bin	Compiler generated executable files
Object codes	.o	Often need linking to execute

File extension and its context of use.

In addition to the file types, a file system must have many other pieces of information that are important. For instance, a file system must know at which location a file is placed in the disk, it should know its size, when was it created, i.e. date and time of creation.

In addition, it should know who owns the files and who else may be permitted access to *read, write* or *execute*. We shall next dwell upon these operational issues.

File operations: As we observed earlier, a file is any organized information. So at that level of abstraction it should be possible for us to have some logical view of files, no matter how these may be stored. Note that the files are stored within the secondary storage. This is a physical view of a file. A file system (as a layer of software) provides a logical view of files to a user or to an application. Yet, at another level the file system offers the physical view to the OS. This means that the OS gets all the information it needs to physically locate, access, and do other file based operations whenever needed. Purely from an operational point of view, a user should be able to create a file. We will also assume that the creator owns the file. In that case he may wish to save or store this file. He should be able to read the contents of the file or even write into this file. Note that a user needs the write capability to update a file. He may wish to display or rename or append this file. He may even wish to make another copy or even delete this file. He may even wish to operate with two or more files. This may entail cut or copy from one file and paste information on the other.

Other management operations are like indicating who else has an authorization of an access to *read* or *write* or *execute* this file. In addition, a user should be able to move this file between his directories. For all of these operations the OS provides the services. These services may even be obtained from within an application like mail or a utility such as an editor. Unix provides a visual editor vi for ASCII file editing. It also provides another editor *sed* for stream editing. MAC OS and PCs provide a range of editors like SimpleText.

Usage	Editor based operation	OS terminology and description
Create	Under FILE menu NEW	A CREATE command is available with explicit read / write option
Open	Under FILE menu OPEN	An OPEN command is available with explicit read / write option
Close	Under FILE menu CLOSE Also when you choose QUIT	A file CLOSE option is available
Read	Open , to read	Specified at the time of open
Write	Save to write	Specified at the time of open
Rename or copy	Use SAVE AS	Can copy using a copy command
Cut and Paste	Via a buffer	Uses desk top environment CDE
Join file:		Concatenation possible or uses an append at shell level
Delete	Under FILE use delete	Use remove or delete command
Relocate		A move command is available
Alias		A symbolic link is possible
List files	OPEN offers selection	Use a list command in a shell

File operations.

With multimedia capabilities now with PCs we have editors for audio and video files too. These often employ MIDI capabilities. MAC OS has Claris works (or Apple works) and MSDOS-based systems have Office 2000 suite of packaged applications which provide the needed file oriented services.

For illustration of many of the basic operations and introduction of shell commands we shall assume that we are dealing with ASCII text files. One may need information on file sizes. More particularly, one may wish to determine the number of lines, words or characters in a file. For such requirements, a shell may have a suite of word counting programs. When there are many files, one often needs longer file names. Often file names may bear a common stem to help us categorize them. For instance, I tend to use "prog" as a prefix to identify my program text files. A programmer derives considerable support through use of regular expressions within file names. Use of regular expressions enhances programmer productivity in checking or accessing file names. For instance, prog* will mean all files prefixed with stem prog, while my file? may mean all the files with prefix my file followed by at most one character within the current directory. Now that we have seen the file operations, we move on to services. Table gives a brief description of the file-oriented services that are made available in a Unix OS. There are similar MS DOS commands. It is a very rewarding experience to try these commands and use regular expression operators like ? and * in conjunction with these commands.

Later we shall discuss some of these commands and other file-related issues in greater depth. Unix, as also the MS environment, allows users to manage the organization of their files. A command which helps viewing current status of files is the *ls* command in Unix (or the *dir* command in MS environment). This command is very versatile. It helps immensely to know various facets and usage options available under the *ls* command. The *ls* command: Unix's *ls* command which lists files and subdirectories in a directory is very revealing. It has many options that offer a wealth of information. It also offers an insight in to what is going on with the files i.e. how the file system is updating the information about files in "inode" which is a short form for an index node in Unix. We shall learn more about inode. In fact, it is very rewarding to study *ls* command in all its details. Table summarizes some of the options and their effects.

Usage	Unix shell command	MS DOS command
Copy a file	cp	COPY
Rename a file	mv	RENAME
Delete a file	rm	DEL
List Files	Is	DIR
Make a directory	mkdir	MKDIR
Change current directory	cd	CHDIR

File oriented Services.

Choose option	To get this information
None chosen	Lists files and directories in a single column list
-I	Lists long reveling file type, permissions, number of links, owner and group ids., file size in bytes, modification date time, name of the file
-d	For each named directory list directory information
-a	List files including those that start with . (period)
-s	Sizes of files in blocks occupied
-t	Print in time sorted order
-u	Print the access time instead of the modification time

Unix is command options.

Using regular expressions: Most operating systems allow use of regular expression operators in conjunction with the commands. This affords enormous flexibility in usage of a command. For instance, one may input a partial pattern and complete the rest by a * or a ? operator. This not only saves on typing but also helps you when you are searching a file after a long time gap and you do not remember the exact file names completely. Suppose a directory has files with names like Comp_page_1.gif, Comp_page_2.gif and Comp_page_1.ps and Comp_page_2.ps. Suppose you wish to list files for page_2. Use a partial name like *ls* C*p*2 or even *2* in *ls* command. We next illustrate the use of operator ?. For instance, use of *ls* my file? in *ls* command will list all files in the current directory with prefix my file followed by at most one character.

Besides these operators, there are command options that make a command structure very flexible. One useful option is to always use the *-i* option with the *rm* command in Unix. A *rm -i* my files* will interrogate a user for each file with prefix my file for a possible removal. This is very useful, as by itself *rm* my file* will remove all the files without any further prompts and this can be very dangerous. A powerful command option within the *rm* command is to use a *-r* option. This results in recursive removal, which means it removes all the files that are linked within a directory tree. It would remove files in the current, as well as, subdirectories all the way down. One should be careful in choosing the options, particularly for remove or delete commands, as information may be lost irretrievably.

It often happens that we may need to use a file in more than one context. For instance, we may need a file in two projects. If each project is in a separate directory then we have two possible solutions. One is to keep two copies, one in each directory or to create a symbolic link and keep one copy. If we keep two unrelated copies we have the problem of consistency because a change in one is not reflected in the other. The symbolic link helps to alleviate this problem. Unix provides the *ln* command to generate a link anywhere regardless of directory locations with the following structure and interpretation: *ln* fileName pseudonym.

Now fileName file has an alias in pseudonym too. Note that the two directories which share a file link should be in the same disk partition. Later, in the chapter on security, we shall observe how this simple facility may also become a security hazard.

File Access Rights

After defining a fairly wide range of possible operations on files we shall now look at the file system which supports all these services on behalf of the OS. In the preamble of this chapter we defined a file system as that software which allows users and applications to organize and manage their files. The organization of information may involve access, updates, and movement of information between devices. Our first major concern is access.

Access permissions: Typically a file may be accessed to read or write or execute.

The usage is determined usually by the context in which the file is created. For instance, a city bus timetable file is created by a transport authority for the benefit of its customers.

So this file may be accessed by all members of public. While they can access it for a read operation, they cannot write into it. An associated file may be available to the supervisor who assigns duties to drivers. He can, not only read but also write in to the files that assign drivers to bus routes. The management at the transport authority can read, write and even execute some files that generate the bus schedules. In other words, a file system must manage access by checking the access rights of users. In general, access is managed by keeping access rights information for each file in a file system.

Who can access files?: Unix recognizes three categories of users of files, e.g. user (usually the user who created it and owns it), the group, and others. The owner may be a person or a program (usually an application or a system-based utility). The notion of "group" comes from software engineering and denotes a team effort. The basic concept is that users in a group may share files for a common project. Group members often need to share files to support each other's activity. Others has the connotation of public usage as in the example above. Unix organizes access as a three bit information for each i.e. owner, group, and others. So the access rights are defined by 9 bits as *rwx rwx rwx* respectively for owner, group and others. The *rwx* can be defined as an octal number too. If all bits are set then we have a pattern 111 111 111 (or 777 in octal) which means the owner has read, write, and execute rights, and the group to which he belongs has also read, write and execute rights, and others have read, write and execute rights as well. A pattern of 111 110 100 (or 764 octal, also denoted as *rwx rw- r-*) means the owner has read, write, and execute permissions; the group has read and write permissions but no execute permission and others have only the read permission. Note that Unix group permissions are for all or none. Windows 2000 and NTFS permit a greater degree of refinement on a group of users. Linux allows individual users to make up groups.

File Access and Security Concerns

The owner of a file can alter the permissions using the *chmod* command in Unix. The commonly used format is *chmod* octalPattern fileName which results in assigning the permission interpreted from the octalPattern to the file named fileName. There are other alternatives to *chmod* command like *chmod* changePattern fileName where changePattern may be of the form *go-rw* to denote withdrawal of read write permission from group and others. Anyone can view all the currently applicable access rights using a *ls* command in Unix with *-l* option. This command lists all the files and subdirectories of the current directory with associated access permissions.

Security concerns: Access permissions are the most elementary and constitute a fairly effective form of security measure in a standalone single user system. In a system which may be connected in a network this can get very complex. We shall for now regard the access control as our first line of security. On a PC which is a single-user system there is no security as such as anyone with an access to the PC has access to all the files.

Windows 2000 and XP systems do permit access restriction amongst all the users of the system. These may have users with system administrator privileges. In Unix too, the super-user (root) has access to all the files of all the users. So there is a need for securing files for individual users. Some systems provide security by having a password for files. However, an enhanced level of security is provided by encryption of important files. Most systems provide some form of encryption facility. A user may use his own encryption key to encrypt his file. When someone else accesses an encrypted file he sees a garbled file which has no pattern or meaning. Unix provides a crypt command to encrypt files.

The format of the crypt command is:

crypt EncryptionKey < inputFileName > outputFileName

The EncryptionKey provides a symmetric key, so that you can use the same key to retrieve the old file (simply reverse the roles of inputFileName and outputFileName) We briefly mention about audit trails which are usually maintained in syslog files in Unix systems. In a chapter on security we shall discuss these issues in detail. So far we have dealt with the logical view of a file. Next, we shall address the issues involved in storage and management of files.

File System

In computing, a file system or filesystem is used to control how data is stored and retrieved. Without a file system, information placed in a storage medium would be one large body of data with no way to tell where one piece of information stops and the next begins. By separating the data into pieces and giving each piece a name, the information is easily isolated and identified. Taking its name from the way paper-based information systems are named, each group of data is called a "file". The structure and logic rules used to manage the groups of information and their names is called a "file system".

There are many different kinds of file systems. Each one has different structure and logic, properties of speed, flexibility, security, size and more. Some file systems have been designed to be used for specific applications. For example, the ISO 9660 file system is designed specifically for optical discs.

File systems can be used on numerous different types of storage devices that use different kinds of media. The most common storage device in use today is a hard disk drive. Other kinds of media that are used include flash memory, magnetic tapes, and optical discs. In some cases, such as with tmpfs, the computer's main memory (random-access memory, RAM) is used to create a temporary file system for short-term use.

Some file systems are used on local data storage devices; others provide file access via a network protocol (for example, NFS, SMB, or 9P clients). Some file systems are "virtual", meaning that the supplied "files" (called virtual files) are computed on request (e.g. procfs) or are merely a mapping into a different file system used as a backing store. The file system manages access to both the content of files and the metadata about those files. It is responsible for arranging storage space; reliability, efficiency, and tuning with regard to the physical storage medium are important design considerations.

Origin of the Term

Before the advent of computers the term *file system* was used to describe a method of storing and retrieving paper documents. By 1961 the term was being applied to computerized filing alongside the original meaning. By 1964 it was in general use.

Architecture

A file system consists of two or three layers. Sometimes the layers are explicitly separated, and sometimes the functions are combined.

The *logical file system* is responsible for interaction with the user application. It provides the application program interface (API) for file operations — OPEN, CLOSE, READ, etc., and passes the requested operation to the layer below it for processing. The logical file system "manage[s] open file table entries and per-process file descriptors." This layer provides "file access, directory operations, [and] security and protection."

The second optional layer is the *virtual file system*. "This interface allows support for multiple concurrent instances of physical file systems, each of which is called a file system implementation."

The third layer is the *physical file system*. This layer is concerned with the physical operation of the storage device (e.g.disk). It processes physical blocks being read or written. It handles buffering and memory management and is responsible for the physical placement of blocks in specific locations on the storage medium. The physical file system interacts with the device drivers or with the channel to drive the storage device.

Aspects of File Systems

Space Management

File systems allocate space in a granular manner, usually multiple physical units on the device.

The file system is responsible for organizing files and directories, and keeping track of which areas of the media belong to which file and which are not being used. For example, in Apple DOS of the early 1980s, 256-byte sectors on 140 kilobyte floppy disk used a *track/sector map*.

Name ▲	Size
99998.txt	1 KB
99999.txt	1 KB
100000.txt	1 KB
mkfile.bat	1 KB
source.txt	1 KB

Type:	File Folder
Location:	C:\
Size:	488 KB (500,059 bytes)
Size on disk:	390 MB (409,608,192 bytes)
Contains:	100,002 Files, 0 Folders

An example of slack space, demonstrated with 4,096-byte NTFS clusters: 100,000 files, each five bytes per file, which equal to 500,000 bytes of actual data but require 409,600,000 bytes of disk space to store.

This results in unused space when a file is not an exact multiple of the allocation unit, sometimes referred to as *slack space*. For a 512-byte allocation, the average unused space is 256 bytes. For 64 KB clusters, the average unused space is 32 KB. The size of the allocation unit is chosen when the file system is created. Choosing the allocation size based on the average size of the files expected to be in the file system can minimize the amount of unusable space. Frequently the default allocation may provide reasonable usage. Choosing an allocation size that is too small results in excessive overhead if the file system will contain mostly very large files.

File systems may become fragmented.

File system fragmentation occurs when unused space or single files are not contiguous. As a file system is used, files are created, modified and deleted. When a file is created the file system allocates space for the data. Some file systems permit or require specifying an initial space allocation and subsequent incremental allocations as the file grows. As files are deleted the space they were allocated eventually is considered available for use by other files. This creates alternating used and unused areas of various sizes. This is free space fragmentation. When a file is created and there is not an area of contiguous space available for its initial allocation the space must be assigned in fragments. When a file is modified such that it becomes larger it may exceed the space initially allocated to it, another allocation must be assigned elsewhere and the file becomes fragmented.

Filenames

A filename (or file name) is used to identify a storage location in the file system. Most file systems have restrictions on the length of filenames. In some file systems, filenames are not case sensitive (i.e., filenames such as FOO and foo refer to the same file); in others, filenames are case sensitive (i.e., the names FOO, Foo and foo refer to three separate files).

Most modern file systems allow filenames to contain a wide range of characters from the Unicode character set. However, they may have restrictions on the use of certain special characters, disallowing them within filenames; those characters might be used to indicate a device, device type, directory prefix, file path separator, or file type.

Directories

File systems typically have directories (also called folders) which allow the user to group files into separate collections. This may be implemented by associating the file name with an index in a table of contents or an inode in a Unix-like file system. Directory structures may be flat (i.e. linear), or allow hierarchies where directories may contain subdirectories. The first file system to support arbitrary hierarchies of directories was used in the Multics operating system. The native file systems of Unix-like systems also support arbitrary directory hierarchies, as do, for example, Apple's Hierarchical File System, and its successor HFS+ in classic Mac OS (HFS+ is still used in macOS), the FAT file system in MS-DOS 2.0 and later versions of MS-DOS and in Microsoft Windows, the NTFS file system in the Windows NT family of operating systems, and the ODS-2 (On-Disk Structure-2) and higher levels of the Files-11 file system in OpenVMS.

Metadata

Other bookkeeping information is typically associated with each file within a file system. The length of the data contained in a file may be stored as the number of blocks allocated for the file or as a byte count. The time that the file was last modified may be stored as the file's timestamp. File systems might store the file creation time, the time it was last accessed, the time the file's metadata was changed, or the time the file was last backed up. Other information can include the file's device type (e.g. block, character, socket, subdirectory, etc.), its owner user ID and group ID, its access permissions and other file attributes (e.g. whether the file is read-only, executable, etc.).

A file system stores all the metadata associated with the file—including the file name, the length of the contents of a file, and the location of the file in the folder hierarchy—separate from the contents of the file.

Most file systems store the names of all the files in one directory in one place—the directory table for that directory—which is often stored like any other file. Many file systems put only some of the metadata for a file in the directory table, and the rest of the metadata for that file in a completely separate structure, such as the inode.

Most file systems also store metadata not associated with any one particular file. Such metadata includes information about unused regions—free space bitmap, block availability map—and information about bad sectors. Often such information about an allocation group is stored inside the allocation group itself.

Additional attributes can be associated on file systems, such as NTFS, XFS, ext2, ext3, some versions of UFS, and HFS+, using extended file attributes. Some file systems provide for user defined attributes such as the author of the document, the character encoding of a document or the size of an image.

Some file systems allow for different data collections to be associated with one file name. These separate collections may be referred to as *streams* or *forks*. Apple has long used a forked file system on the Macintosh, and Microsoft supports streams in NTFS. Some file systems maintain multiple past revisions of a file under a single file name; the filename by itself retrieves the most recent version, while prior saved version can be accessed using a special naming convention such as "filename;4" or "filename(-4)" to access the version four saves ago.

File System as an Abstract User Interface

In some cases, a file system may not make use of a storage device but can be used to organize and represent access to any data, whether it is stored or dynamically generated (e.g. procfs).

Utilities

File systems include utilities to initialize, alter parameters of and remove an instance of the file system. Some include the ability to extend or truncate the space allocated to the file system.

Directory utilities may be used to create, rename and delete *directory entries*, which are also known as *dentries* (singular: *dentry*), and to alter metadata associated with a directory. Directory utilities may also include capabilities to create additional links to a directory (hard links in Unix), to rename parent links (".." in Unix-like operating systems), and to create bidirectional links to files.

File utilities create, list, copy, move and delete files, and alter metadata. They may be able to truncate data, truncate or extend space allocation, append to, move, and modify files in-place. Depending on the underlying structure of the file system, they may provide a mechanism to prepend to, or truncate from, the beginning of a file, insert entries into the middle of a file or delete entries from a file.

Utilities to free space for deleted files, if the file system provides an undelete function, also belong to this category.

Some file systems defer operations such as reorganization of free space, secure erasing of free space, and rebuilding of hierarchical structures by providing utilities to perform these functions at times of minimal activity. An example is the file system defragmentation utilities.

Some of the most important features of file system utilities involve supervisory activities which may involve bypassing ownership or direct access to the underlying device. These include high-performance backup and recovery, data replication and reorganization of various data structures and allocation tables within the file system.

Restricting and Permitting Access

There are several mechanisms used by file systems to control access to data. Usually the intent is to prevent reading or modifying files by a user or group of users. Another reason is to ensure data is modified in a controlled way so access may be restricted to a specific program. Examples include passwords stored in the metadata of the file or elsewhere and file permissions in the form of permission bits, access control lists, or capabilities. The need for file system utilities to be able to access the data at the media level to reorganize the structures and provide efficient backup usually means that these are only effective for polite users but are not effective against intruders.

Methods for encrypting file data are sometimes included in the file system. This is very effective since there is no need for file system utilities to know the encryption seed to effectively manage the data. The risks of relying on encryption include the fact that an attacker can copy the data and use brute force to decrypt the data. Losing the seed means losing the data.

Maintaining Integrity

One significant responsibility of a file system is to ensure that, regardless of the actions by programs accessing the data, the structure remains consistent. This includes actions taken if a program modifying data terminates abnormally or neglects to inform the file system that it has completed its activities. This may include updating the metadata, the directory entry and handling any data that was buffered but not yet updated on the physical storage media.

Other failures which the file system must deal with include media failures or loss of connection to remote systems.

In the event of an operating system failure or "soft" power failure, special routines in the file system must be invoked similar to when an individual program fails.

The file system must also be able to correct damaged structures. These may occur as a result of an operating system failure for which the OS was unable to notify the file system, power failure or reset.

The file system must also record events to allow analysis of systemic issues as well as problems with specific files or directories.

User Data

The most important purpose of a file system is to manage user data. This includes storing, retrieving and updating data.

Some file systems accept data for storage as a stream of bytes which are collected and stored in a manner efficient for the media. When a program retrieves the data, it specifies the size of a memory buffer and the file system transfers data from the media to the buffer. A runtime library routine may sometimes allow the user program to define a *record* based on a library call specifying a length. When the user program reads the data, the library retrieves data via the file system and returns a *record*.

Some file systems allow the specification of a fixed record length which is used for all writes and reads. This facilitates locating the nth record as well as updating records.

An identification for each record, also known as a key, makes for a more sophisticated file system. The user program can read, write and update records without regard to their location. This requires complicated management of blocks of media usually separating key blocks and data blocks. Very efficient algorithms can be developed with pyramid structure for locating records.

Using a File System

Utilities, language specific run-time libraries and user programs use file system APIs to make requests of the file system. These include data transfer, positioning, updating metadata, managing directories, managing access specifications, and removal.

Multiple file Systems within a Single System

Frequently, retail systems are configured with a single file system occupying the entire storage device.

Another approach is to partition the disk so that several file systems with different attributes can be used. One file system, for use as browser cache, might be configured with a small allocation size. This has the additional advantage of keeping the frantic activity of creating and deleting files typical of browser activity in a narrow area of the disk and not interfering with allocations of other files. A similar partition might be created for email. Another partition, and file system might be created for the storage of audio or video files with a relatively large allocation. One of the file systems may normally be set *read-only* and only periodically be set writable.

A third approach, which is mostly used in cloud systems, is to use "disk images" to house additional file systems, with the same attributes or not, within another (host) file system as a file. A common example is virtualization: one user can run an experimental Linux distribution (using the ext4 file system) in a virtual machine under his/her production Windows environment (using NTFS). The ext4 file system resides in a disk image, which is treated as a file (or multiple files, depending on the hypervisor and settings) in the NTFS host file system.

Having multiple file systems on a single system has the additional benefit that in the event of a corruption of a single partition, the remaining file systems will frequently still be intact. This includes virus destruction of the *system* partition or even a system that will not boot. File system utilities which require dedicated access can be effectively completed piecemeal. In addition, defragmentation may be more effective. Several system maintenance utilities, such as virus scans and backups, can also be processed in segments. For example, it is not necessary to backup the file system containing videos along with all the other files if none have been added since the last backup. As for the image files, one can easily "spin off" differential images which contain only "new" data written to the master (original) image. Differential images can be used for both safety concerns (as a "disposable" system - can be quickly restored if destroyed or contaminated by a virus, as the old image can be removed and a new image can be created in matter of seconds, even without automated procedures) and quick virtual machine deployment (since the differential images can be quickly spawned using a script in batches).

Design Limitations

All file systems have some functional limit that defines the maximum storable data capacity within that system. These functional limits are a best-guess effort by the designer based on how large the storage systems are right now and how large storage systems are likely to become in the future. Disk storage has continued to increase at near exponential rates, so after a few years, file systems have kept reaching design limitations that require computer users to repeatedly move to a newer system with ever-greater capacity.

File system complexity typically varies proportionally with the available storage capacity. The file systems of early 1980s home computers with 50 KB to 512 KB of storage would not be a reasonable choice for modern storage systems with hundreds of gigabytes of capacity. Likewise, modern file systems would not be a reasonable choice for these early systems, since the complexity of modern file system structures would quickly consume or even exceed the very limited capacity of the early storage systems.

Types of File Systems

File system types can be classified into disk/tape file systems, network file systems and special-purpose file systems.

Disk File Systems

A *disk file system* takes advantages of the ability of disk storage media to randomly address data in a short amount of time. Additional considerations include the speed of accessing data following that initially requested and the anticipation that the following data may also be requested. This permits multiple users (or processes) access to various data on the disk without regard to the sequential location of the data. Examples include FAT (FAT12, FAT16, FAT32), exFAT, NTFS, HFS and HFS+, HPFS, APFS, UFS, ext2, ext3, ext4, XFS, btrfs, ISO 9660, Files-11, Veritas File System, VMFS, ZFS, ReiserFS and UDF. Some disk file systems are journaling file systems or versioning file systems.

Optical Discs

ISO 9660 and Universal Disk Format (UDF) are two common formats that target Compact Discs, DVDs and Blu-ray discs. Mount Rainier is an extension to UDF supported since 2.6 series of the Linux kernel and since Windows Vista that facilitates rewriting to DVDs.

Flash File Systems

A *flash file system* considers the special abilities, performance and restrictions of flash memory devices. Frequently a disk file system can use a flash memory device as the underlying storage media but it is much better to use a file system specifically designed for a flash device.

Tape File Systems

A *tape file system* is a file system and tape format designed to store files on tape in a self-describing form. Magnetic tapes are sequential storage media with significantly longer random data access times than disks, posing challenges to the creation and efficient management of a general-purpose file system.

In a disk file system there is typically a master file directory, and a map of used and free data regions. Any file additions, changes, or removals require updating the directory and the used/free maps. Random access to data regions is measured in milliseconds so this system works well for disks.

Tape requires linear motion to wind and unwind potentially very long reels of media. This tape motion may take several seconds to several minutes to move the read/write head from one end of the tape to the other.

Consequently, a master file directory and usage map can be extremely slow and inefficient with tape. Writing typically involves reading the block usage map to find free blocks for writing, updating the usage map and directory to add the data, and then advancing the tape to write the data in the correct spot. Each additional file write requires updating the map and directory and writing the data, which may take several seconds to occur for each file.

Tape file systems instead typically allow for the file directory to be spread across the tape intermixed with the data, referred to as *streaming*, so that time-consuming and repeated tape motions are not required to write new data.

However, a side effect of this design is that reading the file directory of a tape usually requires scanning the entire tape to read all the scattered directory entries. Most data archiving software that works with tape storage will store a local copy of the tape catalog on a disk file system, so that adding files to a tape can be done quickly without having to rescan the tape media. The local tape catalog copy is usually discarded if not used for a specified period of time, at which point the tape must be re-scanned if it is to be used in the future.

IBM has developed a file system for tape called the Linear Tape File System. The IBM implementation of this file system has been released as the open-source IBM Linear Tape File System — Single Drive Edition (LTFS-SDE) product. The Linear Tape File System uses a separate partition on the tape to record the index meta-data, thereby avoiding the problems associated with scattering directory entries across the entire tape.

Tape Formatting

Writing data to a tape, erasing, or formatting a tape is often a significantly time-consuming process and can take several hours on large tapes. With many data tape technologies it is not necessary to format the tape before over-writing new data to the tape. This is due to the inherently destructive nature of overwriting data on sequential media.

Because of the time it can take to format a tape, typically tapes are pre-formatted so that the tape user does not need to spend time preparing each new tape for use. All that is usually necessary is to write an identifying media label to the tape before use, and even this can be automatically written by software when a new tape is used for the first time.

Database File Systems

Another concept for file management is the idea of a database-based file system. Instead of, or in addition to, hierarchical structured management, files are identified by their characteristics, like type of file, topic, author, or similar rich metadata.

IBM DB2 for i (formerly known as DB2/400 and DB2 for i5/OS) is a database file system as part of the object based IBM i operating system (formerly known as OS/400 and i5/OS), incorporating a single level store and running on IBM Power Systems (formerly known as AS/400 and iSeries), designed by Frank G. Soltis IBM's former chief scientist for IBM i. Around 1978 to 1988 Frank G. Soltis and his team at IBM Rochester have successfully designed and applied technologies like the database file system where others like Microsoft later failed to accomplish. These technologies are informally known as 'Fortress Rochester' and were in few basic aspects extended from early Mainframe technologies but in many ways more advanced from a technological perspective.

Some other projects that aren't "pure" database file systems but that use some aspects of a database file system:

- Many Web content management systems use a relational DBMS to store and retrieve files. For example, XHTML files are stored as XML or text fields, while image files are stored as blob fields; SQL SELECT (with optional XPath) statements retrieve the files, and allow the use of a sophisticated logic and more rich information associations than "usual file systems". Many CMSs also have the option of storing only metadata within the database, with the standard filesystem used to store the content of files.

- Very large file systems, embodied by applications like Apache Hadoop and Google File System, use some *database file system* concepts.

Transactional File Systems

Some programs need to update multiple files "all at once". For example, a software installation may write program binaries, libraries, and configuration files. If the software installation fails, the program may be unusable. If the installation is upgrading a key system utility, such as the command shell, the entire system may be left in an unusable state.

Transaction processing introduces the isolation guarantee, which states that operations within a transaction are hidden from other threads on the system until the transaction commits, and that interfering operations on the system will be properly serialized with the transaction. Transactions also provide the atomicity guarantee, ensuring that operations inside of a transaction are either all committed or the transaction can be aborted and the system discards all of its partial results. This means that if there is a crash or power failure, after recovery, the stored state will be consistent. Either the software will be completely installed or the failed installation will be completely rolled back, but an unusable partial install will not be left on the system.

Windows, beginning with Vista, added transaction support to NTFS, in a feature called Transactional NTFS, but its use is now discouraged. There are a number of research prototypes of transactional file systems for UNIX systems, including the Valor file system, Amino, LFS, and a transactional ext3 file system on the TxOS kernel, as well as transactional file systems targeting embedded systems, such as TFFS.

Ensuring consistency across multiple file system operations is difficult, if not impossible, without file system transactions. File locking can be used as a concurrency control mechanism for individual files, but it typically does not protect the directory structure or file metadata. For instance, file locking cannot prevent TOCTTOU race conditions on symbolic links. File locking also cannot automatically roll back a failed operation, such as a software upgrade; this requires atomicity.

Journaling file systems are one technique used to introduce transaction-level consistency to file system structures. Journal transactions are not exposed to programs as part of the OS API; they are only used internally to ensure consistency at the granularity of a single system call.

Data backup systems typically do not provide support for direct backup of data stored in a transactional manner, which makes recovery of reliable and consistent data sets difficult. Most backup software simply notes what files have changed since a certain time, regardless of the transactional state shared across multiple files in the overall dataset. As a workaround, some database systems simply produce an archived state file containing all data up to that point, and the backup software only backs that up and does not interact directly with the active transactional databases at all. Recovery requires separate recreation of the database from the state file, after the file has been restored by the backup software.

Network File Systems

A *network file system* is a file system that acts as a client for a remote file access protocol, providing access to files on a server. Programs using local interfaces can transparently create, manage and access hierarchical directories and files in remote network-connected computers. Examples of network file systems include clients for the NFS, AFS, SMB protocols, and file-system-like clients for FTP and WebDAV.

Shared Disk File Systems

A *shared disk file system* is one in which a number of machines (usually servers) all have access to the same external disk subsystem (usually a SAN). The file system arbitrates access to that subsystem, preventing write collisions. Examples include GFS2 from Red Hat, GPFS from IBM, SFS from DataPlow, CXFS from SGI and StorNext from Quantum Corporation.

Special File Systems

A *special file system* presents non-file elements of an operating system as files so they can be acted on using file system APIs. This is most commonly done in Unix-like operating systems, but devices are given file names in some non-Unix-like operating systems as well.

Device File Systems

A *device file system* represents I/O devices and pseudo-devices as files, called device files. Examples in Unix-like systems include devfs and, in Linux 2.6 systems, udev. In non-Unix-like systems, such as TOPS-10 and other operating systems influenced by it, where the full filename or pathname of a file can include a device prefix, devices other than those containing file systems are referred to by a device prefix specifying the device, without anything following it.

Other Special File Systems

- In the Linux kernel, configfs and sysfs provide files that can be used to query the kernel for information and configure entities in the kernel.

- Procfs maps processes and, on Linux, other operating system structures into a filespace.

Minimal File System / audio-cassette Storage

The late 1970s saw the development of the microcomputer. Disk and digital tape devices were too expensive for hobbyists. An inexpensive basic data storage system was devised that used common audio cassette tape.

When the system needed to write data, the user was notified to press "RECORD" on the cassette recorder, then press "RETURN" on the keyboard to notify the system that the cassette recorder was recording. The system wrote a sound to provide time synchronization, then modulated sounds that encoded a prefix, the data, a checksum and a suffix. When the system needed to read data, the user was instructed to press "PLAY" on the cassette recorder. The system would *listen* to the sounds on the tape waiting until a burst of sound could be recognized as the synchronization. The system would then interpret subsequent sounds as data. When the data read was complete, the system would notify the user to press "STOP" on the cassette recorder. It was primitive, but it worked (a lot of the time). Data was stored sequentially, usually in an unnamed format, although some systems (such as the Commodore PET series of computers) did allow the files to be named. Multiple sets of data could be written and located by fast-forwarding the tape and observing at the tape counter to find the approximate start of the next data region on the tape. The user might have to listen to the sounds to find the right spot to begin playing the next data region. Some implementations even included audible sounds interspersed with the data.

Flat File Systems

In a flat file system, there are no subdirectories, directory entries for all files are stored in a single directory.

When floppy disk media was first available this type of file system was adequate due to the relatively small amount of data space available. CP/M machines featured a flat file system, where files could be assigned to one of 16 *user areas* and generic file operations narrowed to work on one instead of defaulting to work on all of them. These user areas were no more than special attributes associated with the files, that is, it was not necessary to define specific quota for each of these areas and files could be added to groups for as long as there was still free storage space on the disk. The early Apple Macintosh also featured a flat file system, the Macintosh File System. It was unusual in that the file management program (Macintosh Finder) created the illusion of a partially hierarchical filing system on top of EMFS. This structure required every file to have a unique name, even if it appeared to be in a separate folder. IBM DOS/360 and OS/360 store entries for all files on a disk pack (*volume*) in a directory on the pack called a *Volume Table of Contents* (VTOC).

While simple, flat file systems become awkward as the number of files grows and makes it difficult to organize data into related groups of files.

A recent addition to the flat file system family is Amazon's S3, a remote storage service, which is intentionally simplistic to allow users the ability to customize how their data is stored. The only constructs are buckets (imagine a disk drive of unlimited size) and objects (similar, but not identical to the standard concept of a file). Advanced file management is allowed by being able to use nearly any character (including '/') in the object's name, and the ability to select subsets of the bucket's content based on identical prefixes.

File Systems and Operating Systems

Many operating systems include support for more than one file system. Sometimes the OS and the file system are so tightly interwoven that it is difficult to separate out file system functions.

There needs to be an interface provided by the operating system software between the user and the file system. This interface can be textual (such as provided by a command line interface, such as the Unix shell, or OpenVMS DCL) or graphical (such as provided by a graphical user interface, such as file browsers). If graphical, the metaphor of the *folder*, containing documents, other files, and nested folders is often used.

Unix and Unix-like Operating Systems

Unix-like operating systems create a virtual file system, which makes all the files on all the devices appear to exist in a single hierarchy. This means, in those systems, there is one root directory, and every file existing on the system is located under it somewhere. Unix-like systems can use a RAM disk or network shared resource as its root directory.

Unix-like systems assign a device name to each device, but this is not how the files on that device are accessed. Instead, to gain access to files on another device, the operating system must first be informed where in the directory tree those files should appear. This process is called mounting a file system. For example, to access the files on a CD-ROM, one must tell the operating system "Take the file system from this CD-ROM and make it appear under such-and-such directory". The directory given to the operating system is called the *mount point* – it might, for example, be /media. The /media directory exists on many Unix systems (as specified in the Filesystem Hierarchy Standard) and is intended specifically for use as a mount point for removable media such as CDs, DVDs, USB drives or floppy disks. It may be empty, or it may contain subdirectories for mounting individual devices. Generally, only the administrator (i.e. root user) may authorize the mounting of file systems.

Unix-like operating systems often include software and tools that assist in the mounting process and provide it new functionality. Some of these strategies have been coined "auto-mounting" as a reflection of their purpose.

- In many situations, file systems other than the root need to be available as soon as the operating system has booted. All Unix-like systems therefore provide a facility for mounting file systems at boot time. System administrators define these file systems in the configuration file fstab (*vfstab* in Solaris), which also indicates options and mount points.

- In some situations, there is no need to mount certain file systems at boot time, although their use may be desired thereafter. There are some utilities for Unix-like systems that allow the mounting of predefined file systems upon demand.

- Removable media have become very common with microcomputer platforms. They allow programs and data to be transferred between machines without a physical connection. Common examples include USB flash drives, CD-ROMs, and DVDs. Utilities have therefore been developed to detect the presence and availability of a medium and then mount that medium without any user intervention.

- Progressive Unix-like systems have also introduced a concept called supermounting the Linux supermount-ng project. For example, a floppy disk that has been super-mounted can be physically removed from the system. Under normal circumstances, the disk should have been synchronized and then unmounted before its removal. Provided synchronization has occurred, a different disk can be inserted into the drive. The system automatically notices that the disk has changed and updates the mount point contents to reflect the new medium.

- An automounter will automatically mount a file system when a reference is made to the directory atop which it should be mounted. This is usually used for file systems on network servers, rather than relying on events such as the insertion of media, as would be appropriate for removable media.

Linux

Linux supports numerous file systems, but common choices for the system disk on a block device include the ext* family (ext2, ext3 and ext4), XFS, JFS, ReiserFS and btrfs. For raw flash without a flash translation layer (FTL) or Memory Technology Device (MTD), there are UBIFS, JFFS2 and YAFFS, among others. SquashFS is a common compressed read-only file system.

Solaris

Solaris in earlier releases defaulted to (non-journaled or non-logging) UFS for bootable and supplementary file systems. Solaris defaulted to, supported, and extended UFS.

Support for other file systems and significant enhancements were added over time, including Veritas Software Corp. (Journaling) VxFS, Sun Microsystems (Clustering) QFS, Sun Microsystems (Journaling) UFS, and Sun Microsystems (open source, poolable, 128 bit compressible, and error-correcting) ZFS.

Kernel extensions were added to Solaris to allow for bootable Veritas VxFS operation. Logging or Journaling was added to UFS in Sun's Solaris 7. Releases of Solaris 10, Solaris Express, OpenSolaris, and other open source variants of the Solaris operating system later supported bootable ZFS.

Logical Volume Management allows for spanning a file system across multiple devices for the purpose of adding redundancy, capacity, and/or throughput. Legacy environments in Solaris may use Solaris Volume Manager (formerly known as Solstice DiskSuite). Multiple operating systems (including Solaris) may use Veritas Volume Manager. Modern Solaris based operating systems eclipse the need for Volume Management through leveraging virtual storage pools in ZFS.

macOS

macOS (formerly Mac OS X) uses a file system inherited from classic Mac OS called HFS Plus. Apple also uses the term "Mac OS Extended". HFS Plus is a metadata-rich and case-preserving but (usually) case-insensitive file system. Due to the Unix roots of macOS, Unix permissions were added to HFS Plus. Later versions of HFS Plus added journaling to prevent corruption of the file system structure and introduced a number of optimizations to the allocation algorithms in an attempt to defragment files automatically without requiring an external defragmenter.

Filenames can be up to 255 characters. HFS Plus uses Unicode to store filenames. On macOS, the filetype can come from the type code, stored in file's metadata, or the filename extension.

HFS Plus has three kinds of links: Unix-style hard links, Unix-style symbolic links and aliases. Aliases are designed to maintain a link to their original file even if they are moved or renamed; they are not interpreted by the file system itself, but by the File Manager code in userland.

macOS also supported the UFS file system, derived from the BSD Unix Fast File System via NeXT-STEP. However, as of Mac OS X Leopard, macOS could no longer be installed on a UFS volume, nor can a pre-Leopard system installed on a UFS volume be upgraded to Leopard. As of Mac OS X Lion UFS support was completely dropped.

Newer versions of macOS are capable of reading and writing to the legacy FAT file systems (16 & 32) common on Windows. They are also capable of *reading* the newer NTFS file systems for Windows. In order to *write* to NTFS file systems on macOS versions prior to Mac OS X Snow Leopard third party software is necessary. Mac OS X 10.6 (Snow Leopard) and later allow writing to NTFS file systems, but only after a non-trivial system setting change (third party software exists that automates this).

Finally, macOS supports reading and writing of the exFAT file system since Mac OS X Snow Leopard, starting from version 10.6.5.

OS/2

OS/2 1.2 introduced the High Performance File System (HPFS). HPFS supports mixed case file names in different code pages, long file names (255 characters), more efficient use of disk space, an architecture that keeps related items close to each other on the disk volume, less fragmentation of data, extent-based space allocation, a B+ tree structure for directories, and the root directory located at the midpoint of the disk, for faster average access. A Journaled filesystem (JFS) was shipped in 1999.

PC-BSD

PC-BSD is a desktop version of FreeBSD, which inherits FreeBSD's ZFS support, similarly to FreeNAS. The new graphical installer of PC-BSD can handle */ (root) on ZFS* and RAID-Z pool installs and disk encryption using Geli right from the start in an easy convenient (GUI) way. The current PC-BSD 9.0+ 'Isotope Edition' has ZFS filesystem version 5 and ZFS storage pool version 28.

Plan 9

Plan 9 from Bell Labs treats everything as a file and accesses all objects as a file would be accessed (i.e., there is no ioctl or mmap): networking, graphics, debugging, authentication, capabilities, encryption, and other services are accessed via I/O operations on file descriptors. The 9P protocol removes the difference between local and remote files. File systems in Plan 9 are organized with the help of private, per-process namespaces, allowing each process to have a different view of the many file systems that provide resources in a distributed system.

The Inferno operating system shares these concepts with Plan 9.

Microsoft Windows

```
C:\Temp> dir
 Volume in drive C is C
 Volume Serial Number is 74F5-B93C

 Directory of C:\Temp

2009-08-25  11:59    <DIR>          .
2009-08-25  11:59    <DIR>          ..
2007-03-01  11:37         2,321,600 AdobeUpdater12345.exe
2009-04-03  10:01            27,988 dd_depcheckdotnetfx30.txt
2009-04-03  10:01               764 dd_dotnetfx3error.txt
2009-04-03  10:01            32,572 dd_dotnetfx3install.txt
2009-06-09  13:46            35,145 GenProfile.log
2009-08-05  12:11               155 KB969856.log
2009-04-20  08:37               402 MSI29e0b.LOG
2009-04-09  16:34            38,895 offcln11.log
2009-04-03  16:02    <DIR>          OfficePatches
2009-07-14  14:30    <DIR>          OHotfix
2009-08-25  10:52            16,384 Perflib_Perfdata_c30.dat
2009-04-03  10:01             1,744 uxeventlog.txt
2009-08-25  11:42        50,245,632 WFV2F.tmp
2009-04-20  10:07             1,397 {AC76BA86-7AD7-1033-7B44-A81200000003}.ini
2009-04-20  10:13               617 {AC76BA86-7AD7-1033-7B44-A81300000003}.ini
              13 File(s)     52,723,295 bytes
               4 Dir(s)  83,570,208,768 bytes free
```

Directory listing in a Windows command shell.

Windows makes use of the FAT, NTFS, exFAT, Live File System and ReFS file systems (the last of these is only supported and usable in Windows Server 2012, Windows Server 2016, Windows 8, Windows 8.1, and Windows 10; Windows cannot boot from it).

Windows uses a *drive letter* abstraction at the user level to distinguish one disk or partition from another. For example, the path C:\WINDOWS represents a directory WINDOWS on the partition represented by the letter C. Drive C: is most commonly used for the primary hard disk drive partition, on which Windows is usually installed and from which it boots. This "tradition" has become so firmly ingrained that bugs exist in many applications which make assumptions that the drive that the operating system is installed on is C. The use of drive letters, and the tradition of using "C" as the drive letter for the primary hard disk drive partition, can be traced to MS-DOS, where the letters A and B were reserved for up to two floppy disk drives. This in turn derived from CP/M in the 1970s, and ultimately from IBM's CP/CMS of 1967.

FAT

The family of FAT file systems is supported by almost all operating systems for personal computers, including all versions of Windows and MS-DOS/PC DOS and DR-DOS. (PC DOS is an OEM version of MS-DOS, MS-DOS was originally based on SCP's 86-DOS. DR-DOS was based on Digital Research's Concurrent DOS, a successor of CP/M-86.) The FAT file systems are therefore well-suited as a universal exchange format between computers and devices of most any type and age.

The FAT file system traces its roots back to an (incompatible) 8-bit FAT precursor in Standalone Disk BASIC and the short-lived MDOS/MIDAS project.

Over the years, the file system has been expanded from FAT12 to FAT16 and FAT32. Various features have been added to the file system including subdirectories, codepage support, extended attributes, and long filenames. Third parties such as Digital Research have incorporated optional support for deletion tracking, and volume/directory/file-based multi-user security schemes to support file and directory passwords and permissions such as read/write/execute/delete access rights. Most of these extensions are not supported by Windows.

The FAT12 and FAT16 file systems had a limit on the number of entries in the root directory of the file system and had restrictions on the maximum size of FAT-formatted disks or partitions.

FAT32 addresses the limitations in FAT12 and FAT16, except for the file size limit of close to 4 GB, but it remains limited compared to NTFS.

FAT12, FAT16 and FAT32 also have a limit of eight characters for the file name, and three characters for the extension (such as .exe). This is commonly referred to as the 8.3 filename limit. VFAT, an optional extension to FAT12, FAT16 and FAT32, introduced in Windows 95 and Windows NT 3.5, allowed long file names (LFN) to be stored in the FAT file system in a backwards compatible fashion.

NTFS

NTFS, introduced with the Windows NT operating system in 1993, allowed ACL-based permission control. Other features also supported by NTFS include hard links, multiple file streams, attribute indexing, quota tracking, sparse files, encryption, compression, and reparse points (directories working as mount-points for other file systems, symlinks, junctions, remote storage links).

exFAT

exFAT is a proprietary and patent-protected file system with certain advantages over NTFS with regard to file system overhead.

exFAT is not backward compatible with FAT file systems such as FAT12, FAT16 or FAT32. The file system is supported with newer Windows systems, such as Windows Server 2003, Windows Vista, Windows 2008, Windows 7, Windows 8, and more recently, support has been added for Windows XP.

exFAT is supported in OS X starting with version 10.6.5 (Snow Leopard). Support in other operating systems is sparse since Microsoft has not published the specifications of the file system and implementing support for exFAT requires a license. exFAT is the only file system that is fully supported on both OS X and Windows that can hold files bigger than 4 GB.

OpenVMS

MVS [IBM Mainframe]

Prior to the introduction of VSAM, OS/360 systems implemented an unusual hybrid file system. The system was designed to easily support removable disk packs, so the information relating to all files on one disk (*volume* in IBM terminology) is stored on that disk in a flat system file called the *Volume Table of Contents* (VTOC). The VTOC stores all metadata for the file. Later a hierarchical directory structure was imposed with the introduction of the *System Catalog*, which can optionally catalog files (datasets) on resident and removable volumes. The catalog only contains information to relate a dataset to a specific volume. If the user requests access to a dataset on an offline volume, and he has suitable privileges, the system will attempt to mount the required volume. Cataloged and non-cataloged datasets can still be accessed using information in the VTOC, bypassing the catalog, if the required volume id is provided to the OPEN request.

Conversational Monitor System

The IBM Conversational Monitor System (CMS) component of VM/370 uses a separate flat file system for each virtual disk (*minidisk*). File data and control information are scattered and intermixed.

The anchor is a record called the *Master File Directory* (MFD), always located in the fourth block on the disk. Originally CMS used fixed-length 800-byte blocks, but later versions used larger size blocks up to 4K. Access to a data record requires two levels of indirection, where the file's directory entry (called a *File Status Table* (FST) entry) points to blocks containing a list of addresses of the individual records.

AS/400 File System

Data on the AS/400 and its successors consists of system objects mapped into the system virtual address space in a single-level store. Many types of AS/400 objects are defined including the directories and files found in other file systems. File objects, along with other types of objects, form the basis of the As/400's support for an integrated relational database.

Other File Systems

- The Prospero File System is a file system based on the Virtual System Model. The system was created by Dr. B. Clifford Neuman of the Information Sciences Institute at the University of Southern California.

- RSRE FLEX file system - written in ALGOL 68.

- The file system of the Michigan Terminal System (MTS) is interesting because: (i) it provides "line files" where record lengths and line numbers are associated as metadata with each record in the file, lines can be added, replaced, updated with the same or different length records, and deleted anywhere in the file without the need to read and rewrite the entire file; (ii) using program keys files may be shared or permitted to commands and programs in addition to users and groups; and (iii) there is a comprehensive file locking mechanism that protects both the file's data and its metadata.

Limitations

Converting the Type of a File System

It may be advantageous or necessary to have files in a different file system than they currently exist. Reasons include the need for an increase in the space requirements beyond the limits of the current file system. The depth of path may need to be increased beyond the restrictions of the file system. There may be performance or reliability considerations. Providing access to another operating system which does not support existing file system is another reason.

In-place Conversion

In some cases conversion can be done in-place, although migrating the file system is more conservative, as it involves a creating a copy of the data and is recommended. On Windows, FAT and FAT32 file systems can be converted to NTFS via the convert.exe utility, but not the reverse. On Linux, ext2 can be converted to ext3 (and converted back), and ext3 can be converted to ext4 (but not back), and both ext3 and ext4 can be converted to btrfs, and converted back until the undo information is deleted. These conversions are possible due to using the same format for the file data itself, and relocating the metadata into empty space, in some cases using sparse file support.

Migrating to a Different File System

Migration has the disadvantage of requiring additional space although it may be faster. The best case is if there is unused space on media which will contain the final file system.

For example, to migrate a FAT32 file system to an ext2 file system. First create a new ext2 file system, then copy the data to the file system, then delete the FAT32 file system.

An alternative, when there is not sufficient space to retain the original file system until the new one is created, is to use a work area (such as a removable media). This takes longer but a backup of the data is a nice side effect.

Long File Paths and Long File Names

In hierarchical file systems, files are accessed by means of a *path* that is a branching list of directories containing the file. Different file systems have different limits on the depth of the path. File systems also have a limit on the length of an individual filename.

Copying files with long names or located in paths of significant depth from one file system to another may cause undesirable results. This depends on how the utility doing the copying handles the discrepancy.

File Storage Management

An operating system needs to maintain several pieces of information that can assist in management of files. For instance, it is important to record when the file was last used and by whom. Also, which are the current processes (recall a process is a program in execution) accessing a particular file. This helps in management of access. One of the important files from the system point of view is the audit trail which indicates who accessed when and did what. As mentioned earlier, these trails are maintained in syslog files under Unix. Audit trail is very useful in recovering from a system crash. It also is useful to detect un-authorized accesses to the system. There is an emerging area within the security community which looks up the audit trails for clues to determine the identity of an intruder.

In Table we list the kind of information which may be needed to perform proper file management. While Unix emphasizes formlessness, it recognizes four basic file types internally. These are ordinary, directory, special, and named. Ordinary files are those that are created by users, programs or utilities. Directory is a file type that organizes files hierarchically, and the system views them differently from ordinary files. All IO communications are conducted as communications to and from special files. For the present we need not concern ourselves with named files. Unix maintains much of this information in a data structure called inode which is a short form for an index node. All file management operations in Unix are controlled and maintained by the information in the inode structure.

We shall now briefly study the structure of inode.

Inode in Unix

In Table we describe typical inode contents. Typically, it offers all the information about access rights, file size, its date of creation, usage and modification. All this information is useful for the management in terms of allocation of physical space, securing information from malicious usage and providing services for legitimate user needs to support applications.

Nature of Information	Its significance	Its use in management
File name	Chosen by its Creator user or a program	To check its uniqueness within a directory
File type	Text, binary, program, etc.	To check its correct usage
Date of creation and last usage	Time and date	Useful for recording identity of user(s)
Current usage	Time and date	identity of all current users
Back-up info.	Time and date	Useful for recovery following a crash
Permissions	rwx information	Controls rw execute + useful for network access
Starting address	Physical mapping	Useful for access
Size	The user must operate within the allocated space	Internal allocation of disk blocks
File structure	Useful in data manipulation	To check its usage

Information required for management of files.

Typically, a disk shall have inode tables which point to data blocks. In Figure we show how a disk may have data and inode tables organized. We also show how a typical Unix-based system provides for a label on the disk.

Organistion of inodes.

Item	Description
File type	16 bit information
	Bits 14 - 12 : file type (ordinary; directory; character, etc.)
	Bits 11 - 9 : Execution flags
	Bits 8 - 6 : Owner's rwx information
	Bits 5 - 3 : group's rwx information
	Bits 2 - 0 : other's rwx information
Link count	Number of symbolic references to this file
Owner's id	Login id of the individual who owns this file

Group's id	Group id of the user
File size	Expressed in number of bytes
File address	39 bytes of addressing information
Last access to File	Date and time of last access
Last modified	Date and time of last modification
Last inode modification	Date and time of last inode modification

Inode structure in unix.

File Control Blocks

In MS environment the counterpart of inode is FCB, which is a short form for File Control Block. The FCBs store file name, location of secondary storage, length of file in bytes, date and time of its creation, last access, etc. One clear advantage MS has over Unix is that it usually maintains file type by noting which application created it. It uses extension names like *doc, txt, dll,* etc. to identify how the file was created. Of course, notepad may be used to open any file (one can make sense out of it when it is a text file). MS environment uses a simple chain of clusters which is easy to manage files.

The Root File System

At this stage it would be worthwhile to think about the organization and management of files in the root file system. When an OS is installed initially, it creates a root file system. The OS not only ensures, but also specifies how the system and user files shall be distributed for space allocation on the disk storage. Almost always the root file system has a directory tree structure. This is just like the users file organization which we studied earlier in Figure. In OSs with Unix flavors the root of the root file system is a directory. The root is identified by the directory '/'. In MS environment it is identified by 'n'. The root file system has several subdirectories. OS creates disk partitions to allocate files for specific usages. A certain disk partition may have system files and some others may have other user files or utilities. The system files are usually programs that are executable with . bin in Unix and .EXE extension in MS environment.

Under Unix the following convention is commonly employed.

- Subdirectory usr contain shareable binaries. These may be used both by users and the system. Usually these are used in read-only mode.

- Under subdirectories bin (found at any level of directory hierarchy) there are executables. For instance, the Unix commands are under /usr/bin. Clearly, these are shareable executables.

- Subdirectory sbin contains some binaries for system use. These files are used during boot time and on power-on.

- Subdirectories named lib anywhere usually contain libraries. A lib subdirectory may appear at many places. For example, as we explain a little later the graphics library which supports the graphics user interface (GUI) uses the X11 graphics library, and there shall be a lib subdirectory under directory X11.

- Subdirectory etc contains the host related files. It usually has many subdirectories to store device, internet and configuration related information. Subdirectory hosts stores internet addresses of hosts machines which may access this host. Similarly, config subdirectory maintains system configuration information and inet subdirectory maintains internet configuration related information. Under subdirectory dev, we have all the IO device related utilities.

- Subdirectories mnt contain the device mount information (in Linux).

- Subdirectories tmp contain temporary files created during file operation. When you use an editor the OS maintains a file in this directory keeping track of all the edits. Clearly this is its temporary residence.

- Subdirectories var contain files which have variable data. For instance, mail and system log information keeps varying over time. It may also have subdirectories for spools. Spools are temporary storages. For instance, a file given away for printing may be spooled to be picked up by the printer. Even mails may be spooled temporarily.

- All X related file support is under a special directory X11. One finds all X11 library files under a lib directory within this directory.

- A user with name u name would find that his files are under /home/u name. This is also the home directory for the user u name.

- Subdirectories include contain the C header include files.

- A subdirectory marked as yp (a short form for yellow pages) has network information. Essentially, it provides a database support for network operations.

One major advantage of the root file system is that the system knows exactly where to look for some specific routines. For instance, when we give a command, the system looks for a path starting from the root directory and looks for an executable file with the command name specified (usually to find it under one of the bin directories). Users can customize their operational environment by providing a definition for an environment variable PATH which guides the sequence in which the OS searches for the commands. Unix, as also the MS environment, allows users to manage the organization of their files.

One of the commands which helps to view the current status of files is the *ls* command in Unix or the command dir in MS environment.

Block-based File Organization

Recall we observed in chapter 1 that disks are bulk data transfer devices (as opposed to character devices like a keyboard). So data transfer takes place from disks in blocks as large as 512 or 1024 bytes at a time. Any file which a user generates (or retrieves), therefore, moves in blocks. Each operating system has its own block management policy. We shall study the general principles underlying allocation policies. These policies map each linear byte stream into disk blocks. We consider a very simple case where we need to support a file system on one disk. Note a policy on storage management can heavily influence the performance of a file system (which in turn affects the throughput of an OS). File Storage allocation policy: Let us assume we know apriori the sizes of files before their creation. So this information can always be given to OS before a file is created. Consequently, the OS can simply make space available. In such a situation it is possible to follow a pre-allocation policy: find a suitable starting block so that the file can be accommodated in a contiguous sequence of disk blocks. A simple solution would be to allocate a sequence of contiguous blocks as shown in Figure.

The numbers 1, 2, 3 and 4 denote the starting blocks for the four files. One clear advantage of such a policy is that the retrieval of information is very fast. However, note that pre-allocation policy requires apriori knowledge. Also, it is a static policy. Often users' needs develop over time and files undergo changes. Therefore, we need a dynamic policy.

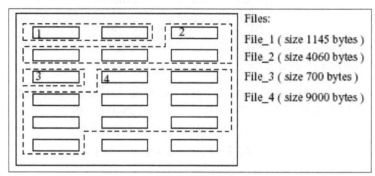

Contiguous allocation

Chained list Allocation : There are two reasons why a dynamic block allocation policy is needed. The first is that in most cases it is not possible to know apriori the size of a file being created. The second is that there are some files that already exist and it is not easy to find contiguous regions. For instance, even though there may be enough space in the disk, yet it may not be possible to find a single large enough chunk to accommodate an incoming file. Also, users' needs evolve and a file during its lifetime undergoes changes. Contiguous blocks leave no room for such changes. That is because there may be already allocated files occupying the contiguous space.

In a dynamic situation, a list of free blocks is maintained. Allocation is made as the need arises. We may even allocate one block at a time from a free space list. The OS maintains a chain of free blocks and allocates next free block in the chain to an incoming file. This way the finally allocated files may be located at various positions on the disk. The obvious overhead is the maintenance of chained links. But then we now have a dynamically allocated disk space. An example is shown in Figure.

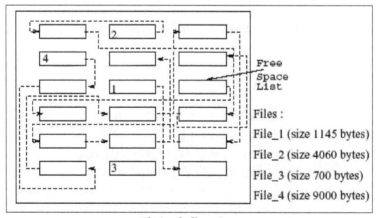

Chained allocation

Chained list allocation does not require apriori size information. Also, it is a dynamic allocation method. However, it has one major disadvantage: random access to blocks is not possible.

Indexed allocation: In an indexed allocation we maintain an index table for each file in its very first block. Thus it is possible to obtain the address information for each of the blocks with only one level of indirection, i.e. from the index. This has the advantage that there is a direct access to every block of the file. This means we truly operate in the direct access mode at the block level.

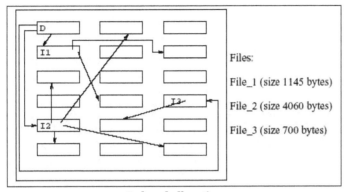

Indexed allocation

In Figure we see that File-2 occupies four blocks. Suppose we use a block I2 to store the starting addresses of these four blocks, then from this index we can access any of the four parts of this file. In a chained list arrangement we would have to traverse the links. In Figure we have also shown D to denote the file's current directory. All files have their own index blocks. In terms of storage the overhead of storing the indices is more than the overhead of storing the links in the chained list arrangements. However, the speed of access compensates for the extra overhead.

Internal and external Fragmentation: In mapping byte streams to blocks we assumed a block size of 1024 bytes. In our example, a file (File 1) of size 1145 bytes was allocated two blocks. The two blocks together have 2048 bytes capacity. We will fill the first block completely but the second block will be mostly empty. This is because only 121 bytes out of 1024 bytes are used. As the assignment of storage is by blocks in size of 1024 bytes the remaining bytes in the second block can not be used. Such non-utilization of space caused internally (as it is within a file's space) is termed as internal fragmentation. We note that initially the whole disk is a free-space list of connected blocks. After a number of file insertions and deletion or modifications the free-space list becomes smaller in size. This can be explained as follows. For instance, suppose we have a file which was initially spread over 7 blocks. Now after a few edits the file needs only 4 blocks. This space of 3 blocks which got released is now not connected anywhere. It is not connected with the free storage list either. As a result, we end up with a hole of 3 blocks which is not connected anywhere. After many file edits and operations many such holes of various sizes get created. Suppose we now wish to insert a moderately large sized file thinking that adequate space should be still available. Then it may happen that the free space list has shrunk so much that enough space is not available. This may be because there are many unutilized holes in the disk. Such non-utilization, which is outside of file space, is regarded as external fragmentation. A file system, therefore, must periodic all perform an operation to rebuild free storage list by collecting all the unutilized holes and linking them back to free storage list. This process is called compaction. When you boot a system, often the compaction gets done automatically. This is usually a part of file system management check. Some run-time systems, like LISP and Java, support periodic automatic compaction. This is also referred to as run-time garbage collection.

Policies In Practice

MS DOS and OS2 (the PC-based systems) use a FAT (file allocation table) strategy. FAT is a table that has entries for files for each directory. The file name is used to get the starting address of the first block of a file. Each file block is chain linked to the next block till an EOF (end of file) is stored in some block. MS uses the notion of a cluster in place of blocks, i.e. the concept of cluster in MS is same as that of blocks in Unix. The cluster size is different for different sizes of disks. For instance, for a 256 MB disk the cluster may have a size of 4 KB and for a disk with size of 1 GB it may be 32 KB. The formula used for determining the cluster size in MS environment is disk-size/64K.

FAT was created to keep track of all the file entries. To that extent it also has the information similar to the index node in Unix. Since MS environment uses chained allocation, FAT also maintains a list of "free" block chains. Earlier, the file names under MS DOS were restricted to eight characters and a three letter extension often indicating the file type like BAT or EXE, etc. Usually FAT is stored in the first few blocks of disk space.

An updated version of FAT, called FAT32, is used in Windows 98 and later systems. FAT32 additionally supports longer file names and file compression. File compression may be used to save on storage space for less often used files. Yet another version of the Windows is available under the Windows NT. This file system is called NTFS. Rather than having one FAT in the beginning of disk, the NTFS file system spreads file tables throughout the disks for efficient management. Like FAT32, it also supports long file names and file compression. Windows 2000 uses NTFS. Other characteristics worthy of note are the file access permissions supported by NTFS.

Unix always supported long file names and most Unix based systems such as Solaris and almost all Linux versions automatically compress the files that have not been used for long. Unix uses indexed allocation. Unix was designed to support truly large files. We next describe how large can be large files in Unix.

Unix file sizes: Unix was designed to support large-scale program development with team effort. Within this framework, it supports group access to very large files at very high speeds. It also has a very flexible organization for files of various sizes. The information about files is stored in two parts. The first part has information about the mode of access, the symbolic links, owner and times of creation and last modification. The second part is a 39 byte area within the inode structure. These 39 bytes are 13, 3 byte address pointers. Of the 39 bytes, first 10 point to the first 10 blocks of a file. If the files are longer then the other 3, 3 byte addresses are used for indirect indexing. So the 11th 3 byte address points to a block that has pointers to real data. In case the file is still larger then the 12th 3 byte address points to an index. This index in turn points to another index table which finally point to data. If the files are still larger then the 13th 3 byte address is used to support a triple indirect indexing. Obviously, Unix employs the indexed allocation.

In Figure we assume a data block size of 1024 bytes. We show the basic scheme and also show the size of files supported as the levels of indirection increase. Physical Layout of Information on Media: In our discussions on file storage and management we have concentrated on logical storage of files. We, however, ignored one very important aspect. And that concerns the physical layout of information on the disk media. Of course, we shall revisit aspects of information map on physical medium later in the chapter on IO device management. For now, we let us examine Figures to see how information is stored, read, and written in to a disk.

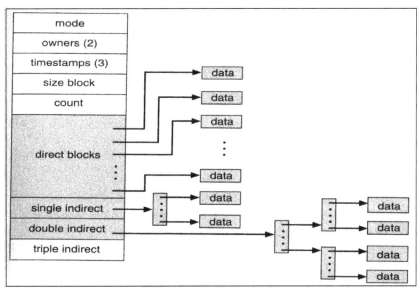

Storage allocation in unix.

In Figure, tracks may be envisaged as rings on a disk platter. Each ring on a platter is capable of storing 1 bit along its width. These 1 bit wide rings are broken into sectors, which serve as blocks. We essentially referred to these as blocks.

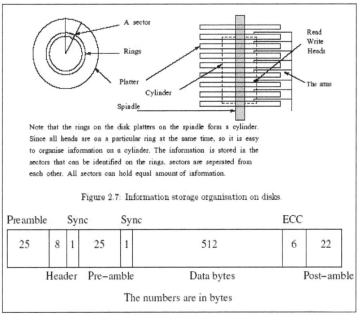

Information storage in sectors.

This break up into sectors is necessitated because of the physical nature of control required to let the system recognize, where within the tracks blocks begin in a disk. With disks moving at a very high speed, it is not possible to identify individual characters as they are laid out. Only the beginning of a block of information can be detected by hardware control to initiate a stream of bits for either input or output. The read-write heads on the tracks read or write a stream of data along the track in the identified sectors. With multiple disks mounted on a spindle as shown in Figure, it helps to think of a cylinder formed by tracks that are equidistant from the center. Just imagine a large number of tracks, one above the other, and you begin to see a cylinder. These cylinders can be given contiguous block sequence numbers to store information. In fact, this is desirable because then one can access these blocks in sequence without any additional head movement in a head per track disk. The question of our interest for now is: where is inode (or FAT block) located and how it helps to locate the physical file which is mapped on to sectors on tracks which form cylinders.

Disk Partitions

Disk-partitioning is an important notion. It allows a better management of disk space. The basic idea is rather simple. If you think of a disk as a large space then simply draw some boundaries to keep things in specific areas for specific purposes. In most cases the disk partitions are created at the time the disc is formatted. So a formatted disk has information about the partition size.

In Unix oriented systems, a physical partition of a disk houses a file system. Unix also allows creating a logical partition of disk space which may extend over multiple disk drives. In either case, every partition has its own file system management information.

This information is about the files in that partition which populate the file system. Unix ensures that the partitions for the system kernel and the users files are located in different partitions (or file systems). Unix systems identify specific partitions to store the root file system, usually in root partition. The root partition may also co-locate other system functions with variable storage requirements which we discussed earlier. The user files may be in another file system, usually called home. Under Linux, a proc houses all the executable processes.

Under the Windows system too, a hard disk is partitioned. One interesting conceptual notion is to make each such partition that can be taken as a logical drive. In fact, one may have one drive and by partitioning, a user can make the OS offer a possibility to write into each partition as if it was writing in to a separate drive. There are many third-party tools for personal computer to help users to create partitions on their disks. Yet another use in the PC world is to house two operating system, one in each partition. For instance, using two partitions it is possible to have Linux on one and Windows on another partition in the disk. This gives enormous flexibility of operations. Typically, a 80 GB disk in modern machines may be utilized to house Windows XP and Linux with nearly 40 GB disk available for each.

Yet another associated concept in this context, is the way the disk partitions are mounted on a file system. Clearly, a disk partition, with all its contents, is essentially a set of organized information. It has its own directory structure. Hence, it is a tree by itself. This tree gets connected to some node in the overall tree structure of the file system and forks out. This is precisely what mounting means. The partition is regarded to be mounted in the file system. This basic concept is also carried to the file servers on a network. The network file system may have remote partitions which are mounted on it. It offers seamless file access as if all of the storage was on the local disk. In modern systems, the file servers are located on networks somewhere without the knowledge of the user. From a user's standpoint all that is important to note is that as a user, his files are a part of a large tree structure which is a file system.

Portable Storage

There are external media like tapes, disks, and floppies. These storage devices can be physically ported. Most file systems recognize these as on-line files when these are mounted on an IO device like a tape drive or a floppy drive. Unix treats these as special files. PCs and MAC OS recognize these as external files and provide an icon when these are mounted.

In this chapter we have covered considerable ground. Files are the entities that users deal with all the time. Users create files, manage them and seek system support in their file management activity. The discussion here has been to help build up a conceptual basis and leaves much to be covered with respect to specific instructions. For specifics, one should consult manuals. In this very rapidly advancing field, while the concept does not change, the practice does and does at a phenomenal pace.

File System Fragmentation

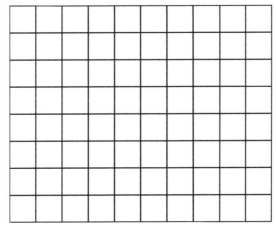

Visualization of fragmentation and then of defragmentation.

In computing, file system fragmentation, sometimes called file system aging, is the tendency of a file system to lay out the contents of files non-contiguously to allow in-place modification of their contents. It is a special case of data fragmentation. File system fragmentation increases disk head movement or seek time, which are known to hinder throughput. In addition, file systems cannot sustain unlimited fragmentation. The correction to existing fragmentation is to reorganize files and free space back into contiguous areas, a process called defragmentation.

Causes

When a file system is first initialized on a partition, it contains only a few small internal structures and is otherwise one contiguous block of empty space. This means that the file system is able to place newly created files anywhere on the partition. For some time after creation, files can be laid out near-optimally. When the operating system and applications are installed or archives are unpacked, separate files end up occurring sequentially so related files are positioned close to each other.

As existing files are deleted or truncated, new regions of free space are created. When existing files are appended to, it is often impossible to resume the write exactly where the file used to end, as another file may already be allocated there; thus, a new fragment has to be allocated. As time goes on, and the same factors are continuously present, free space as well as frequently appended files tend to fragment more. Shorter regions of free space also mean that the file system is no longer able to allocate new files contiguously, and has to break them into fragments. This is especially true when the file system becomes full and large contiguous regions of free space are unavailable.

Example

(1)	A	B	C	D	E	Free Space
(2)	A		C	D	E	Free Space
(3)	A	F	C	D	E	Free Space
(4)	A	F	G	C	D	E	Free Space
(5)	A	F	G	C	D	E	Free Space

F (Second *extent*, or allocation)

Oversimplified example of how free space fragmentation and file fragmentation occur.

The following example is a simplification of an otherwise complicated subject. Consider the following scenario: A new disk has had five files, named A, B, C, D and E, saved continuously and sequentially in that order. Each file is using 10 *blocks* of space. (Here, the block size is unimportant.) The remainder of the disk space is one free block. Thus, additional files can be created and saved after the file E.

If the file B is deleted, a second region of ten blocks of free space is created, and the disk becomes fragmented. The empty space is simply left there, marked as and available for later use, then used again as needed. The file system *could* defragment the disk immediately after a deletion, but doing so would incur a severe performance penalty at unpredictable times.

Now, a new file called F, which requires seven blocks of space, can be placed into the first seven blocks of the newly freed space formerly holding the file B, and the three blocks following it will remain available. If another new file called G, which needs only three blocks, is added, it could then occupy the space after F and before C.

If subsequently F needs to be expanded, since the space immediately following it is occupied, there are three options for the file system:

1. Adding a new block somewhere else and indicating that F has a second extent.

2. Moving files in the way of the expansion elsewhere, to allow F to remain contiguous.

3. Moving file F so it can be one contiguous file of the new, larger size.

The second option is probably impractical for performance reasons, as is the third when the file is very large. The third option is impossible when there is no single contiguous free space large enough to hold the new file. Thus the usual practice is simply to create an *extent* somewhere else and chain the new extent onto the old one.

Material added to the end of file F would be part of the same extent. But if there is so much material that no room is available after the last extent, then *another* extent would have to be created, and so on. Eventually the file system has free segments in many places and some files may be spread over many extents. Access time for those files (or for all files) may become excessively long.

Necessity

Some early file systems were unable to fragment files. One such example was the Acorn DFS file system used on the BBC Micro. Due to its inability to fragment files, the error message *can't extend* would at times appear, and the user would often be unable to save a file even if the disk had adequate space for it.

DFS used a very simple disk structure and files on disk were located only by their length and starting sector. This meant that all files had to exist as a continuous block of sectors and fragmentation was not possible. Using the example in the table above, the attempt to expand file F in step five would have failed on such a system with the *can't extend* error message. Regardless of how much free space might remain on the disk in total, it was not available to extend the data file.

Standards of error handling at the time were primitive and in any case programs squeezed into the limited memory of the BBC Micro could rarely afford to waste space attempting to handle errors gracefully. Instead, the user would find themselves dumped back at the command prompt with the *Can't extend* message and all the data which had yet to be appended to the file would be lost. The resulting frustration would be greater if the user had taken the trouble to check the free space on the disk beforehand and found free space. While free space on the disk may exist, the fact that it was not in the place where it was needed was not apparent without analyzing the numbers presented by the disk catalog and so would escape the user's notice. In addition, DFS users had almost without exception previously been accustomed to cassette file storage, which does not suffer from this error. The upgrade to a floppy disk system was expensive performance upgrade, and it was a shock to make the sudden and unpleasant discovery that the upgrade might without warning cause data loss.

Types

File system fragmentation may occur on several levels:

- Fragmentation within individual files.

- Free space fragmentation.

- The decrease of locality of reference between separate, but related files.

File Fragmentation

Individual file fragmentation occurs when a single file has been broken into multiple pieces (called extents on extent-based file systems). While disk file systems attempt to keep individual files contiguous, this is not often possible without significant performance penalties. File system check and defragmentation tools typically only account for file fragmentation in their "fragmentation percentage" statistic.

Free Space Fragmentation

Free (unallocated) space fragmentation occurs when there are several unused areas of the file system where new files or metadata can be written to. Unwanted free space fragmentation is generally caused by deletion or truncation of files, but file systems may also intentionally insert fragments ("bubbles") of free space in order to facilitate extending nearby files.

File Scattering

File segmentation, also called related-file fragmentation, or application-level (file) fragmentation, refers to the lack of locality of reference (within the storing medium) between related files. Unlike the previous two types of fragmentation, file scattering is a much more vague concept, as it heavily depends on the access pattern of specific applications. This also makes objectively measuring or estimating it very difficult. However, arguably, it is the most critical type of fragmentation, as studies have found that the most frequently accessed files tend to be small compared to available disk throughput per second.

To avoid related file fragmentation and improve locality of reference (in this case called *file contiguity*), assumptions or active observations about the operation of applications have to be made. A very frequent assumption made is that it is worthwhile to keep smaller files within a single directory together, and lay them out in the natural file system order. While it is often a reasonable assumption, it does not always hold. For example, an application might read several different files, perhaps in different directories, in exactly the same order they were written. Thus, a file system that simply orders all writes successively, might work faster for the given application.

Negative Consequences

File system fragmentation is more problematic with consumer-grade hard disk drives because of the increasing disparity between sequential access speed and rotational latency (and to a lesser extent seek time) on which file systems are usually placed. Thus, fragmentation is an important problem in file system research and design. The containment of fragmentation not only depends on the on-disk format of the file system, but also heavily on its implementation. File system fragmentation has less performance impact upon solid-state drives, as there is no mechanical seek time involved. However, the file system needs to store one additional piece of metadata for the corresponding file. Each piece of metadata itself occupies space and requires processing power and processor time. If the maximum fragmentation limit is reached, write requests fail.

In simple file system benchmarks, the fragmentation factor is often omitted, as realistic aging and fragmentation is difficult to model. Rather, for simplicity of comparison, file system benchmarks are often run on empty file systems. Thus, the results may vary heavily from real-life access patterns.

Mitigation

Several techniques have been developed to fight fragmentation. They can usually be classified into two categories: *preemptive* and *retroactive*. Due to the difficulty of predicting access patterns these techniques are most often heuristic in nature and may degrade performance under unexpected workloads.

Preventing Fragmentation

Preemptive techniques attempt to keep fragmentation at a minimum at the time data is being written on the disk. The simplest is appending data to an existing fragment in place where possible, instead of allocating new blocks to a new fragment.

Many of today's file systems attempt to preallocate longer chunks, or chunks from different free space fragments, called extents to files that are actively appended to. This largely avoids file fragmentation when several files are concurrently being appended to, thus avoiding their becoming excessively intertwined.

If the final size of a file subject to modification is known, storage for the entire file may be preallocated. For example, the Microsoft Windows swap file (page file) can be resized dynamically under normal operation, and therefore can become highly fragmented. This can be prevented by specifying a page file with the same minimum and maximum sizes, effectively preallocating the entire file.

BitTorrent and other peer-to-peer filesharing applications limit fragmentation by preallocating the full space needed for a file when initiating downloads.

A relatively recent technique is delayed allocation in XFS, HFS+ and ZFS; the same technique is also called allocate-on-flush in reiser4 and ext4. When the file system is being written to, file system blocks are reserved, but the locations of specific files are not laid down yet. Later, when the file system is forced to flush changes as a result of memory pressure or a transaction commit, the allocator will have much better knowledge of the files' characteristics. Most file systems with this approach try to flush files in a single directory contiguously. Assuming that multiple reads from a single directory are common, locality of reference is improved. Reiser4 also orders the layout of files according to the directory hash table, so that when files are being accessed in the natural file system order (as dictated by readdir), they are always read sequentially.

Defragmentation

Retroactive techniques attempt to reduce fragmentation, or the negative effects of fragmentation, after it has occurred. Many file systems provide defragmentation tools, which attempt to reorder fragments of files, and sometimes also decrease their scattering (i.e. improve their contiguity, or locality of reference) by keeping either smaller files in directories, or directory trees, or even file sequences close to each other on the disk.

The HFS Plus file system transparently defragments files that are less than 20 MiB in size and are broken into 8 or more fragments, when the file is being opened.

The now obsolete Commodore Amiga Smart File System (SFS) defragmented itself while the filesystem was in use. The defragmentation process is almost completely stateless (apart from the location it is working on), so that it can be stopped and started instantly. During defragmentation data integrity is ensured for both metadata and normal data.

Memory Management

The von Neumann principle for the design and operation of computers requires that a program has to be primary memory resident to execute. Also, a user requires to revisit his programs often during its evolution. However, due to the fact that primary memory is volatile, a user needs to store his program in some non-volatile store. All computers provide a non-volatile secondary memory available as an online storage. Programs and files may be disk resident and downloaded whenever their execution is required. Therefore, some form of memory management is needed at both primary and secondary memory levels.

Secondary memory may store program scripts, executable process images and data files. It may store applications, as well as, system programs. In fact, a good part of all OS, the system programs which provide services (the utilities for instance) are stored in the secondary memory. These are requisitioned as needed.

The main motivation for management of main memory comes from the support for multi- programming. Several executables processes reside in main memory at any given time. In other words, there are several programs using the main memory as their address space. Also, programs move into, and out of, the main memory as they terminate, or get suspended for some IO, or new executables are required to be loaded in main memory.

So, the OS has to have some strategy for main memory management. In this chapter we shall discuss the management issues and strategies for both main memory and secondary memory.

Main Memory Management

Let us begin by examining the issues that prompt the main memory management.

- Allocation: First of all the processes that are scheduled to run must be resident in the memory. These processes must be allocated space in main memory.

- Swapping, fragmentation and compaction: If a program is moved out or terminates, it creates a hole, (i.e. a contiguous unused area) in main memory. When a new process is to be moved in, it may be allocated one of the available holes. It is quite possible that main memory has far too many small holes at a certain time. In such a situation none of these holes is really large enough to be allocated to a new process that may be moving in. The main memory is too fragmented. It is, therefore, essential to attempt compaction. Compaction means OS re-allocates the existing programs in contiguous regions and creates a large enough free area for allocation to a new process.

- Garbage collection: Some programs use dynamic data structures. These programs dynamically use and discard memory space. Technically, the deleted data items (from a dynamic data structure) release memory locations. However, in practice the OS does not collect such free space immediately for allocation. This is because that affects performance. Such areas, therefore, are called garbage. When such garbage exceeds a certain threshold, the OS would not have enough memory available for any further allocation. This entails compaction (or garbage collection), without severely affecting performance.

- Protection: With many programs residing in main memory it can happen that due to a programming error (or with malice) some process writes into data or instruction area of some other process. The OS ensures that each process accesses only to its own allocated area, i.e. each process is protected from other processes.

- Virtual memory: Often a processor sees a large logical storage space (a virtual storage space) though the actual main memory may not be that large. So some facility needs to be provided to translate a logical address available to a processor into a physical address to access the desired data or instruction.

- IO support: Most of the block-oriented devices are recognized as specialized files. Their buffers need to be managed within main memory alongside the other processes. The considerations stated above motivate the study of main memory management.

One of the important considerations in locating an executable program is that it should be possible to relocate it any where in the main memory. We shall dwell upon the concept of relocation next.

Memory Relocation Concept

Relocation is an important concept. To understand this concept we shall begin with a linear map (one-dimensional view) of main memory. If we know an address we can fetch its contents. So, a process residing in the main memory, we set the program counter to an absolute address of its first instruction and can initiate its run. Also, if we know the locations of data then we can fetch those too. All of this stipulates that we know the absolute addresses for a program, its data and process context etc. This means that we can load a process with only absolute addresses for instructions and data, only when those specific addresses are free in main memory. This would mean we loose flexibility with regard to loading a process. For instance, we cannot load a process, if some other process is currently occupying that area which is needed by this process. This may happen even though we may have enough space in the memory. To avoid such a catastrophe, processes are generated to be relocatable. In Figure we see a process resident in main memory.

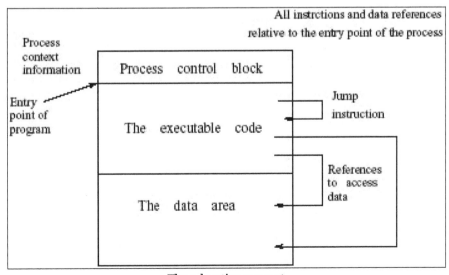

The relocation concept.

Initially, all the addresses in the process are relative to the start address. With this flexibility we can allocate any area in the memory to load this process. Its instruction, data, process context (process control block) and any other data structure required by the process can be accessed easily if the addresses are relative. This is most helpful when processes move in and out of main memory. Suppose a process created a hole on moving out. In case we use non-relocatable addresses, we have the following very severe problem.

When the process moves back in, that particular hole (or area) may not be available any longer. In case we can relocate, moving a process back in creates no problem. This is so because the process can be relocated in some other free area. We shall next examine the linking and loading of programs to understand the process of relocation better.

Compiler Generated Bindings

The advantage of relocation can also be seen in the light of binding of addresses to variables in a program. Suppose we have a program variable x in a program P. Suppose the compiler allocated a fixed address to x. This address allocation by the compiler is called binding. If x is bound to a fixed location then we can execute program P only when x could be put in its allocated memory location. Otherwise, all address references to x will be incorrect.

If, however, the variable can be assigned a location relative to an assumed origin (or first address in program P) then, on relocating the program's origin anywhere in main memory, we will still be able to generate a proper relative address reference for x and execute the program. In fact, compilers generate relocatable code.

Linking and Loading Concepts

In Figure we depict the three stages of the way a HLL program gets processed.

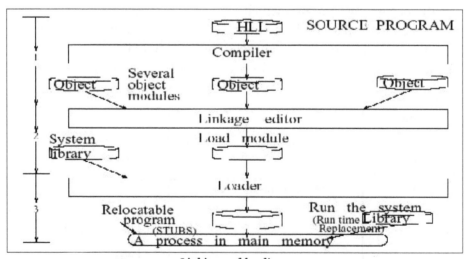

Linking and loading.

The three stages of the processing are:

- Stage 1: In the first stage the HLL source program is compiled and an object code is produced. Technically, depending upon the program, this object code may by itself be sufficient to generate a relocatable process. However many programs are compiled in parts, so this object code may have to link up with other object modules. At this stage the compiler may also insert stub at points where run time library modules may be linked.

- Stage 2: All those object modules which have sufficient linking information (generated by the compiler) for static linking are taken up for linking. The linking editor generates a re-locatable code. At this stage, however, we still do not replace the stubs placed by compilers for a run time library link up.

- Stage3: The final step is to arrange to make substitution for the stubs with run time library code which is a relocatable code.

When all the three stages are completed we have an executable. When this executable is resident in the main memory it is a runnable process.

The compiler uses a symbol table to generate addresses. These addresses are not bound, i.e. these do not have absolute values but do have information on sizes of data. The binding produced at compile time is generally relative. Some OSs support a linking loader which translates the relative addresses to relocatable addresses. In any event, the relocatable process is finally formed as an output of a loader.

Process and Main Memory Management

Once processes have been created, the OS organizes their execution. This requires interaction between process management and main memory management. To understand this interaction better, we shall create a scenario requiring memory allocations. For the operating environment we assume the following:

- A uni-processor, multi-programming operation.

- A Unix like operating system environment.

With a Unix like OS, we can assume that main memory is partitioned in two parts. One part is for user processes and the other is for OS. We will assume that we have a main memory of 20 units (for instance it could be 2 or 20 or 200 MB). We show the requirements and time of arrival and processing requirements for 6 processes in Table.

	P1	P2	P3	P4	P5	P6
Time of arrival	0	0	0	0	10	15
Processing time required	8	5	20	12	10	5
Memory required	3 units	7 units	2 units	4 units	2 units	2 units

The given data.

We shall assume that OS requires 6 units of space. To be able to compare various policies, we shall repeatedly use the data in table for every policy option.

With these requirements we can now trace the emerging scenario for the given data. We shall assume round robin allocation of processor time slots with no context switching over-heads. We shall trace the events as they occur giving reference to the corresponding part in Table. This table also shows a memory map as the processes move in and out of the main memory.

Time units	Programs in main memory	Programs on disk	Holes with sizes	Figures	Comments
0	P1, P2, P3	P4	H1=2	(a)	P4 requires more space than H1
5	P1, P4, P3		H1=2; H2=3	(b)	P2 is finished P4 is loaded Hole H2 is Created
8	P4, P3		H1=2; H2=3; H3=3	(c)	New hole created
10	P4, P3	P5			P5 arrives
10+	P5, P4, P3		H1=2; H2=3; H3=1	(d)	P5 is allocated P1's space
15	P5, P4, P3	P6	H1=2; H2=3; H3=1		P6 has arrived
15+	P5, P4, P6, P3		H1=2; H2=1; H3=1	(e)	P6 is allocated

FCFS memory allocation.

The First Fit Policy: Memory Allocation

In this example we make use of a policy called first fit memory allocation policy. The first fit policy suggests that we use the first available hole, which is large enough to accommodate an incoming process. In Figure, it is important to note that we are following first-come first-served (process management) and first fit (memory allocation) policies. The process index denotes its place in the queue. As per first-come first-served policies the queue order determines the order in which the processes are allocated areas. In addition, as per first-fit policy allocation we scan the memory always from one end and find the first block of free space which is large enough to accommodate the incoming process.

In our example, initially, processes P1, P2, P3 and P4 are in the queue. The allocations for processes P1, P2, P3 are shown in 4.3(a). At time 5, process P2 terminates. So, process P4 is allocated in the hole created by process P2. This is shown at 4.3(b) in the figure. It still leaves a hole of size 3. Now on advancing time further we see that at time 8, process P1 terminates. This creates a hole of size 3 as shown at 4.3(c) in the figure.

This hole too is now available for allocation. We have 3 holes at this stage. Two of these 3 holes are of size 3 and one is of size 2. When process P5 arrives at time 10, we look for the first hole which can accommodate it. This is the one created by the departure of process P1. Using the first-fit argument this is the hole allocated to process P5 as shown in Figure(d). The final allocation status is shown in Figure. The first-fit allocation policy is very easy to implement and is fast in execution.

Program P1	Program P1	Hole 3 units	Program P5	Program P5
			Hole 1 unit	Hole 1 unit
Program P2	Program P4	Program P4	Program P4	Program P4
	Hole 3 units	Hole 3 units	Hole 3 units	Program P6
				Hole 1 unit
Program P3	Program P3	Program P3	Program P3	Program P3
Hole 2 units	Hole 2 units	Hole 2 units	Hole 2 units	Hole 2 units
Operting system's area	Operting system's area	Operting system's area	Operting system's area	Operting system's area
(a)	(b)	(c)	(d)	(e)

First-fit policy allocation.

The Best Fit Policy: Memory Allocation

The main criticism of first-fit policy is that it may leave many smaller holes. For instance, let us trace the allocation for process P5. It needs 2 units of space. At the time it moves into the main memory there is a hole with 2 units of space. But this is the last hole when we scan the main memory from the top (beginning). The first hole is 3 units. Using the first-fit policy process P5 is allocated this hole. So when we used this hole we also created a still smaller hole. Note that smaller holes are less useful for future allocations.

In the best-fit policy we scan the main memory for all the available holes. Once we have information about all the holes in the memory then we choose the one which is closest to the size of the requirement of the process. In our example we allocate the hole with size 2 as there is one available. Table follows best-fit policy for the current example.

Also, as we did for the previous example, we shall again assume round-robin allocation of the processor time slots. With these considerations we can now trace the possible emerging scenario.

In Figure, we are following first-come first-served (process management) and best fit (memory allocation) policies. The process index denotes its place in the queue. Initially, processes P1, P2, P3 and P4 are in the queue. Processes P1, P2 and P3 are allocated as shown in Figure (a). At time 5, P2 terminates and process P4 is allocated in the hole so created. This is shown in Figure (b). This is the best fit. It leaves a space of size 3 creating a new hole. At time 8, process P1 terminates. We now have 3 holes. Two of these holes are of size 3 and one is of size 2. When process P5 arrives at time 10, we look for a hole whose size is nearest to 2 and can accommodate P5. This is the last hole.

Best-fit policy allocation

Clearly, the best-fit (and also the worst-fit) policy should be expected to be slow in execution. This is so because the implementation requires a time consuming scan of all of main memory. There is another method called the next-fit policy. In the next-fit method the search pointer does not start at the top (beginning), instead it begins from where it ended during the previous search. Like the first-fit policy it locates the next first-fit hole that can be used. Note that unlike the first-fit policy the next-fit policy can be expected to distribute small holes uniformly in the main memory. The first-fit policy would have a tendency to create small holes towards the beginning of the main memory scan. Both first-fit and next-fit methods are very fast and easy to implement.

In conclusion, first-fit and next-fit are the fastest and seem to be the preferred methods. One of the important considerations in main memory management is: how should an OS allocate a chunk of main memory required by a process. One simple approach would be to somehow create partitions and then different processes could reside in different partitions. We shall next discuss how the main memory partitions may be created.

Time units	Programs in Main memory	Programs on disk	Holes with sizes	Figure 4.4	Comments
0	P1, P2, P3	P4	H1=2	(a)	P4 requires more space than H1
5	P1, P4, P3		H1=2; H2=3	(b)	P2 is finished P4 is loaded Hole H2 is created
8	P4, P3		H1=2; H2=3; H3=3	(c)	Creates a new hole
10	P4, P3	P5			P5 arrives
10+	P4, P3, P5		H2=3; H3=3	(d)	P5 is allocated the best fit hole
15	P4, P3, P5	P6	H2=3; H3=3		P6 arrives
15+	P6, P4, P3, P5		H2=3; H4=1	(e)	P6 takes the hole left by P1

Best-fit policy memory allocation.

Fixed and Variable Partitions

In a fixed size partitioning of the main memory all partitions are of the same size. The memory resident processes can be assigned to any of these partitions. Fixed sized partitions are relatively simple to implement. However, there are two problems. This scheme is not easy to use when a program requires more space than the partition size. In this situation the programmer has to resort to overlays. Overlays involve moving data and program segments in and out of memory essentially reusing the area in main memory. The second problem has to do with internal fragmentation. No matter what the size of the process is, a fixed size of memory block is allocated as shown in Figure (a). So there will always be some space which will remain unutilized within the partition.

In a variable-sized partition, the memory is partitioned into partitions with different sizes. Processes are loaded into the size nearest to its requirements. It is easy to always ensure the best-fit. One may organize a queue for each size of the partition as shown in the Figure (b). With best-fit policy, variable partitions minimize internal fragmentation.

However, such an allocation may be quite slow in execution. This is so because a process may end up waiting (queued up) in the best-fit queue even while there is space available elsewhere. For example, we may have several jobs queued up in a queue meant for jobs that require 1 unit of memory, even while no jobs are queued up for jobs that require say 4 units of memory.

Both fixed and dynamic partitions suffer from external fragmentation whenever there are partitions that have no process in it. One of techniques that have been used to keep both internal and external fragmentations low is dynamic partitioning. It is basically a variable partitioning with a variable number of partitions determined dynamically (i.e. at run time).

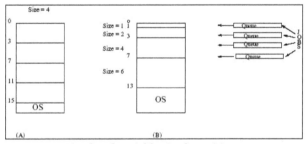

Fixed and variable sized partitions.

Such a scheme is difficult to implement. Another scheme which falls between the fixed and dynamic partitioning is a buddy system described next.

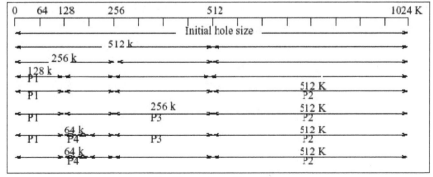

Buddy system allocation.

The Buddy system of partitioning: The buddy system of partitioning relies on the fact that space allocations can be conveniently handled in sizes of power of 2. There are two ways in which the buddy system allocates space. Suppose we have a hole which is the closest power of two. In that case, that hole is used for allocation. In case we do not have that situation then we look for the next power of 2 hole size, split in two equal halves and allocate one of these. Because we always split the holes in two equal sizes, the two are \buddies". Hence, the name buddy system. We shall illustrate allocation using a buddy system We assume that initially we have a space of 1024 K. We also assume that processes arrive and are allocated following a time sequence as shown in figure.

With 1024 K or (1 M) storage space we split it into buddies of 512 K, splitting one of them to two 256 K buddies and so on till we get the right size. Also, we assume scan of memory from the beginning. We always use the first hole which accommodates the process. Otherwise, we split the next sized hole into buddies. Note that the buddy system begins search for a hole as if we had a fixed number of holes of variable sizes but turns into a dynamic partitioning scheme when we do not find the best-fit hole. The buddy system has the advantage that it minimizes the internal fragmentation. However, it is not popular because it is very slow. In Figure we assume the requirements as (P1:80 K); (P2:312 K); (P3:164 K); (P4:38 K). These processes arrive in the order of their index and P1 and P3 finish at the same time.

Virtual Storage Space and Main Memory Partitions

Programming models assume the presence of main memory only. Therefore, ideally we would like to have an unlimited (infinite) main memory available. In fact, an unlimited main memory shall give us a Turing machine capability. However, in practice it is infeasible. So the next best thing is attempted. CPU designers support and generate a very large logical addressable space to support programming concerns. However, the directly addressable main memory is limited and is quite small in comparison to the logical addressable space. The actual size of main memory is referred as the physical memory. The logical addressable space is referred to as virtual memory. The notion of virtual memory is a bit of an illusion. The OS supports and makes this illusion possible. It does so by copying chunks of disk memory into the main memory as shown in Figure. In other words, the processor is fooled into believing that it is accessing a large addressable space. Hence, the name virtual storage space. The disk area may map to the virtual space requirements and even beyond.

Besides the obvious benefit that virtual memory offers a very large address space, there is one other major benefit derived from the use of virtual storage. We now can have many more main memory resident active processes. This can be explained as follows. During much of the lifetime of its execution, a process operates on a small set of instructions within a certain neighborhood. The same applies for the data as well. In other words a process makes use of a very small memory area for doing most of the instructions and making references to the data. This is primarily due to the locality of reference. So, technically, at any time we need a very small part of a process to really be memory resident. For a moment, let us suppose that this small part is only 1/10th of the process's overall requirements. Note in that case, for the same size of physical main memory, we can service 10 times as many memory resident programs. The next question then is how do we organize and allocate these small chunks of often required areas to be in memory. In fact, this is where paging and segmentation become important. In this context we need to understand some of the techniques of partitioning of main memory into pages or segments.

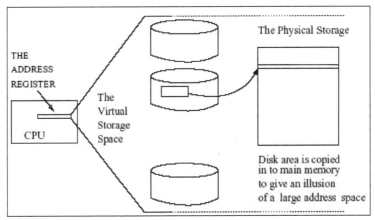

Virtual storage concept.

In addition, we need to understand virtual addressing concepts with paging and/or segmentation. We begin with some simple techniques of partitioning both these memories and management of processes.

Virtual Memory: Paging

In some sense, paging of virtual memory has an underlying mechanism which resembles reading of a book. When we read a book we only need to open only the current page to read. All the other pages are not visible to us. In the same manner, we can argue that even when we may have a large online main memory available, the processor only needs a small set of instructions to execute at any time. In fact, it often happens that for a brief while, all the instructions which the processor needs to execute are within a small proximity of each other. That is like a page we are currently reading in a book. Clearly, this kind of situation happens quite frequently.

Essentially virtual memory is a large addressable space supported by address generating mechanisms in modern CPUs. Virtual address space is much larger than the physical main memory in a computer system. During its execution, a process mostly generates instruction and data references from within a small range. This is referred to as the locality of reference. Examples of locality of reference abound. For instance, we have locality of reference during execution of a *for* or *while* loop, or a call to a procedure. Even in a sequence of assignment statements, the references to instructions and data are usually within a very small range. Which means, during bursts of process execution, only small parts of all of the instruction and data space are needed, i.e. only these parts need be in the main memory. The remaining process, instructions and data, can be anywhere in the virtual space (i.e. it must remain accessible by CPU but not necessarily in main memory). If we are able to achieve that, then we can actually follow a schedule, in which we support a large address space and keep bringing in that part of process which is needed. This way we can comfortably support (a) multi-programming (b) a large logical addressable space giving enormous freedom to a programmer. Note, however, that this entails mapping of logical addresses into physical address space. Such a mapping assures that the instruction in sequence is fetched or the data required in computation is correctly used.

If this translation were to be done in software, it would be very slow. In fact, nowadays this address translation support is provided by hardware in CPUs. Paging is one of the popular memory management schemes to implement such virtual memory management schemes. OS software and the hardware address translation between them achieve this.

Mapping the Pages

Paging stipulates that main memory is partitioned into frames of sufficiently small sizes. Also, we require that the virtual space is divided into pages of the same size as the frames. This equality facilitates movement of a page from anywhere in the virtual space (on disks) to a frame anywhere in the physical memory. The capability to map "any page" to "any frame" gives a lot of flexibility of operation as shown in Figure.

Division of main memory into frames is like fixed partitioning. So keeping the frame size small helps to keep the internal fragmentation small. Often, the page to frame movement is determined by a convenient size (usually a power of two) which disks also use for their own DMA data transfer. The usual frame size is 1024 bytes, though it is not unusual to have 4 K frame sizes as well. Paging supports multi-programming. In general there can be many processes in main memory, each with a different number of pages. To that extent, paging is like dynamic variable partitioning.

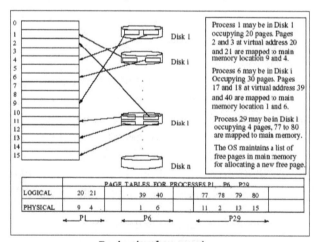

Paging implementation.

Paging: Implementation

Paging implementation requires CPU (HW) and OS (SW) support. In Figure, we assume presence of three active processes. These processes need to have their pages mapped to the main memory page frames. The OS maintains a page table for every process to translate its logical to physical addresses. The page table may itself be resident in main memory.

For a process, which is presently active, there are a number of pages that are in the main memory. This set of pages (being used by the process) forms its resident set. With the locality of reference generally observed, most of the time, the processes make reference within the resident set. We define the set of pages needed by a process at any time as the working set. The OS makes every effort to have the resident set to be the same as the working set. However, it does happen (and happens quite often), that a page required for continuing the process is not in the resident set. This is called a page fault. In normal course of operation, though whenever a process makes virtual address reference, its page table is looked up to find if that page is in main memory. Often it is there. Let us now suppose that the page is not in main memory, i.e. a page fault has occurred. In that case, the OS accesses the required page on the disk and loads it in a free page frame. It then makes an entry for this page in process page table. Similarly, when a page is swapped out, the OS deletes its entry from the page table. Sometimes it may well happen that all the page frames in main memory are in use. If a process now needs a page which is not in main memory, then a page must be forced out to make way for the new page. This is done using a page replacement policy discussed next.

Paging: Replacement

Page replacement policies are based on the way the processes use page frames. In our example shown in Figure, process P29 has all its pages present in main memory. Process P6 does not have all its pages in main memory. If a page is present we record 1 against its entry. The OS also records if a page has been referenced to read or to write. In both these cases a reference is recorded. If a page frame is written into, then a modified bit is set. In our example frames 4, 9, 40, 77, 79 have been referenced and page frames 9 and 13 have been modified. Sometimes OS may also have some information about protection using *rwe* information. If a reference is made to a certain virtual address and its corresponding page is not present in main memory, then we say a page fault has occurred. Typically, a page fault is followed by moving in a page. However, this may require that we move a page out to create a space for it. Usually this is done by using an appropriate page replacement policy to ensure that the throughput of a system does not suffer. We shall later see how a page replacement policy can affect performance of a system.

	Page tables for processes P1, .. P6, .. P29 ...											
	P1			P6				P29				
Logical	20	21			39	40			77	78	79	80
Physical	9	4			1	6			11	2	13	15
Present	0 1	1 0		0 0 1		1 0	1	1	1	1	1	1 1
Referenced	1	1		0		1			1	0	1	0
Modified	1	0		0		0			0	0	1	0
Protection	rw—	rw—							r—		r—	

Replacement policy.

Page Replacement Policy

Towards understanding page replacement policies we shall consider a simple example of a process P which gets an allocation of four pages to execute. Further, we assume that the OS collects some information about the use of these pages as this process progresses in execution. Let us examine the information depicted in figure.

- In some detail to determine how this may help in evolving a page replacement policy. Note that we have the following information available about P.

- The time of arrival of each page. We assume that the process began at some time with value of time unit 100. During its course of progression we now have pages that have been loaded at times 112, 117 119, and 120.

- The time of last usage. This indicates when a certain page was last used. This entirely depends upon which part of the process P is being executed at any time.

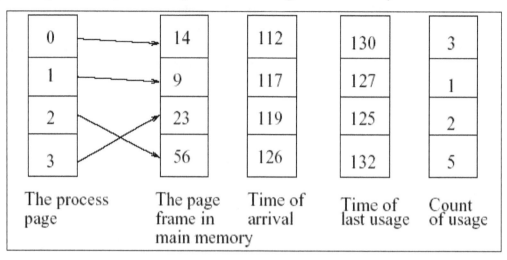

The process page	The page frame in main memory	Time of arrival	Time of last usage	Count of usage
0	14	112	130	3
1	9	117	127	1
2	23	119	125	2
3	56	126	132	5

Information on page usage policy.

- The frequency of use. We have also maintained the frequency of use over some fixed interval of time T in the immediate past. This clearly depends upon the nature of control flow in process P.

As an example we may say that page located at 23 which was installed at time 119, was last used at time unit 125 and over the time period T the process P made two references to it. Based on the above pieces of information if we now assume that at time unit 135 the process P experiences a page-fault, what should be done. Based on the choice of the policy and the data collected for P, we shall be able to decide which page to swap out to bring in a new page.

FIFO policy: This policy simply removes pages in the order they arrived in the main memory. Using this policy we simply remove a page based on the time of its arrival in the memory. Clearly, use of this policy would suggest that we swap page located at 14 as it arrived in the memory earliest.

LRU policy: LRU expands to least recently used. This policy suggests that we remove a page whose last usage is farthest from current time. Note that the current time is 135 and the least recently used page is the page located at 23. It was used last at time unit 125 and every other page is more recently used. So, page 23 is the least recently used page and so it should be swapped if LRU replacement policy is employed.

NFU policy: NFU expands to not frequently used. This policy suggests to use the criterion of the count of usage of page over the interval T. Note that process P has not made use of page located at 9. Other pages have a count of usage like 2, 3 or even 5 times. So the basic argument is that these pages may still be needed as compared to the page at 9. So page 9 should be swapped.

Let us briefly discuss the merits of choices that one is offered. FIFO is a very simple policy and it is relatively easy to implement. All it needs is the time of arrival. However, in following such a policy we may end up replacing a page frame that is referred often during the lifetime of a process. In other words, we should examine how useful a certain page is before we decide to replace it. LRU and NFU policies are certainly better in that regard but as is obvious we need to keep the information about the usage of the pages by the process. In following the not frequently used (NFU) and least recently used (LRU) page replacement policies, the OS needs to define *recency*. As we saw recency is defined as a fixed time interval proceeding the current time. With a definition of recency, we can implement the policy framework like least recently used (LRU). So one must choose a proper interval of time. Depending upon the nature of application environment and the work load a choice of duration of recency will give different throughput from the system. Also, this means that the OS must keep a tab on the pages which are being used and how often these are in use. It is often the case that the most recently used pages are likely to be the ones used again. On the whole one can sense that the LRU policy should be statistically better than FIFO.

A more advanced technique of page replacement policy may look-up the likely future references to pages. Such a policy frame would require use of some form of predictive techniques. In that case, one can prevent too many frequent replacements of pages which prevents thrashing as discussed in the subsection.

Let us for now briefly pay our attention to page references resulting in a page hit and a page miss. When we find that a page frame reference is in the main memory then we have a page hit and when page fault occurs we say we have a page miss. As is obvious from the discussion, a poor choice of policy may result in lot of page misses. We should be able to determine how it influences the throughput of a system. Let us assume that we have a system with the following characteristics.

- Time to look-up page table: 10 time units.

- Time to look-up the information from a page frame (case of a page hit): 40 time units.

- Time to retrieve a page from disk and load it and finally access the page frame (case of a page miss): 190 time units.

Now let us consider the following two cases when we have 50% and 80% page hits. We shall compute the average time to access.

- Case 1: With 50% page hits the average access time is $((10+40) * 0{:}5) + (10+190)$

  $*$ $0{:}5 = 125$ time units.

- Case 2: With 80% page hits the average access time is $(10+40) * 0{:}8) + (10+190)$

  $*$ $0{:}2 = 80$ time units.

Clearly, the case 2 is better. The OS designers attempt to offer a page replacement policy which will try to minimize the page miss. Also, sometimes the system programmers have to tune an OS to achieve a high efficacy in performance by ensuring that page miss cases are within some tolerable limits. It is not unusual to be able to achieve over 90% page hits when the application profile is very well known.

There is one other concern that may arise with regard to page replacement. It may be that while a certain process is operative, some of the information may be often required. These may be definitions globally defined in a program, or some terminal related IO information in a monitoring program. If this kind of information is stored in certain pages then these have to be kept at all times during the lifetime of the process. Clearly, this requires that we have these pages identified. Some programming environments allow directives like keep to specify such information to be available at all the time during the lifetime of the process. In Windows there is a keep function that allows one to specify which programs must be kept at all the time. The Windows environment essentially uses the keep function to load TSR (terminate and stay resident) programs to be loaded in the memory 1. Recall, earlier we made a reference to thrashing which arises from the overheads generated from frequent page replacement. We shall next study that.

Thrashing

Suppose there is a process with several pages in its resident set. However, the page replacement policy results in a situation such that two pages alternatively move in and out of the resident set. Note that because pages are moved between main memory and disk, this has an enormous overhead. This can adversely affect the throughput of a system. The drop in the level of system throughput resulting from frequent page replacement is called thrashing. Let us try to comprehend when and how it manifests. Statistically, on introducing paging we can hope to enhance multi-programming as well as locality of reference. The main consequence of this shall be enhanced processor utilization and hence, better throughput. Note that the page size influences the number of pages and hence it determines the number of resident sets we may support. With more programs in main memory or more pages of a program we hope for better locality of reference. This is seen to happen (at least initially) as more pages are available. This is because, we may have more effective locality of reference as well as multi-programming. However, when the page size becomes too small we may begin to witness more page-faults.

Incidentally, a virus writer may employ this to mount an attack. For instance, the keep facility may be used to have a periodic display of some kind on the victim's screen. More page-faults would result in more frequent disk IO. As disk IO happens more often the throughput would drop. The point when this begins to happen, we say thrashing has occurred. In other words, the basic advantage of higher throughput from a greater level of utilization of processor and more effective multi-programming does not accrue any more. When the advantage derived from locality of reference and multi-programming begins to vanish, we are at the point when thrashing manifests. This is shown in Figure.

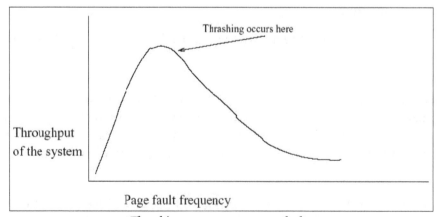

Thrashing on numerous page fault.

Paging: HW support

Recall we emphasized that we need HW within CPU to support paging. The CPU generates a logical address which must get translated to a physical address. In figure we indicate the basic address generation and translation.

Let us trace the sequence of steps in the generation of address.

- The process generates a logical address. This address is interpreted in two parts.
- The first part of the logical address identifies the virtual page.
- The second part of the logical address gives the offset within this page.
- The first part is used as an input to the page table to find out the following:
  * Is the page in the main memory?
  * What is the page frame number for this virtual page?
- The page frame number is the first part of the physical memory address.
- The offset is the second part of the correct physical memory location.

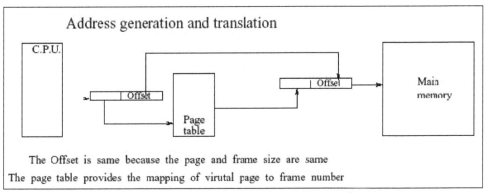

Hardware support for paging.

If the page is not in the physical memory, a page-fault is generated. This is treated as a trap. The trap then suspends the regular sequence of operations and fetches the required page from the disk into main memory.

We next discuss a relatively simple extension of the basic paging scheme with hardware support. This scheme results in considerable improvement in page frame access.

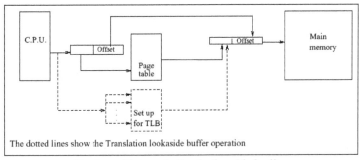

Paging with translation look-aside buffer.

The TLB scheme

The basic idea in the translation look-aside buffer access is quite simple. The scheme is very effective in improving the performance of page frame access. The scheme employs a cache buffer to keep copies of some of the page frames in a cache buffer. This buffer is also interrogated for the presence of page frame copy. Note that a cache buffer is implemented in a technology which is faster than the main memory technology. So, a retrieval from the cache buffer is faster than that from the main memory. The hardware signal which looks up the page table is also used to look up (with address translation) to check if the cache buffer on a side has the desired page. This nature of look-up explains why this scheme is called Translation Look-aside Buffer (TLB) scheme. The basic TLB buffering scheme is shown in Figure. Note that the figure replicates the usual hardware support for page table look-up. So, obviously the scheme cannot be worse than the usual page table look-up schemes. However, since a cache buffer is additionally maintained to keep some of the frequently accessed pages, one can expect to achieve an improvement in the access time required for those pages which obtain a page hit for presence in the buffer. Suppose we wish to access page frame p. The following three possibilities may arise:

1. Cache presence: There is a copy of the page frame p. In this case it is procured from the look-aside buffer which is the cache.

2. Page table presence: The cache does not have a copy of the page frame p, but page table access results in a page hit. The page is accessed from the main memory.

3. Not in page table: This is a case when the copy of the page frame is neither in the cache buffer nor does it have an entry in the page table. Clearly, this is a case of page-fault. It is handled exactly as the page-fault is normally handled.

Note that if a certain page frame copy is available in the cache then the cache look-up takes precedence and the page frame is fetched from the cache instead of fetching it from the main memory. This obviously saves time to access the page frame. In the case the page hit occurs for a page not in cache then the scheme ensures its access from the main memory. So it is at least as good as the standard paging scheme with a possibility of improvement whenever a page frame copy is in cache buffer.

Some Additional Points

Since page frames can be loaded anywhere in the main memory, we can say that paging mechanism supports dynamic relocation. Also, there are other schemes like multi-level page support systems which support page tables at multiple levels of hierarchy. In addition, there are methods to identify pages that may be shared amongst more than one process. Clearly, such shareable pages involve additional considerations to maintain consistency of data when multiple processes try to have read and write access. These are usually areas of research and beyond the scope of this book.

Segmentation

Like paging, segmentation is also a scheme which supports virtual memory concept. Segmentation can be best understood in the context of a program's storage requirements. One view could be that each part like its code segment, its stack requirements (of data, nested procedure calls), its different object modules, etc. has a contiguous space. This space would then define a process's space requirement as an integrated whole (or complete space). As a view, this is very uni-dimensional.

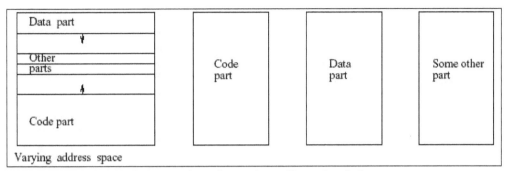

Segmentation scheme: A two dimensional view.

In using segmentation, one recognizes various segments such as the stack, object code, data area etc. Each segment has requirements that vary over time. For instance, stacks grow and shrink the memory requirements of object and data segments may change during the lifetime of the process. This may depend on which functions have been called and are currently active. It is, therefore, best to take a two-dimensional view of a process's memory requirement. In this view, each of the process segments has an opportunity to acquire a variable amount of space over time. This ensures that one area does not run into the space of any other segment. The basic scheme is shown in Figure. The implementation of segmentation is similar to paging, except that we now have segment table (in place of a page table) look-ups to identify addresses in each of the segments. HW supports a table look-up for a segment and an offset within that segment. We may now compare paging with segmentation.

- Paging offers the simplest mechanism to effect virtual addressing.

- While paging suffers from internal fragmentation, segmentation suffers from external fragmentation.

- One of the advantages segmentation clearly offers is separate compilation of each segment with a view to link up later. This has another advantage. A user may develop a code segment and share it amongst many applications. He generates the required links at the time of launching the application. However, note that this also places burden on the programmer to manage linking. To that extent paging offers greater transparency in usage.

- In paging, a process address space is linear. Hence, it is uni-dimensional. In a segment based scheme each procedure and data segment has its own virtual space mapping. Thus the segmentation assures a much greater degree of protection.

- In case a program's address space fluctuates considerably, paging may result in frequent page faults. Segmentation does not suffer from such problems.

- Paging partitions a program and data space uniformly and is, therefore, much simpler to manage. However, one cannot easily distinguish data space from program space in paging. Segmentation partitions process space requirements according to a logical division of the segments that make up the process. Generally, this simplifies protection.

Clearly, a clever scheme with advantages of both would be: segmentation with paging. In such a scheme each segment would have a descriptor with its pages identified. Such a scheme is shown in Figure. Note that we have to now use three sets of offsets. First, a segment offset helps to identify the set of pages. Next, within the corresponding page table (for the segment), we need to identify the exact page table. This is done by using the page table part of the virtual address. Once the exact page has been identified, the offset is used to obtain main memory address reference.

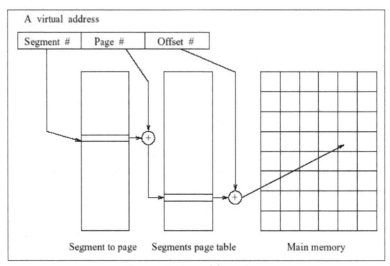

Segmentation with paging.

In practice, there are segments for the code(s), data, and stack. Each segment carries the *rwe* information as well. Usually the stack and data have read write permissions but no execute permissions. Code rarely has write permission but would have a read and execute permission.

References

- Reiser, Hans (2006-02-06). "The Reiser4 Filesystem". Google TechTalks. Archived from the original on 22 August 2012. Retrieved 2006-12-14

- Singh, Amit (2007). "12 The HFS Plus File System". Mac OS X Internals: A Systems Approach. Addison Wesley. ISBN 0321278542

- Smith, Keith Arnold (January 2001). "Workload-Specific File System Benchmarks" (PDF). Cambridge, Massachusetts: Harvard University. Retrieved 2006-12-14

- Disc File Applications: Reports Presented at the Nation's First Disc File Symposium. American Data Processing. 1964. Retrieved August 1, 2016

- Douceur, John R.; Bolosky, William J. (June 1999). "A Large-Scale Study of File-System Contents". ACM SIGMETRICS Performance Evaluation Review. Association for Computing Machinery. 27 (1): 59–70. doi:10.1145/301464.301480

- "OS X Mountain Lion: What is a Mac OS Extended (Journaled) volume?". Apple. August 8, 2013. Retrieved February 7, 2014

5

Diverse Aspects of Operating Systems

There are various components which make up operating systems such as kernel, process, memory management, virtual memory, preemption, device driver, etc. The computer program that is the core of operating systems and controls everything in the system is known as the kernel. The chapter closely examines these key aspects of operating systems to provide an extensive understanding of the subject.

Kernel

The kernel (also called nucleus) is a computer program that constitutes the central core of a computer's operating system. It has complete control over everything that occurs in the system. As such, it is the first program loaded on startup, and then manages the remainder of the startup, as well as input/output requests from software, translating them into data processing instructions for the central processing unit. It is also responsible for managing memory, and for managing and communicating with computing peripherals, like printers, speakers, etc. The kernel is a fundamental part of a modern computer's operating system.

The critical code of the kernel is usually loaded into a *protected area* of memory, which prevents it from being overwritten by other, less frequently used parts of the operating system or by applications. The kernel performs its tasks, such as executing processes and handling interrupts, in *kernel space*, whereas everything a user normally does, such as writing text in a text editor or running programs in a GUI (graphical user interface), is done in *user space*. This separation prevents user data and kernel data from interfering with each other and thereby diminishing performance or causing the system to become unstable (and possibly crashing).

When a *process* makes requests of the kernel, the request is called a system call. Various kernel designs differ in how they manage system calls and resources. For example, a monolithic kernel executes all the operating system instructions in the same address space in order to improve the performance of the system. A microkernel runs most of the operating system's background processes in user space, to make the operating system more modular and, therefore, easier to maintain.

The kernel's interface is a low-level abstraction layer.

Functions of the Kernel

The kernel's primary function is to mediate access to the computer's resources, including:

The central processing unit:

> This central component of a computer system is responsible for *running* or *executing* programs. The kernel takes responsibility for deciding at any time which of the many running

programs should be allocated to the processor or processors (each of which can usually run only one program at a time).

Random-access memory:

> Random-access memory is used to store both program instructions and data. Typically, both need to be present in memory in order for a program to execute. Often multiple programs will want access to memory, frequently demanding more memory than the computer has available. The kernel is responsible for deciding which memory each process can use, and determining what to do when not enough memory is available.

Input/output (I/O) devices:

> I/O devices include such peripherals as keyboards, mice, disk drives, printers, network adapters, and display devices. The kernel allocates requests from applications to perform I/O to an appropriate device and provides convenient methods for using the device (typically abstracted to the point where the application does not need to know implementation details of the device).

Key aspects necessary in resource management are the definition of an execution domain (address space) and the protection mechanism used to mediate the accesses to the resources within a domain.

Kernels also usually provide methods for synchronization and communication between processes called inter-process communication (IPC).

A kernel may implement these features itself, or rely on some of the processes it runs to provide the facilities to other processes, although in this case it must provide some means of IPC to allow processes to access the facilities provided by each other.

Finally, a kernel must provide running programs with a method to make requests to access these facilities.

Memory Management

The kernel has full access to the system's memory and must allow processes to safely access this memory as they require it. Often the first step in doing this is virtual addressing, usually achieved by paging and/or segmentation. Virtual addressing allows the kernel to make a given physical address appear to be another address, the virtual address. Virtual address spaces may be different for different processes; the memory that one process accesses at a particular (virtual) address may be different memory from what another process accesses at the same address. This allows every program to behave as if it is the only one (apart from the kernel) running and thus prevents applications from crashing each other.

On many systems, a program's virtual address may refer to data which is not currently in memory. The layer of indirection provided by virtual addressing allows the operating system to use other data stores, like a hard drive, to store what would otherwise have to remain in main memory (RAM). As a result, operating systems can allow programs to use more memory than the system has physically available. When a program needs data which is not currently in RAM, the CPU signals to the kernel that this has happened, and the kernel responds by writing the contents of an inactive memory block to disk (if necessary) and replacing it with the data requested by the program. The program can then be resumed from the point where it was stopped. This scheme is generally known as demand paging.

Virtual addressing also allows creation of virtual partitions of memory in two disjointed areas, one being reserved for the kernel (kernel space) and the other for the applications (user space). The applications are not permitted by the processor to address kernel memory, thus preventing an application from damaging the running kernel. This fundamental partition of memory space has contributed much to the current designs of actual general-purpose kernels and is almost universal in such systems, although some research kernels (e.g. Singularity) take other approaches.

Device Management

To perform useful functions, processes need access to the peripherals connected to the computer, which are controlled by the kernel through device drivers. A device driver is a computer program that enables the operating system to interact with a hardware device. It provides the operating system with information of how to control and communicate with a certain piece of hardware. The driver is an important and vital piece to a program application. The design goal of a driver is abstraction; the function of the driver is to translate the OS-mandated function calls (programming calls) into device-specific calls. In theory, the device should work correctly with the suitable driver. Device drivers are used for such things as video cards, sound cards, printers, scanners, modems, and LAN cards. The common levels of abstraction of device drivers are:

1. On the hardware side:

    - Interfacing directly.

    - Using a high level interface (Video BIOS).

    - Using a lower-level device driver (file drivers using disk drivers).

    - Simulating work with hardware, while doing something entirely different.

2. On the software side:

    - Allowing the operating system direct access to hardware resources.

    - Implementing only primitives.

    - Implementing an interface for non-driver software (Example: TWAIN).

    - Implementing a language, sometimes high-level (Example PostScript).

For example, to show the user something on the screen, an application would make a request to the kernel, which would forward the request to its display driver, which is then responsible for actually plotting the character/pixel.

A kernel must maintain a list of available devices. This list may be known in advance (e.g. on an embedded system where the kernel will be rewritten if the available hardware changes), configured by the user (typical on older PCs and on systems that are not designed for personal use) or detected by the operating system at run time (normally called plug and play). In a plug and play system, a device manager first performs a scan on different hardware buses, such as Peripheral Component Interconnect (PCI) or Universal Serial Bus (USB), to detect installed devices, then searches for the appropriate drivers.

As device management is a very OS-specific topic, these drivers are handled differently by each kind of kernel design, but in every case, the kernel has to provide the I/O to allow drivers to physically access their devices through some port or memory location. Very important decisions have to be made when designing the device management system, as in some designs accesses may involve context switches, making the operation very CPU-intensive and easily causing a significant performance overhead.

System Calls

In computing, a system call is how a program requests a service from an operating system's kernel that it does not normally have permission to run. System calls provide the interface between a process and the operating system. Most operations interacting with the system require permissions not available to a user level process, e.g. I/O performed with a device present on the system, or any form of communication with other processes requires the use of system calls.

A system call is a mechanism that is used by the application program to request a service from the operating system. They use a machine-code instruction that causes the processor to change mode. An example would be from supervisor mode to protected mode. This is where the operating system performs actions like accessing hardware devices or the memory management unit. Generally the operating system provides a library that sits between the operating system and normal programs. Usually it is a C library such as Glibc or Windows API. The library handles the low-level details of passing information to the kernel and switching to supervisor mode. System calls include close, open, read, wait and write.

To actually perform useful work, a process must be able to access the services provided by the kernel. This is implemented differently by each kernel, but most provide a C library or an API, which in turn invokes the related kernel functions.

The method of invoking the kernel function varies from kernel to kernel. If memory isolation is in use, it is impossible for a user process to call the kernel directly, because that would be a violation of the processor's access control rules. A few possibilities are:

- Using a software-simulated interrupt. This method is available on most hardware, and is therefore very common.

- Using a call gate. A call gate is a special address stored by the kernel in a list in kernel memory at a location known to the processor. When the processor detects a call to that address, it instead redirects to the target location without causing an access violation. This requires hardware support, but the hardware for it is quite common.

- Using a special system call instruction. This technique requires special hardware support, which common architectures (notably, x86) may lack. System call instructions have been added to recent models of x86 processors, however, and some operating systems for PCs make use of them when available.

- Using a memory-based queue. An application that makes large numbers of requests but does not need to wait for the result of each may add details of requests to an area of memory that the kernel periodically scans to find requests.

Kernel Design Decisions

Issues of Kernel Support for Protection

An important consideration in the design of a kernel is the support it provides for protection from faults (fault tolerance) and from malicious behaviours (security). These two aspects are usually not clearly distinguished, and the adoption of this distinction in the kernel design leads to the rejection of a hierarchical structure for protection.

The mechanisms or policies provided by the kernel can be classified according to several criteria, including: static (enforced at compile time) or dynamic (enforced at run time); pre-emptive or post-detection; according to the protection principles they satisfy (e.g. Denning); whether they are hardware supported or language based; whether they are more an open mechanism or a binding policy; and many more.

Support for hierarchical protection domains is typically implemented using CPU modes.

Many kernels provide implementation of "capabilities", i.e. objects that are provided to user code which allow limited access to an underlying object managed by the kernel. A common example occurs in file handling: a file is a representation of information stored on a permanent storage device. The kernel may be able to perform many different operations (e.g. read, write, delete or execute the file content's) but a user level application may only be permitted to perform some of these operations (e.g. it may only be allowed to read the file). A common implementation of this is for the kernel to provide an object to the application (typically called a "file handle") which the application may then invoke operations on, the validity of which the kernel checks at the time the operation is requested. Such a system may be extended to cover all objects that the kernel manages, and indeed to objects provided by other user applications.

An efficient and simple way to provide hardware support of capabilities is to delegate the MMU the responsibility of checking access-rights for every memory access, a mechanism called capability-based addressing. Most commercial computer architectures lack such MMU support for capabilities.

An alternative approach is to simulate capabilities using commonly supported hierarchical domains; in this approach, each protected object must reside in an address space that the application does not have access to; the kernel also maintains a list of capabilities in such memory. When an application needs to access an object protected by a capability, it performs a system call and the kernel then checks whether the application's capability grants it permission to perform the requested action, and if it is permitted performs the access for it (either directly, or by delegating the request to another user-level process). The performance cost of address space switching limits the practicality of this approach in systems with complex interactions between objects, but it is used in current operating systems for objects that are not accessed frequently or which are not expected to perform quickly. Approaches where protection mechanism are not firmware supported but are instead simulated at higher levels (e.g. simulating capabilities by manipulating page tables on hardware that does not have direct support), are possible, but there are performance implications. Lack of hardware support may not be an issue, however, for systems that choose to use language-based protection.

An important kernel design decision is the choice of the abstraction levels where the security mechanisms and policies should be implemented. Kernel security mechanisms play a critical role in supporting security at higher levels.

One approach is to use firmware and kernel support for fault tolerance, and build the security policy for malicious behavior on top of that (adding features such as cryptography mechanisms where necessary), delegating some responsibility to the compiler. Approaches that delegate enforcement of security policy to the compiler and/or the application level are often called *language-based security*.

The lack of many critical security mechanisms in current mainstream operating systems impedes the implementation of adequate security policies at the application abstraction level. In fact, a common misconception in computer security is that any security policy can be implemented in an application regardless of kernel support.

Hardware-based or Language-based Protection

Typical computer systems today use hardware-enforced rules about what programs are allowed to access what data. The processor monitors the execution and stops a program that violates a rule (e.g., a user process that is about to read or write to kernel memory, and so on). In systems that lack support for capabilities, processes are isolated from each other by using separate address spaces. Calls from user processes into the kernel are regulated by requiring them to use one of the above-described system call methods.

An alternative approach is to use language-based protection. In a language-based protection system, the kernel will only allow code to execute that has been produced by a trusted language compiler. The language may then be designed such that it is impossible for the programmer to instruct it to do something that will violate a security requirement.

Advantages of this approach include:

- No need for separate address spaces. Switching between address spaces is a slow operation that causes a great deal of overhead, and a lot of optimization work is currently performed in order to prevent unnecessary switches in current operating systems. Switching is completely unnecessary in a language-based protection system, as all code can safely operate in the same address space.

- Flexibility. Any protection scheme that can be designed to be expressed via a programming language can be implemented using this method. Changes to the protection scheme (e.g. from a hierarchical system to a capability-based one) do not require new hardware.

Disadvantages include:

- Longer application start up time. Applications must be verified when they are started to ensure they have been compiled by the correct compiler, or may need recompiling either from source code or from bytecode.

- Inflexible type systems. On traditional systems, applications frequently perform operations that are not type safe. Such operations cannot be permitted in a language-based protection system, which means that applications may need to be rewritten and may, in some cases, lose performance.

Examples of systems with language-based protection include JX and Microsoft's Singularity.

Process Cooperation

Edsger Dijkstra proved that from a logical point of view, atomic lock and unlock operations operating on binary semaphores are sufficient primitives to express any functionality of process cooperation. However this approach is generally held to be lacking in terms of safety and efficiency, whereas a message passing approach is more flexible. A number of other approaches (either lower- or higher-level) are available as well, with many modern kernels providing support for systems such as shared memory and remote procedure calls.

I/O Devices Management

The idea of a kernel where I/O devices are handled uniformly with other processes, as parallel co-operating processes, was first proposed and implemented by Brinch Hansen (although similar ideas were suggested in 1967). In Hansen's description of this, the "common" processes are called *internal processes*, while the I/O devices are called *external processes*.

Similar to physical memory, allowing applications direct access to controller ports and registers can cause the controller to malfunction, or system to crash. With this, depending on the complexity of the device, some devices can get surprisingly complex to program, and use several different controllers. Because of this, providing a more abstract interface to manage the device is important. This interface is normally done by a Device Driver or Hardware Abstraction Layer. Frequently, applications will require access to these devices. The Kernel must maintain the list of these devices by querying the system for them in some way. This can be done through the BIOS, or through one of the various system buses (such as PCI/PCIE, or USB). When an application requests an operation on a device (Such as displaying a character), the kernel needs to send this request to the current active video driver. The video driver, in turn, needs to carry out this request. This is an example of Inter Process Communication (IPC).

Kernel-wide Design Approaches

Naturally, the above listed tasks and features can be provided in many ways that differ from each other in design and implementation.

The principle of *separation of mechanism and policy* is the substantial difference between the philosophy of micro and monolithic kernels. Here a *mechanism* is the support that allows the implementation of many different policies, while a policy is a particular "mode of operation". For instance, a mechanism may provide for user log-in attempts to call an authorization server to determine whether access should be granted; a policy may be for the authorization server to request a password and check it against an encrypted password stored in a database. Because the mechanism is generic, the policy could more easily be changed (e.g. by requiring the use of a security token) than if the mechanism and policy were integrated in the same module.

In minimal microkernel just some very basic policies are included, and its mechanisms allows what is running on top of the kernel (the remaining part of the operating system and the other applications) to decide which policies to adopt (as memory management, high level process scheduling, file system management, etc.). A monolithic kernel instead tends to include many policies, therefore restricting the rest of the system to rely on them.

Per Brinch Hansen presented arguments in favour of separation of mechanism and policy. The failure to properly fulfill this separation is one of the major causes of the lack of substantial innovation in existing operating systems, a problem common in computer architecture. The monolithic design is induced by the "kernel mode"/"user mode" architectural approach to protection (technically called hierarchical protection domains), which is common in conventional commercial systems; in fact, every module needing protection is therefore preferably included into the kernel. This link between monolithic design and "privileged mode" can be reconducted to the key issue of mechanism-policy separation; in fact the "privileged mode" architectural approach melts together the protection mechanism with the security policies, while the major alternative architectural approach, capability-based addressing, clearly distinguishes between the two, leading naturally to a microkernel design.

While monolithic kernels execute all of their code in the same address space (kernel space) microkernels try to run most of their services in user space, aiming to improve maintainability and modularity of the codebase. Most kernels do not fit exactly into one of these categories, but are rather found in between these two designs. These are called hybrid kernels. More exotic designs such as nanokernels and exokernels are available, but are seldom used for production systems. The Xen hypervisor, for example, is an exokernel.

Monolithic Kernels

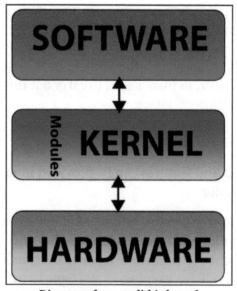

Diagram of a monolithic kernel.

In a monolithic kernel, all OS services run along with the main kernel thread, thus also residing in the same memory area. This approach provides rich and powerful hardware access. Some developers, such as UNIX developer Ken Thompson, maintain that it is "easier to implement a monolithic kernel" than microkernels. The main disadvantages of monolithic kernels are the dependencies between system components – a bug in a device driver might crash the entire system – and the fact that large kernels can become very difficult to maintain.

Monolithic kernels, which have traditionally been used by Unix-like operating systems, contain all the operating system core functions and the device drivers (small programs that allow the operating system to interact with hardware devices, such as disk drives, video cards and printers). This is the traditional design of UNIX systems. A monolithic kernel is one single program that contains all of the code necessary to perform every kernel related task. Every part which is to be accessed by most programs which cannot be put in a library is in the kernel space: Device drivers, Scheduler, Memory handling, File systems, Network stacks. Many system calls are provided to applications, to allow them to access all those services. A monolithic kernel, while initially loaded with subsystems that may not be needed, can be tuned to a point where it is as fast as or faster than the one that was specifically designed for the hardware, although more relevant in a general sense. Modern monolithic kernels, such as those of Linux and FreeBSD, both of which fall into the category of Unix-like operating systems, feature the ability to load modules at runtime, thereby allowing easy extension of the kernel's capabilities as required, while helping to minimize the amount of code running in kernel space. In the monolithic kernel, some advantages hinge on these points:

- Since there is less software involved it is faster.

- As it is one single piece of software it should be smaller both in source and compiled forms.

- Less code generally means fewer bugs which can translate to fewer security problems.

Most work in the monolithic kernel is done via system calls. These are interfaces, usually kept in a tabular structure, that access some subsystem within the kernel such as disk operations. Essentially calls are made within programs and a checked copy of the request is passed through the system call. Hence, not far to travel at all. The monolithic Linux kernel can be made extremely small not only because of its ability to dynamically load modules but also because of its ease of customization. In fact, there are some versions that are small enough to fit together with a large number of utilities and other programs on a single floppy disk and still provide a fully functional operating system (one of the most popular of which is muLinux). This ability to miniaturize its kernel has also led to a rapid growth in the use of Linux in embedded systems.

These types of kernels consist of the core functions of the operating system and the device drivers with the ability to load modules at runtime. They provide rich and powerful abstractions of the underlying hardware. They provide a small set of simple hardware abstractions and use applications called servers to provide more functionality. This particular approach defines a high-level virtual interface over the hardware, with a set of system calls to implement operating system services such as process management, concurrency and memory management in several modules that run in supervisor mode. This design has several flaws and limitations:

- Coding in kernel can be challenging, in part because one cannot use common libraries (like a full-featured libc), and because one needs to use a source-level debugger like gdb. Rebooting the computer is often required. This is not just a problem of convenience to the developers. When debugging is harder, and as difficulties become stronger, it becomes more likely that code will be "buggier".

- Bugs in one part of the kernel have strong side effects; since every function in the kernel has all the privileges, a bug in one function can corrupt data structure of another, totally unrelated part of the kernel, or of any running program.

- Kernels often become very large and difficult to maintain.

- Even if the modules servicing these operations are separate from the whole, the code integration is tight and difficult to do correctly.

- Since the modules run in the same address space, a bug can bring down the entire system.

- Monolithic kernels are not portable; therefore, they must be rewritten for each new architecture that the operating system is to be used on.

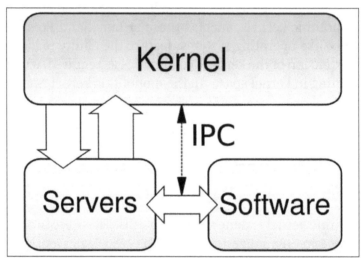

In the microkernel approach, the kernel itself only provides basic functionality that allows the execution of servers, separate programs that assume former kernel functions, such as device drivers, GUI servers, etc.

Microkernels

Microkernel (also abbreviated μK or uK) is the term describing an approach to operating system design by which the functionality of the system is moved out of the traditional "kernel", into a set of "servers" that communicate through a "minimal" kernel, leaving as little as possible in "system space" and as much as possible in "user space". A microkernel that is designed for a specific platform or device is only ever going to have what it needs to operate. The microkernel approach consists of defining a simple abstraction over the hardware, with a set of primitives or system calls to implement minimal OS services such as memory management, multitasking, and inter-process communication. Other services, including those normally provided by the kernel, such as networking, are implemented in user-space programs, referred to as *servers*. Microkernels are easier to maintain than monolithic kernels, but the large number of system calls and context switches might slow down the system because they typically generate more overhead than plain function calls.

Only parts which really require being in a privileged mode are in kernel space: IPC (Inter-Process Communication), basic scheduler, or scheduling primitives, basic memory handling, basic I/O primitives. Many critical parts are now running in user space: The complete scheduler, memory handling, file systems, and network stacks. Micro kernels were invented as a reaction to traditional "monolithic" kernel design, whereby all system functionality was put in a one static program running in a special "system" mode of the processor. In the microkernel, only the most fundamental of tasks are performed such as being able to access some (not necessarily all) of the hardware, manage memory and coordinate message passing between the processes. Some systems that use micro kernels are QNX and the HURD. In the case of QNX and Hurd user sessions can be entire snapshots of the system itself or views as it is referred to. The very essence of the microkernel architecture illustrates some of its advantages:

- Maintenance is generally easier.

- Patches can be tested in a separate instance, and then swapped in to take over a production instance.

- Rapid development time and new software can be tested without having to reboot the kernel.

- More persistence in general, if one instance goes hay-wire, it is often possible to substitute it with an operational mirror.

Most micro kernels use a message passing system of some sort to handle requests from one server to another. The message passing system generally operates on a port basis with the microkernel. As an example, if a request for more memory is sent, a port is opened with the microkernel and the request sent through. Once within the microkernel, the steps are similar to system calls. The rationale was that it would bring modularity in the system architecture, which would entail a cleaner system, easier to debug or dynamically modify, customizable to users' needs, and more performing. They are part of the operating systems like AIX, BeOS, Hurd, Mach, macOS, MINIX, QNX. Etc. Although micro kernels are very small by themselves, in combination with all their required auxiliary code they are, in fact, often larger than monolithic kernels. Advocates of monolithic kernels also point out that the two-tiered structure of microkernel systems, in which most of the operating system does not interact directly with the hardware, creates a not-insignificant cost in terms of system efficiency. These types of kernels normally provide only the minimal services such as defining memory address spaces, Inter-process communication (IPC) and the process management. The other functions such as running the hardware processes are not handled directly by micro kernels. Proponents of micro kernels point out those monolithic kernels have the disadvantage that an error in the kernel can cause the entire system to crash. However, with a microkernel, if a kernel process crashes, it is still possible to prevent a crash of the system as a whole by merely restarting the service that caused the error.

Other services provided by the kernel such as networking are implemented in user-space programs referred to as *servers*. Servers allow the operating system to be modified by simply starting and stopping programs. For a machine without networking support, for instance, the networking server is not started. The task of moving in and out of the kernel to move data between the various applications and servers creates overhead which is detrimental to the efficiency of micro kernels in comparison with monolithic kernels.

Disadvantages in the microkernel exist however. Some are:

- Larger running memory footprint.

- More software for interfacing is required, there is a potential for performance loss.

- Messaging bugs can be harder to fix due to the longer trip they have to take versus the one off copy in a monolithic kernel.

- Process management in general can be very complicated.

The disadvantages for micro kernels are extremely context based. As an example, they work well for small single purpose (and critical) systems because if not many processes need to run, then the complications of process management are effectively mitigated.

A microkernel allows the implementation of the remaining part of the operating system as a normal application program written in a high-level language, and the use of different operating systems on top of the same unchanged kernel. It is also possible to dynamically switch among operating systems and to have more than one active simultaneously.

Monolithic Kernels vs. Microkernels

As the computer kernel grows, so grows the size and vulnerability of its trusted computing base; and, besides reducing security, there is the problem of enlarging the memory footprint. This is mitigated to some degree by perfecting the virtual memory system, but not all computer architectures have virtual memory support. To reduce the kernel's footprint, extensive editing has to be performed to carefully remove unneeded code, which can be very difficult with non-obvious interdependencies between parts of a kernel with millions of lines of code.

By the early 1990s, due to the various shortcomings of monolithic kernels versus microkernels, monolithic kernels were considered obsolete by virtually all operating system researchers. As a result, the design of Linux as a monolithic kernel rather than a microkernel was the topic of a famous debate between Linus Torvalds and Andrew Tanenbaum. There is merit on both sides of the argument presented in the Tanenbaum–Torvalds debate.

Performance

Monolithic kernels are designed to have all of their code in the same address space (kernel space), which some developers argue is necessary to increase the performance of the system. Some developers also maintain that monolithic systems are extremely efficient if well written. The monolithic model tends to be more efficient through the use of shared kernel memory, rather than the slower IPC system of microkernel designs, which is typically based on message passing.

The performance of microkernels was poor in both the 1980s and early 1990s. However, studies that empirically measured the performance of these microkernels did not analyze the reasons of such inefficiency. The explanations of this data were left to "folklore", with the assumption that they were due to the increased frequency of switches from "kernel-mode" to "user-mode", to the increased frequency of inter-process communication and to the increased frequency of context switches.

In fact, as guessed in 1995, the reasons for the poor performance of microkernels might as well have been: (1) an actual inefficiency of the whole microkernel *approach*, (2) the particular *concepts* implemented in those microkernels, and (3) the particular *implementation* of those concepts. Therefore it remained to be studied if the solution to build an efficient microkernel was, unlike previous attempts, to apply the correct construction techniques.

On the other end, the hierarchical protection domains architecture that leads to the design of a monolithic kernel has a significant performance drawback each time there's an interaction between different levels of protection (i.e. when a process has to manipulate a data structure both in 'user mode' and 'supervisor mode'), since this requires message copying by value.

By the mid-1990s, most researchers had abandoned the belief that careful tuning could reduce this overhead dramatically, but recently, newer microkernels, optimized for performance, such as L4 and K42 have addressed these problems.

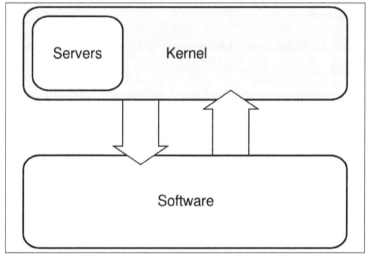

The hybrid kernel approach combines the speed and simpler design of
a monolithic kernel with the modularity and execution safety of a microkernel.

Hybrid (or Modular) Kernels

Hybrid kernels are used in most commercial operating systems such as Microsoft Windows NT 3.1, NT 3.5, NT 3.51, NT 4.0, 2000, XP, Vista, 7, 8, 8.1 and 10. Apple Inc's own macOS uses a hybrid kernel called XNU which is based upon code from Carnegie Mellon's Mach kernel and FreeBSD's monolithic kernel. They are similar to micro kernels, except they include some additional code in kernel-space to increase performance. These kernels represent a compromise that was implemented by some developers before it was demonstrated that pure micro kernels can provide high performance. These types of kernels are extensions of micro kernels with some properties of monolithic kernels. Unlike monolithic kernels, these types of kernels are unable to load modules at runtime on their own. Hybrid kernels are micro kernels that have some "non-essential" code in kernel-space in order for the code to run more quickly than it would were it to be in user-space. Hybrid kernels are a compromise between the monolithic and microkernel designs. This implies running some services (such as the network stack or the filesystem) in kernel space to reduce the performance overhead of a traditional microkernel, but still running kernel code (such as device drivers) as servers in user space.

Many traditionally monolithic kernels are now at least adding (if not actively exploiting) the module capability. The most well known of these kernels is the Linux kernel. The modular kernel essentially can have parts of it that are built into the core kernel binary or binaries that load into memory on demand. It is important to note that a code tainted module has the potential to destabilize a running kernel. Many people become confused on this point when discussing micro kernels. It is possible to write a driver for a microkernel in a completely separate memory space and test it before "going" live. When a kernel module is loaded, it accesses the monolithic portion's memory space by adding to it what it needs, therefore, opening the doorway to possible pollution. A few advantages to the modular (or) Hybrid kernel are:

- Faster development time for drivers that can operate from within modules. No reboot required for testing (provided the kernel is not destabilized).

- On demand capability versus spending time recompiling a whole kernel for things like new drivers or subsystems.

- Faster integration of third party technology (related to development but pertinent unto itself nonetheless).

Modules, generally, communicate with the kernel using a module interface of some sort. The interface is generalized (although particular to a given operating system) so it is not always possible to use modules. Often the device drivers may need more flexibility than the module interface affords. Essentially, it is two system calls and often the safety checks that only have to be done once in the monolithic kernel now may be done twice. Some of the disadvantages of the modular approach are:

- With more interfaces to pass through, the possibility of increased bugs exists (which implies more security holes).

- Maintaining modules can be confusing for some administrators when dealing with problems like symbol differences.

Nanokernels

A nanokernel delegates virtually all services – including even the most basic ones like interrupt controllers or the timer – to device drivers to make the kernel memory requirement even smaller than a traditional microkernel.

Exokernels

Exokernels are a still-experimental approach to operating system design. They differ from the other types of kernels in that their functionality is limited to the protection and multiplexing of the raw hardware, providing no hardware abstractions on top of which to develop applications. This separation of hardware protection from hardware management enables application developers to determine how to make the most efficient use of the available hardware for each specific program.

Exokernels in themselves are extremely small. However, they are accompanied by library operating systems, providing application developers with the functionalities of a conventional operating system. A major advantage of exokernel-based systems is that they can incorporate multiple library operating systems, each exporting a different API, for example one for high level UI development and one for real-time control.

History of Kernel Development

Early Operating System Kernels

Strictly speaking, an operating system (and thus, a kernel) is not *required* to run a computer. Programs can be directly loaded and executed on the "bare metal" machine, provided that the authors of those programs are willing to work without any hardware abstraction or operating system support. Most early computers operated this way during the 1950s and early 1960s, which were reset and reloaded between the execution of different programs. Eventually, small ancillary programs such as program loaders and debuggers were left in memory between runs, or loaded from ROM. As these were developed, they formed the basis of what became early operating system kernels. The "bare metal" approach is still used today on some video game consoles and embedded systems, but in general, newer computers use modern operating systems and kernels.

In 1969, the RC 4000 Multiprogramming System introduced the system design philosophy of a small nucleus "upon which operating systems for different purposes could be built in an orderly manner", what would be called the microkernel approach.

Time-sharing Operating Systems

In the decade preceding Unix, computers had grown enormously in power – to the point where computer operators were looking for new ways to get people to use their spare time on their machines. One of the major developments during this era was time-sharing, whereby a number of users would get small slices of computer time, at a rate at which it appeared they were each connected to their own, slower, machine.

The development of time-sharing systems led to a number of problems. One was that users, particularly at universities where the systems were being developed, seemed to want to hack the system to get more CPU time. For this reason, security and access control became a major focus of the Multics project in 1965. Another ongoing issue was properly handling computing resources: users spent most of their time staring at the screen and thinking instead of actually using the resources of the computer, and a time-sharing system should give the CPU time to an active user during these periods. Finally, the systems typically offered a memory hierarchy several layers deep, and partitioning this expensive resource led to major developments in virtual memory systems.

Amiga

The Commodore Amiga was released in 1985, and was among the first – and certainly most successful – home computers to feature an advanced kernel architecture. The AmigaOS kernel's executive component, *exec.library*, uses a microkernel message-passing design, but there are other kernel components, like *graphics.library*, that have direct access to the hardware. There is no memory protection, and the kernel is almost always running in user mode. Only special actions are executed in kernel mode, and user-mode applications can ask the operating system to execute their code in kernel mode.

Unix

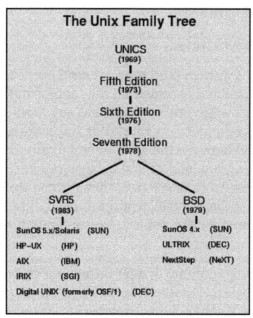

The Unix Family Tree

A diagram of the predecessor/successor family relationship for Unix-like systems.

During the design phase of Unix, programmers decided to model every high-level device as a file, because they believed the purpose of computation was data transformation.

For instance, printers were represented as a "file" at a known location – when data was copied to the file, it printed out. Other systems, to provide a similar functionality, tended to virtualize devices at a lower level – that is, both devices *and* files would be instances of some lower level concept. Virtualizing the system at the file level allowed users to manipulate the entire system using their existing file management utilities and concepts, dramatically simplifying operation. As an extension of the same paradigm, Unix allows programmers to manipulate files using a series of small programs, using the concept of pipes, which allowed users to complete operations in stages, feeding a file through a chain of single-purpose tools. Although the end result was the same, using smaller programs in this way dramatically increased flexibility as well as ease of development and use, allowing the user to modify their workflow by adding or removing a program from the chain.

In the Unix model, the *operating system* consists of two parts; first, the huge collection of utility programs that drive most operations, the other the kernel that runs the programs. Under Unix, from a programming standpoint, the distinction between the two is fairly thin; the kernel is a program, running in supervisor mode, that acts as a program loader and supervisor for the small utility programs making up the rest of the system, and to provide locking and I/O services for these programs; beyond that, the kernel didn't intervene at all in user space.

Over the years the computing model changed, and Unix's treatment of everything as a file or byte stream no longer was as universally applicable as it was before. Although a terminal could be treated as a file or a byte stream, which is printed to or read from, the same did not seem to be true for a graphical user interface. Networking posed another problem. Even if network communication can be compared to file access, the low-level packet-oriented architecture dealt with discrete chunks of data and not with whole files. As the capability of computers grew, Unix became increasingly cluttered with code. It is also because the modularity of the Unix kernel is extensively scalable. While kernels might have had 100,000 lines of code in the seventies and eighties, kernels of modern Unix successors like Linux have more than 13 million lines.

Modern Unix-derivatives are generally based on module-loading monolithic kernels. Examples of this are the QNX, a microkernel owned by BlackBerry, Linux kernel in its many distributions as well as the Berkeley software distribution variant kernels such as FreeBSD, DragonflyBSD, OpenBSD, NetBSD,and macOS. Apart from these alternatives, amateur developers maintain an active operating system development community, populated by self-written hobby kernels which mostly end up sharing many features with Linux, FreeBSD, DragonflyBSD, OpenBSD or NetBSD kernels and/or being compatible with them.

Mac OS

Apple first launched its classic Mac OS in 1984, bundled with its Macintosh personal computer. Apple moved to a nanokernel design in Mac OS 8.6. Against this, the modern macOS (originally named Mac OS X) is based on Darwin, which uses a hybrid kernel called XNU, which was created combining the 4.3BSD kernel and the Mach kernel.

Microsoft Windows

Microsoft Windows was first released in 1985 as an add-on to MS-DOS. Because of its dependence on another operating system, initial releases of Windows, prior to Windows 95, were considered an operating environment). This product line continued to evolve through the 1980s and 1990s, culminating with release of the Windows 9x series (upgrading the system's capabilities to 32-bit addressing and pre-emptive multitasking) through the mid-1990s and ending with the release of Windows Me in 2000. Microsoft also developed Windows NT, an operating system intended for high-end and business users. This line started with the release of Windows NT 3.1 in 1993, and has continued through the years of 2010 with Windows 8 and Windows Server 2012.

The release of Windows XP in October 2001 brought the NT kernel version of Windows to general users, replacing Windows 9x with a completely different operating system. The architecture of Windows NT's kernel is considered a hybrid kernel because the kernel itself contains tasks such as the Window Manager and the IPC Managers, with a client/server layered subsystem model.

Development of Microkernels

Although Mach, developed at Carnegie Mellon University from 1985 to 1994, is the best-known general-purpose microkernel, other microkernels have been developed with more specific aims. The L4 microkernel family (mainly the L3 and the L4 kernel) was created to demonstrate that microkernels are not necessarily slow. Newer implementations such as Fiasco and Pistachio are able to run Linux next to other L4 processes in separate address spaces.

Additionally, QNX is a microkernel which is principally used in embedded systems.

Process

A list of processes as displayed by htop

In computing, a process is an instance of a computer program that is being executed. It contains the program code and its current activity. Depending on the operating system (OS), a process may be made up of multiple threads of execution that execute instructions concurrently.

A computer program is a passive collection of instructions, while a process is the actual execution of those instructions. Several processes may be associated with the same program; for example, opening up several instances of the same program often means more than one process is being executed.

Multitasking is a method to allow multiple processes to share processors (CPUs) and other system resources. Each CPU executes a single task at a time. However, multitasking allows each processor to switch between tasks that are being executed without having to wait for each task to finish. Depending on the operating system implementation, switches could be performed when tasks perform input/output operations, when a task indicates that it can be switched, or on hardware interrupts.

A common form of multitasking is time-sharing. Time-sharing is a method to allow fast response for interactive user applications. In time-sharing systems, context switches are performed rapidly, which makes it seem like multiple processes are being executed simultaneously on the same processor. This seeming execution of multiple processes simultaneously is called concurrency.

For security and reliability, most modern operating systems prevent direct communication between independent processes, providing strictly mediated and controlled inter-process communication functionality.

Representation

In general, a computer system process consists of (or is said to *own*) the following resources:

- An *image* of the executable machine code associated with a program.

- Memory (typically some region of virtual memory); which includes the executable code, process-specific data (input and output), a call stack (to keep track of active subroutines and/or other events), and a heap to hold intermediate computation data generated during run time.

- Operating system descriptors of resources that are allocated to the process, such as file descriptors (Unix terminology) or handles (Windows), and data sources and sinks.

- Security attributes, such as the process owner and the process' set of permissions (allowable operations).

- Processor state (context), such as the content of registers and physical memory addressing. The *state* is typically stored in computer registers when the process is executing, and in memory otherwise.

The operating system holds most of this information about active processes in data structures called process control blocks. Any subset of the resources, typically at least the processor state, may be associated with each of the process' threads in operating systems that support threads or *child* (*daughter*) processes.

The operating system keeps its processes separate and allocates the resources they need, so that they are less likely to interfere with each other and cause system failures (e.g., deadlock or thrashing). The operating system may also provide mechanisms for inter-process communication to enable processes to interact in safe and predictable ways.

Multitasking and Process Management

A multitasking operating system may just switch between processes to give the appearance of many processes executing simultaneously (that is, in parallel), though in fact only one process can be executing at any one time on a single CPU (unless the CPU has multiple cores, then multithreading or other similar technologies can be used).

It is usual to associate a single process with a main program, and child processes with any spinoff, parallel processes, which behave like asynchronous subroutines. A process is said to *own* resources, of which an *image* of its program (in memory) is one such resource. However, in multiprocessing systems *many* processes may run off of, or share, the same reentrant program at the same location in memory, but each process is said to own its own *image* of the program.

Processes are often called "tasks" in embedded operating systems. The sense of "process" (or task) is "something that takes up time", as opposed to "memory", which is "something that takes up space".

The above description applies to both processes managed by an operating system, and processes as defined by process calculi.

If a process requests something for which it must wait, it will be blocked. When the process is in the blocked state, it is eligible for swapping to disk, but this is transparent in a virtual memory system, where regions of a process's memory may be really on disk and not in main memory at any time. Note that even *unused* portions of active processes/tasks (executing programs) are eligible for swapping to disk. *All parts of an executing program and its data do not have to be in physical memory for the associated process to be active.*

Process States

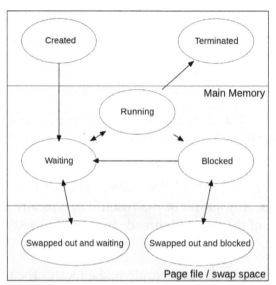

The various process states, displayed in a state diagram, with arrows indicating possible transitions between states.

An operating system kernel that allows multitasking needs processes to have certain states. Names for these states are not standardised, but they have similar functionality.

- First, the process is "created" by being loaded from a secondary storage device (hard disk drive, CD-ROM, etc.) into main memory. After that the process scheduler assigns it the "waiting" state.

- While the process is "waiting", it waits for the scheduler to do a so-called context switch and load the process into the processor. The process state then becomes "running", and the processor executes the process instructions.

- If a process needs to wait for a resource (wait for user input or file to open, for example), it is assigned the "blocked" state. The process state is changed back to "waiting" when the process no longer needs to wait (in a blocked state).

- Once the process finishes execution, or is terminated by the operating system, it is no longer needed. The process is removed instantly or is moved to the "terminated" state. When removed, it just waits to be removed from main memory.

Inter-process Communication

When processes communicate with each other it is called "Inter-process communication" (IPC). Processes frequently need to communicate, for instance in a shell pipeline, the output of the first process need to pass to the second one, and so on to the other process. It is preferred in a well-structured way not using interrupts.

It is even possible for the two processes to be running on different machines. The operating system

(OS) may differ from one process to the other, therefore some mediator(s) (called protocols) are needed.

History

By the early 1960s, computer control software had evolved from monitor control software, for example IBSYS, to executive control software. Over time, computers got faster while computer time was still neither cheap nor fully utilized; such an environment made multiprogramming possible and necessary. Multiprogramming means that several programs run concurrently. At first, more than one program ran on a single processor, as a result of underlying uniprocessor computer architecture, and they shared scarce and limited hardware resources; consequently, the concurrency was of a *serial* nature. On later systems with multiple processors, multiple programs may run concurrently in *parallel*.

Programs consist of sequences of instructions for processors. A single processor can run only one instruction at a time: it is impossible to run more programs at the same time. A program might need some resource, such as an input device, which has a large delay, or a program might start some slow operation, such as sending output to a printer. This would lead to processor being "idle" (unused). To keep the processor busy at all times, the execution of such a program is halted and the operating system switches the processor to run another program. To the user, it will appear that the programs run at the same time (hence the term "parallel").

Shortly thereafter, the notion of a "program" was expanded to the notion of an "executing program and its context". The concept of a process was born, which also became necessary with the invention of re-entrant code. Threads came somewhat later. However, with the advent of concepts such as time-sharing, computer networks, and multiple-CPU shared memory computers, the old "multiprogramming" gave way to true multitasking, multiprocessing and, later, multithreading.

Interrupt

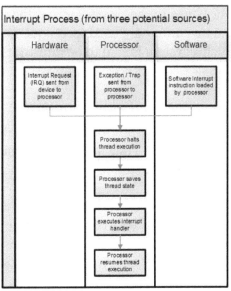

interrupt sources and processor handling.

In system programming, an interrupt is a signal to the processor emitted by hardware or software indicating an event that needs immediate attention. An interrupt alerts the processor to a high-priority condition requiring the interruption of the current code the processor is executing. The processor responds by suspending its current activities, saving its state, and executing a function called an *interrupt handler* (or an interrupt service routine, ISR) to deal with the event. This interruption is temporary, and, after the interrupt handler finishes, the processor resumes normal activities. There are two types of interrupts: hardware interrupts and software interrupts.

Hardware interrupts are used by devices to communicate that they require attention from the operating system. Internally, hardware interrupts are implemented using electronic alerting signals that are sent to the processor from an external device, which is either a part of the computer itself, such as a disk controller, or an external peripheral. For example, pressing a key on the keyboard or moving the mouse triggers hardware interrupts that cause the processor to read the keystroke or mouse position. Unlike the software type (described below), hardware interrupts are asynchronous and can occur in the middle of instruction execution, requiring additional care in programming. The act of initiating a hardware interrupt is referred to as an interrupt request (IRQ).

A software interrupt is caused either by an exceptional condition in the processor itself, or a special instruction in the instruction set which causes an interrupt when it is executed. The former is often called a *trap* or *exception* and is used for errors or events occurring during program execution that are exceptional enough that they cannot be handled within the program itself. For example, a divide-by-zero exception will be thrown if the processor's arithmetic logic unit is commanded to divide a number by zero as this instruction is in error and impossible. The operating system will catch this exception, and can choose to abort the instruction. Software interrupt instructions can also function similarly to subroutine calls and be used for a variety of purposes, such as to request services from device drivers, like interrupts sent to and from a disk controller to request reading or writing of data to and from the disk.

Each interrupt has its own interrupt handler. The number of hardware interrupts is limited by the number of interrupt request (IRQ) lines to the processor, but there may be hundreds of different software interrupts. Interrupts are a commonly used technique for computer multitasking, especially in real-time computing. Such a system is said to be interrupt-driven.

Overview

Hardware interrupts were introduced as an optimization, eliminating unproductive waiting time in polling loops, waiting for external events. They may be implemented in hardware as a distinct system with control lines, or they may be integrated into the memory subsystem.

If implemented in hardware, an interrupt controller circuit such as the IBM PC's Programmable Interrupt Controller (PIC) may be connected between the interrupting device and the processor's interrupt pin to multiplex several sources of interrupt onto the one or two CPU lines typically available. If implemented as part of the memory controller, interrupts are mapped into the system's memory address space.

Interrupts can be categorized into these different types:

- *Maskable interrupt* (IRQ): a hardware interrupt that may be ignored by setting a bit in an interrupt mask register's (IMR) bit-mask.

- *Non-maskable interrupt* (NMI): a hardware interrupt that lacks an associated bit-mask, so that it can never be ignored. NMIs are used for the highest priority tasks such as timers, especially watchdog timers.

- *Inter-processor interrupt* (IPI): a special case of interrupt that is generated by one processor to interrupt another processor in a multiprocessor system.

- *Software interrupt*: an interrupt generated within a processor by executing an instruction. Software interrupts are often used to implement system calls because they result in a subroutine call with a CPU ring level change.

- *Spurious interrupt*: a hardware interrupt that is unwanted. They are typically generated by system conditions such as electrical interference on an interrupt line or through incorrectly designed hardware.

Processors typically have an internal *interrupt mask* which allows software to ignore all external hardware interrupts while it is set. Setting or clearing this mask may be faster than accessing an interrupt mask register (IMR) in a PIC or disabling interrupts in the device itself. In some cases, such as the x86 architecture, disabling and enabling interrupts on the processor itself act as a memory barrier; however, it may actually be slower.

An interrupt that leaves the machine in a well-defined state is called a *precise interrupt*. Such an interrupt has four properties:

- The Program Counter (PC) is saved in a known place.

- All instructions before the one pointed to by the PC have fully executed.

- No instruction beyond the one pointed to by the PC has been executed (that is no prohibition on instruction beyond that in PC, it is just that any changes they make to registers or memory must be undone before the interrupt happens).

- The execution state of the instruction pointed to by the PC is known.

An interrupt that does not meet these requirements is called an *imprecise interrupt*.

The phenomenon where the overall system performance is severely hindered by excessive amounts of processing time spent handling interrupts is called an interrupt storm.

Types of Interrupts

Level-triggered

A *level-triggered interrupt* is an interrupt signalled by maintaining the interrupt line at a high or low level. A device wishing to signal a Level-triggered interrupt drives the interrupt request line to its active level (high or low), and then holds it at that level until it is serviced. It ceases asserting the line when the CPU commands it to or otherwise handles the condition that caused it to signal the interrupt.

Typically, the processor samples the interrupt input at predefined times during each bus cycle such as state T2 for the Z80 microprocessor. If the interrupt isn't active when the processor samples it, the CPU doesn't see it. One possible use for this type of interrupt is to minimize spurious signals from a noisy interrupt line: a spurious pulse will often be so short that it is not noticed.

Multiple devices may share a level-triggered interrupt line if they are designed to. The interrupt line must have a pull-down or pull-up resistor so that when not actively driven it settles to its inactive state. Devices actively assert the line to indicate an outstanding interrupt, but let the line float (do not actively drive it) when not signalling an interrupt. The line is then in its asserted state when any (one or more than one) of the sharing devices is signalling an outstanding interrupt.

Level-triggered interrupt is favored by some because it is easy to share the interrupt request line without losing the interrupts, when multiple shared devices interrupt at the same time. Upon detecting assertion of the interrupt line, the CPU must search through the devices sharing the interrupt request line until one who triggered the interrupt is detected. After servicing this device, the CPU may recheck the interrupt line status to determine whether any other devices also needs service. If the line is now de-asserted, the CPU avoids checking the remaining devices on the line. Since some devices interrupt more frequently than others, and other device interrupts are particularly expensive, a careful ordering of device checks is employed to increase efficiency. The original PCI standard mandated level-triggered interrupts because of this advantage of sharing interrupts.

There are also serious problems with sharing level-triggered interrupts. As long as any device on the line has an outstanding request for service the line remains asserted, so it is not possible to detect a change in the status of any other device. Deferring servicing a low-priority device is not an option, because this would prevent detection of service requests from higher-priority devices. If there is a device on the line that the CPU does not know how to service, then any interrupt from that device permanently blocks all interrupts from the other devices.

Edge-triggered

An *edge-triggered interrupt* is an interrupt signalled by a level transition on the interrupt line, either a falling edge (high to low) or a rising edge (low to high). A device, wishing to signal an interrupt, drives a pulse onto the line and then releases the line to its inactive state. If the pulse is too short to be detected by polled I/O then special hardware may be required to detect the edge.

Multiple devices may share an edge-triggered interrupt line if they are designed to. The interrupt line must have a pull-down or pull-up resistor so that when not actively driven it settles to one particular state. Devices signal an interrupt by briefly driving the line to its non-default state, and let the line float (do not actively drive it) when not signalling an interrupt. This type of connection is also referred to as open collector. The line then carries all the pulses generated by all the devices. (This is analogous to the pull cord on some buses and trolleys that any passenger can pull to signal the driver that they are requesting a stop.) However, interrupt pulses from different devices may merge if they occur close in time. To avoid losing interrupts the CPU must trigger on the trailing edge of the pulse (e.g. the rising edge if the line is pulled up and driven low). After detecting an interrupt the CPU must check all the devices for service requirements.

Edge-triggered interrupts do not suffer the problems that level-triggered interrupts have with sharing. Service of a low-priority device can be postponed arbitrarily, and interrupts will continue to be received from the high-priority devices that are being serviced. If there is a device that the CPU does not know how to service, it may cause a spurious interrupt, or even periodic spurious interrupts, but it does not interfere with the interrupt signalling of the other devices. However, it is fairly easy for an edge triggered interrupt to be missed - for example if interrupts have to be masked for a period - and unless there is some type of hardware latch that records the event it is impossible to recover. Such problems caused many "lockups" in early computer hardware because the processor did not know it was expected to do something. More modern hardware often has one or more interrupt status registers that latch the interrupt requests; well written edge-driven interrupt software often checks such registers to ensure events are not missed.

The elderly Industry Standard Architecture (ISA) bus uses edge-triggered interrupts, but does not mandate that devices be able to share them. The parallel port also uses edge-triggered interrupts. Many older devices assume that they have exclusive use of their interrupt line, making it electrically unsafe to share them. However, ISA motherboards include pull-up resistors on the IRQ lines, so well-behaved devices share ISA interrupts just fine.

Hybrid

Some systems use a hybrid of level-triggered and edge-triggered signalling. The hardware not only looks for an edge, but it also verifies that the interrupt signal stays active for a certain period of time.

A common use of a hybrid interrupt is for the NMI (non-maskable interrupt) input. Because NMIs generally signal major – or even catastrophic – system events, a good implementation of this signal tries to ensure that the interrupt is valid by verifying that it remains active for a period of time. This 2-step approach helps to eliminate false interrupts from affecting the system.

Message-signaled

A *message-signalled interrupt* does not use a physical interrupt line. Instead, a device signals its request for service by sending a short message over some communications medium, typically a computer bus. The message might be of a type reserved for interrupts, or it might be of some pre-existing type such as a memory write.

Message-signalled interrupts behave very much like edge-triggered interrupts, in that the interrupt is a momentary signal rather than a continuous condition. Interrupt-handling software treats the two in much the same manner. Typically, multiple pending message-signalled interrupts with the same message (the same virtual interrupt line) are allowed to merge, just as closely spaced edge-triggered interrupts can merge.

Message-signalled interrupt vectors can be shared, to the extent that the underlying communication medium can be shared. No additional effort is required.

Because the identity of the interrupt is indicated by a pattern of data bits, not requiring a separate physical conductor, many more distinct interrupts can be efficiently handled. This reduces the need for sharing. Interrupt messages can also be passed over a serial bus, not requiring any additional lines.

PCI Express, a serial computer bus, uses message-signalled interrupts exclusively.

Doorbell

In a push button analogy applied to computer systems, the term *doorbell* or *doorbell interrupt* is often used to describe a mechanism whereby a software system can signal or notify a computer hardware device that there is some work to be done. Typically, the software system will place data in some well-known and mutually agreed upon memory location(s), and "ring the doorbell" by writing to a different memory location. This different memory location is often called the doorbell region, and there may even be multiple doorbells serving different purposes in this region. It is this act of writing to the doorbell region of memory that "rings the bell" and notifies the hardware device that the data are ready and waiting. The hardware device would now know that the data are valid and can be acted upon. It would typically write the data to a hard disk drive, or send them over a network, or encrypt them, etc.

The term *doorbell interrupt* is usually a misnomer. It's similar to an interrupt, because it causes some work to be done by the device; however, the doorbell region is sometimes implemented as a polled region, sometimes the doorbell region writes through to physical device registers, and sometimes the doorbell region is hardwired directly to physical device registers. When either writing through or directly to physical device registers, this may cause a real interrupt to occur at the device's central processor unit (CPU), if it has one.

Doorbell interrupts can be compared to Message Signaled Interrupts, as they have some similarities.

Difficulty with Sharing Interrupt Lines

Multiple devices sharing an interrupt line (of any triggering style) all act as spurious interrupt sources with respect to each other. With many devices on one line the workload in servicing interrupts grows in proportion to the square of the number of devices. It is therefore preferred to spread devices evenly across the available interrupt lines. Shortage of interrupt lines is a problem in older system designs where the interrupt lines are distinct physical conductors. Message-signalled interrupts, where the interrupt line is virtual, are favored in new system architectures (such as PCI Express) and relieve this problem to a considerable extent.

Some devices with a poorly designed programming interface provide no way to determine whether they have requested service. They may lock up or otherwise misbehave if serviced when they do not want it. Such devices cannot tolerate spurious interrupts, and so also cannot tolerate sharing an interrupt line. ISA cards, due to often cheap design and construction, are notorious for this problem. Such devices are becoming much rarer, as hardware logic becomes cheaper and new system architectures mandate shareable interrupts.

Performance Issues

Interrupts provide low overhead and good latency at low load, but degrade significantly at high interrupt rate unless care is taken to prevent several pathologies. These are various forms of livelocks, when the system spends all of its time processing interrupts to the exclusion of other required tasks. Under extreme conditions, a large number of interrupts (like very high network traffic) may completely stall the system. To avoid such problems, an operating system must schedule network interrupt handling as carefully as it schedules process execution.

With multi-core processors, additional performance improvements in interrupt handling can be achieved through receive-side scaling (RSS) when multiqueue NICs are used. Such NICs provide multiple receive queues associated to separate interrupts; by routing each of those interrupts to different cores, processing of the interrupt requests triggered by the network traffic received by a single NIC can be distributed among multiple cores. Distribution of the interrupts among cores can be performed automatically by the operating system, or the routing of interrupts (usually referred to as *IRQ affinity*) can be manually configured.

A purely software-based implementation of the receiving traffic distribution, known as *receive packet steering* (RPS), distributes received traffic among cores later in the data path, as part of the interrupt handler functionality. Advantages of RPS over RSS include no requirements for specific hardware, more advanced traffic distribution filters, and reduced rate of interrupts produced by a NIC. As a downside, RPS increases the rate of inter-processor interrupts (IPIs). *Receive flow steering* (RFS) takes the software-based approach further by accounting for application locality; further performance improvements are achieved by processing interrupt requests by the same cores on which particular network packets will be consumed by the targeted application.

Typical Uses

Typical uses of interrupts include the following: system timers, disk I/O, power-off signals, and traps. Other interrupts exist to transfer data bytes using UARTs or Ethernet; sense key-presses; control motors; or anything else the equipment must do.

Another typical use is to generate periodic interrupts by dividing the output of a crystal oscillator and having an interrupt handler count the interrupts in order for a processor to keep time. These periodic interrupts are often used by the OS's task scheduler to reschedule the priorities of running processes. Some older computers generated periodic interrupts from the power line frequency because it was controlled by the utilities to eliminate long-term drift of electric clocks.

For example, a disk interrupt signals the completion of a data transfer from or to the disk peripheral; a process waiting to read or write a file starts up again. As another example, a power-off interrupt predicts or requests a loss of power, allowing the computer equipment to perform an orderly shut-down. Also, interrupts are used in typeahead features for buffering events like keystrokes.

Protected Mode

In computing, protected mode, also called protected virtual address mode, is an operational mode of x86-compatible central processing units (CPUs). It allows system software to use features such as virtual memory, paging and safe multi-tasking designed to increase an operating system's control over application software.

When a processor that supports x86 protected mode is powered on, it begins executing instructions in real mode, in order to maintain backward compatibility with earlier x86 processors. Protected mode may only be entered after the system software sets up several descriptor tables and enables the Protection Enable (PE) bit in the control register 0 (CR0).

Protected mode was first added to the x86 architecture in 1982, with the release of Intel's 80286 (286) processor, and later extended with the release of the 80386 (386) in 1985. Due to the enhancements added by protected mode, it has become widely adopted and has become the foundation for all subsequent enhancements to the x86 architecture, although many of those enhancements, such as added instructions and new registers, also brought benefits to the real mode.

History

The Intel 8086, the predecessor to the 286, was originally designed with a 20-bit address bus for its memory. This allowed the processor to access 2^{20} bytes of memory, equivalent to 1 megabyte. At the time, 1 megabyte was considered a relatively large amount of memory, so the designers of the IBM Personal Computer reserved the first 640 kilobytes for use by applications and the operating system and the remaining 384 kilobytes for the BIOS (Basic Input/Output System) and memory for add-on devices.

As the cost of memory decreased and memory use increased, the 1 MB limitation became a significant problem. Intel intended to solve this limitation along with others with the release of the 286.

The 286

The initial protected mode, released with the 286, was not widely used; for example, it was used by Microsoft Xenix (around 1984), Coherent and Minix. Several shortcomings such as the inability to access the BIOS or DOS calls due to inability to switch back to real mode without resetting the processor prevented widespread usage. Acceptance was additionally hampered by the fact that the 286 only allowed memory access in 16 bit segments via each of four segment registers, meaning only $4*2^{16}$ bytes, equivalent to 256 kilobytes, could be accessed at a time. Because changing a segment register in protected mode caused a 6-byte segment descriptor to be loaded into the CPU from memory, the segment register load instruction took many tens of processor cycles, making it much slower than on the 8086; therefore, the strategy of computing segment addresses on-the-fly in order to access data structures larger than 128 kilobytes (the combined size of the two data segments) became impractical, even for those few programmers who had mastered it on the 8086/8088.

The 286 maintained backwards compatibility with its precursor the 8086 by initially entering real mode on power up. Real mode functioned virtually identically to the 8086, allowing the vast majority of existing 8086 software to run unmodified on the newer 286. Real mode also served as a more basic mode in which protected mode could be set up, solving a sort of chicken-and-egg problem. To access the extended functionality of the 286, the operating system would set up some tables in memory that controlled memory access in protected mode, set the addresses of those tables into some special registers of the processor, and then set the processor into protected mode. This enabled 24 bit addressing which allowed the processor to access 2^{24} bytes of memory, equivalent to 16 megabytes.

The 386

With the release of the 386 in 1985, many of the issues preventing widespread adoption of the previous protected mode were addressed. The 386 was released with an address bus size of 32 bits, which allows for 2^{32} bytes of memory accessing, equivalent to 4 gigabytes. The segment sizes were also increased to 32 bits, meaning that the full address space of 4 gigabytes could be accessed without the need to switch between multiple segments. In addition to the increased size of the address bus and segment registers, many other new features were added with the intention of increasing operational security and stability. Protected mode is now used in virtually all modern operating systems which run on the x86 architecture, such as Microsoft Windows, Linux, and many others.

An Intel 80386 microprocessor.

Furthermore, learning from the failures of the 286 protected mode to satisfy the needs for multiuser DOS, Intel added a separate virtual 8086 mode, which allowed multiple virtualized 8086 processors to be emulated on the 386. Hardware support required for virtualizing the protected mode itself, however, had to wait for another 20 years.

386 Additions to Protected Mode

With the release of the 386, the following additional features were added to protected mode:

- Paging.

- 32-bit physical and virtual address space (The 32-bit physical address space is not present on the 80386SX, and other 386 processor variants which use the older 286 bus.).

- 32-bit segment offsets.

- Ability to switch back to real mode without resetting.

- Virtual 8086 mode.

Entering and Exiting Protected Mode

Until the release of the 386, protected mode did not offer a direct method to switch back into real mode once protected mode was entered. IBM devised a workaround (implemented in the IBM

AT) which involved resetting the CPU via the keyboard controller and saving the system registers, stack pointer and often the interrupt mask in the real-time clock chip's RAM. This allowed the BIOS to restore the CPU to a similar state and begin executing code before the reset. Later, a triple fault was used to reset the 286 CPU, which was a lot faster and cleaner than the keyboard controller method (and does not depend on IBM AT-compatible hardware, but will work on any 80286 CPU in any system).

To enter protected mode, the Global Descriptor Table (GDT) must first be created with a minimum of three entries: a null descriptor, a code segment descriptor and data segment descriptor. In an IBM-compatible machine, the A20 line (21st address line) also must be enabled to allow the use of all the address lines so that the CPU can access beyond 1 megabyte of memory (Only the first 20 are allowed to be used after power-up, to guarantee compatibility with older software written for the Intel 8088-based IBM PC and PC/XT models). After performing those two steps, the PE bit must be set in the CR0 register and a far jump must be made to clear the prefetch input queue.

```
; set PE bit

mov eax, cr0

or eax, 1

mov cr0, eax

; far jump (cs = selector of code segment)

jmp cs:@pm

@pm:

; Now we are in PM.
```

With the release of the 386, protected mode could be exited by loading the segment registers with real mode values, disabling the A20 line and clearing the PE bit in the CR0 register, without the need to perform the initial setup steps required with the 286.

Features

Protected mode has a number of features designed to enhance an operating system's control over application software, in order to increase security and system stability. These additions allow the operating system to function in a way that would be significantly more difficult or even impossible without proper hardware support.

Privilege Levels

In protected mode, there are four privilege levels or rings, numbered from 0 to 3, with ring 0 being the most privileged and 3 being the least. The use of rings allows for system software to restrict tasks from accessing data, call gates or executing privileged instructions. In most environments, the operating system and some device drivers run in ring 0 and applications run in ring 3.

Real Mode Application Compatibility

According to the *Intel 80286 Programmer's Reference Manual,*

> ...the 80286 remains upwardly compatible with most 8086 and 80186 application programs. Most 8086 application programs can be re-compiled or re-assembled and executed on the 80286 in Protected Mode.

For the most part, the binary compatibility with real-mode code, the ability to access up to 16 MB of physical memory, and 1 GB of virtual memory, were the most apparent changes to application programmers. This was not without its limitations, if an application utilized or relied on any of the techniques below it wouldn'trun:

- Segment arithmetic.

- Privileged instructions.

- Direct hardware access.

- Writing to a code segment.

- Executing data.

- Overlapping segments.

- Use of BIOS functions, due to the BIOS interrupts being reserved by Intel.

In reality, almost all DOS application programs violated these rules. Due to these limitations, virtual 8086 mode was introduced with the 386. Despite such potential setbacks, Windows 3.0 and its successors can take advantage of the binary compatibility with real mode to run many Windows 2.x (Windows 2.0 and Windows 2.1x) applications, which run in real mode in Windows 2.x, in protected mode.

Virtual 8086 Mode

With the release of the 386, protected mode offers what the Intel manuals call *virtual 8086 mode*. Virtual 8086 mode is designed to allow code previously written for the 8086 to run unmodified and concurrently with other tasks, without compromising security or system stability.

Virtual 8086 mode, however, is not completely backwards compatible with all programs. Programs that require segment manipulation, privileged instructions, direct hardware access, or use self-modifying code will generate an exception that must be served by the operating system. In addition, applications running in virtual 8086 mode generate a trap with the use of instructions that involve input/output (I/O), which can negatively impact performance.

Due to these limitations, some programs originally designed to run on the 8086 cannot be run in virtual 8086 mode. As a result, system software is forced to either compromise system security or backwards compatibility when dealing with legacy software. An example of such a compromise can be seen with the release of Windows NT, which dropped backwards compatibility for "ill-behaved" DOS applications.

Segment Addressing

In real mode each logical address points directly into physical memory location, every logical address consists of two 16 bit parts: The segment part of the logical address contains the base address of a segment with a granularity of 16 bytes, i.e. a segments may start at physical address

0, 16, 32, ..., 2^{20}-16. The offset part of the logical address contains an offset inside the segment, i.e. the physical address can be calculated as physical_address : = segment_part × 16 + offset (if the address line A20 is enabled), respectively (segment_part × 16 + offset) mod 2^{20} (if A20 is off) Every segment has a size of 2^{16} bytes.

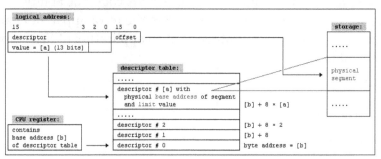

Virtual segments of 80286.

Protected Mode

In protected mode, the segment_part is replaced by a 16-bit *selector*, in which the 13 upper bits (bit 3 to bit 15) contain the index of an *entry* inside a *descriptor table*. The next bit (bit 2) specifies whether the operation is used with the GDT or the LDT. The lowest two bits (bit 1 and bit 0) of the selector are combined to define the privilege of the request, where the values of 0 and 3 represent the highest and the lowest priority, respectively. This means that the byte offset of descriptors in the descriptor table is the same as the 16-bit selector, provided the lower three bits are zeroed.

The descriptor table entry defines the real *linear* address of the segment, a limit value for the segment size, and some attribute bits (flags).

286

The segment address inside the descriptor table entry has a length of 24 bits so every byte of the physical memory can be defined as bound of the segment. The limit value inside the descriptor table entry has a length of 16 bits so segment length can be between 1 byte and 2^{16} byte. The calculated linear address equals the physical memory address.

386

The segment address inside the descriptor table entry is expanded to 32 bits so every byte of the physical memory can be defined as bound of the segment. The limit value inside the descriptor table entry is expanded to 20 bits and completed with a granularity flag (G-bit, for short):

- If G-bit is zero limit has a granularity of 1 byte, i.e. segment size may be 1, 2, ..., 2^{20} bytes.

- If G-bit is one limit has a granularity of 2^{12} bytes, i.e. segment size may be 1×2^{12}, 2×2^{12}, ..., $2^{20} \times 2^{12}$ bytes. If paging is off, the calculated linear address equals the physical memory address. If paging is on, the calculated linear address is used as input of paging.

The 386 processor also uses 32 bit values for the address offset.

For maintaining compatibility with 286 protected mode a new default flag (D-bit, for short) was added. If the D-bit of a code segment is off (0) all commands inside this segment will be interpreted as 16-bit commands by default; if it is on (1), they will be interpreted as 32-bit commands.

Structure of Segment Descriptor Entry

B	Bits	80286	80386	B			Attribute flags #2
0	00..07, 0..7	limit	bits 0..15 of limit	0	52	4	unused, available for operating system
1	08..15, 0..7			1	53	5	reserved, should be zero
2	16..23, 0..7	base address	bits 0..23 of base address	2	54	6	default flag / D-bit
3	24..31, 0..7			3	55	7	granularity flag / G-bit
4	32..39, 0..7			4			
5	40..47, 0..7	attribute flags #1		5			
6	48..51, 0..3	unused	bits 16..19 of limit	6			
	52..55, 4..7		attribute flags #2				
7	56..63, 0..7		bits 24..31 of base address	7			

a. Byte offset inside entry.

b. First range is the bit offset inside entry; second range is the bit offset inside byte.

Paging

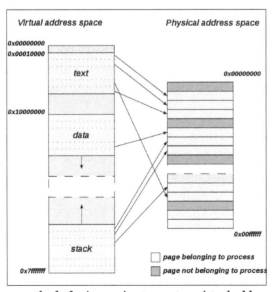

Common method of using paging to create a virtual address space.

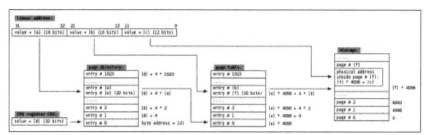

Paging (on Intel 80386) with page size of 4K.

In addition to adding virtual 8086 mode, the 386 also added paging to protected mode. Through paging, system software can restrict and control a task's access to pages, which are sections of memory. In many operating systems, paging is used to create an independent virtual address space for each task, preventing one task from manipulating the memory of another. Paging also allows for pages to be moved out of primary storage and onto a slower and larger secondary storage, such as a hard disk drive. This allows for more memory to be used than physically available in primary storage.

The x86 architecture allows control of pages through two arrays: page directories and page tables. Originally, a page directory was the size of one page, four kilobytes, and contained 1,024 page directory entries (PDE), although subsequent enhancements to the x86 architecture have added the ability to use larger page sizes. Each PDE contained a pointer to a page table. A page table was also originally four kilobytes in size and contained 1,024 page table entries (PTE). Each PTE contained a pointer to the actual page's physical address and are only used when the four-kilobyte pages are used. At any given time, only one page directory may be in active use.

Multitasking

Through the use of the rings, privileged call gates, and the Task State Segment (TSS), introduced with the 286, preemptive multitasking was made possible on the x86 architecture. The TSS allows general-purpose registers, segment selector fields, and stacks to all be modified without affecting those of another task. The TSS also allows a task's privilege level, and I/O port permissions to be independent of another task's.

In many operating systems, the full features of the TSS are not used. This is commonly due to portability concerns or due to the performance issues created with hardware task switches. As a result, many operating systems use both hardware and software to create a multitasking system.

Operating Systems

Operating systems like OS/2 1.x try to switch the processor between protected and real modes. This is both slow and unsafe, because a real mode program can easily crash a computer. OS/2 1.x defines restrictive programming rules allowing a *Family API* or *bound* program to run in either real or protected mode. Some early Unix operating systems, OS/2 1.x, and Windows used this mode.

Windows 3.0 was able to run real mode programs in 16-bit protected mode; when switching to protected mode, it decided to preserve the single privilege level model that was used in real mode, which is why Windows applications and DLLs can hook interrupts and do direct hardware access. That lasted through the Windows 9x series. If a Windows 1.x or 2.x program is written properly and avoids segment arithmetic, it will run the same way in both real and protected modes. Windows programs generally avoid segment arithmetic because Windows implements a software virtual memory scheme, moving program code and data in memory when programs are not running, so manipulating absolute addresses is dangerous; programs should only keep handles to memory blocks when not running. Starting an old program while Windows 3.0 is running in protected mode triggers a warning dialog, suggesting to either run Windows in real mode or to obtain an updated version of the application. Updating well-behaved programs using the MARK utility with the MEMORY parameter avoids this dialog. It is not possible to have some GUI programs running in 16-bit protected mode and other GUI programs running in real mode. In Windows 3.1, real mode was no longer supported and could not be accessed.

In modern operating systems, 16-bit protected mode is still used for running applications, e.g. DPMI compatible DOS extender programs (through virtual DOS machines) or Windows 3.x applications (through the Windows on Windows subsystem) and certain classes of device drivers (e.g. for changing the screen-resolution using BIOS functionality) in OS/2 2.0 and later, all under control of a 32-bit kernel.

Memory Management

Memory management is a form of resource management applied to computer memory. The essential requirement of memory management is to provide ways to dynamically allocate portions of memory to programs at their request, and free it for reuse when no longer needed. This is critical to any advanced computer system where more than a single process might be underway at any time.

Several methods have been devised that increase the effectiveness of memory management. Virtual memory systems separate the memory addresses used by a process from actual physical addresses, allowing separation of processes and increasing the size of the virtual address space beyond the available amount of RAM using paging or swapping to secondary storage. The quality of the virtual memory manager can have an extensive effect on overall system performance.

Levels

Modern general-purpose computer systems manage memory at two levels:

- Operating system level, and

- Application level.

Application

Application-level memory management is generally categorized as either automatic memory management, usually involving garbage collection (computer science), or manual memory management.

Dynamic Memory Allocation

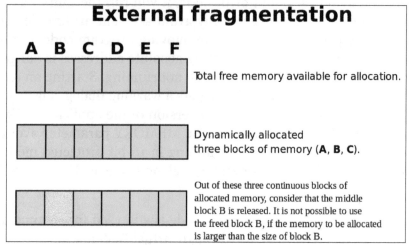

An example of external fragmentation.

Details

The task of fulfilling an allocation request consists of locating a block of unused memory of suffi-cient size. Memory requests are satisfied by allocating portions from a large pool of memory called the *heap* or *free store*.[a] At any given time, some parts of the heap are in use, while some are "free" (unused) and thus available for future allocations.

Several issues complicate the implementation, such as external fragmentation, which arises when there are many small gaps between allocated memory blocks, which invalidates their use for an allocation request. The allocator's metadata can also inflate the size of (individually) small alloca-tions. This is often managed by chunking. The memory management system must track outstand-ing allocations to ensure that they do not overlap and that no memory is ever "lost" as a memory leak.

Efficiency

The specific dynamic memory allocation algorithm implemented can impact performance signifi-cantly. A study conducted in 1994 by Digital Equipment Corporation illustrates the overheads in-volved for a variety of allocators. The lowest average instruction path length required to allocate a single memory slot was 52 (as measured with an instruction level profiler on a variety of software).

Implementations

Since the precise location of the allocation is not known in advance, the memory is accessed in-directly, usually through a pointer reference. The specific algorithm used to organize the memory area and allocate and deallocate chunks is interlinked with the kernel, and may use any of the following methods:

Fixed-size Blocks Allocation

Fixed-size blocks allocation, also called memory pool allocation, uses a free list of fixed-size blocks of memory (often all of the same size). This works well for simple embedded systems where no large objects need to be allocated, but suffers from fragmentation, especially with long memory addresses. However, due to the significantly reduced overhead this method can substantially improve performance for objects that need frequent allocation / de-allocation and is often used in video games.

Buddy Blocks

In this system, memory is allocated into several pools of memory instead of just one, where each pool represents blocks of memory of a certain power of two in size, or blocks of some other convenient size progression. All blocks of a particular size are kept in a sorted linked list or tree and all new blocks that are formed during allocation are added to their respective memory pools for later use. If a smaller size is requested than is available, the smallest available size is selected and split. One of the resulting parts is selected, and the process repeats until the request is complete. When a block is allocated, the allocator will start with the smallest sufficiently large block to avoid needlessly breaking blocks. When a block is freed, it is compared to its buddy. If they are both free, they are combined and placed in the correspondingly larger-sized buddy-block list.

Systems with Virtual Memory

Virtual memory is a method of decoupling the memory organization from the physical hardware. The applications operate memory via *virtual addresses*. Each time an attempt to access stored data is made, virtual memory data orders translate the virtual address to a *physical address*. In this way addition of virtual memory enables granular control over memory systems and methods of access.

In virtual memory systems the operating system limits how a process can access the memory. This feature, called memory protection, can be used to disallow a process to read or write to memory that is not allocated to it, preventing malicious or malfunctioning code in one program from interfering with the operation of another.

Even though the memory allocated for specific processes is normally isolated, processes sometimes need to be able to share information. Shared memory is one of the fastest techniques for inter-process communication.

Memory is usually classified by access rate into primary storage and secondary storage. Memory management systems, among other operations, also handle the moving of information between these two levels of memory.

Virtual Memory

In computing, virtual memory is a memory management technique that is implemented using both hardware and software. It maps memory addresses used by a program, called *virtual addresses*, into *physical addresses* in computer memory. Main storage as seen by a process or task appears as a contiguous address space or collection of contiguous segments. The operating system manages virtual address spaces and the assignment of real memory to virtual memory. Address translation hardware in the CPU, often referred to as a memory management unit or *MMU*, automatically translates virtual addresses to physical addresses. Software within the operating system may extend these capabilities to provide a virtual address space that can exceed the capacity of real memory and thus reference more memory than is physically present in the computer.

The primary benefits of virtual memory include freeing applications from having to manage a shared memory space, increased security due to memory isolation, and being able to conceptually use more memory than might be physically available, using the technique of paging.

Properties

Virtual memory makes application programming easier by hiding fragmentation of physical memory; by delegating to the kernel the burden of managing the memory hierarchy (eliminating the need for the program to handle overlays explicitly); and, when each process is run in its own dedicated address space, by obviating the need to relocate program code or to access memory with relative addressing.

Memory virtualization can be considered a generalization of the concept of virtual memory.

Usage

Virtual memory is an integral part of a modern computer architecture; implementations usually require hardware support, typically in the form of a memory management unit built into the CPU. While not necessary, emulators and virtual machines can employ hardware support to increase performance of their virtual memory implementations. Consequently, older operating systems, such as those for the mainframes of the 1960s, and those for personal computers of the early to mid-1980s (e.g., DOS), generally have no virtual memory functionality, though notable exceptions for mainframes of the 1960s include:

- The Atlas Supervisor for the Atlas.

- THE multiprogramming system for the Electrologica X8 (software based virtual memory without hardware support).

- MCP for the Burroughs B5000.

- MTS, TSS/360 and CP/CMS for the IBM System/360 Model 67.

- Multics for the GE 645.

- The Time Sharing Operating System for the RCA Spectra 70/46.

The operating system for the Apple Lisa is an example of a personal computer operating system of the 1980s that features virtual memory.

During the 1960s and early 70s, computer memory was very expensive. The introduction of virtual memory provided an ability for software systems with large memory demands to run on computers with less real memory. The savings from this provided a strong incentive to switch to virtual memory for all systems. The additional capability of providing virtual address spaces added another level of security and reliability, thus making virtual memory even more attractive to the market place.

Most modern operating systems that support virtual memory also run each process in its own dedicated address space. Each program thus appears to have sole access to the virtual memory. However, some older operating systems (such as OS/VS1 and OS/VS2 SVS) and even modern ones (such as IBM i) are single address space operating systems that run all processes in a single address space composed of virtualized memory.

Embedded systems and other special-purpose computer systems that require very fast and/or very consistent response times may opt not to use virtual memory due to decreased determinism; virtual memory systems trigger unpredictable traps that may produce unwanted "jitter" during I/O operations. This is because embedded hardware costs are often kept low by implementing all such operations with software (a technique called bit-banging) rather than with dedicated hardware.

History

In the 1940s and 1950s, all larger programs had to contain logic for managing primary and secondary storage, such as overlaying. Virtual memory was therefore introduced not only to extend primary memory, but to make such an extension as easy as possible for programmers to use. To allow for multiprogramming and multitasking, many early systems divided memory between multiple programs without virtual memory, such as early models of the PDP-10 via registers.

The concept of virtual memory was first developed by German physicist Fritz-Rudolf Güntsch at the Technische Universität Berlin in 1956 in his doctoral thesis, *Logical Design of a Digital Computer with Multiple Asynchronous Rotating Drums and Automatic High Speed Memory Operation*; it described a machine with 6 100-word blocks of primary core memory and an address space of 1,000 100-word blocks, with hardware automatically moving blocks between primary memory and secondary drum memory. Paging was first implemented at the University of Manchester as a way to extend the Atlas Computer's working memory by combining its 16 thousand words of primary core memory with an additional 96 thousand words of secondary drum memory. The first Atlas was commissioned in 1962 but working prototypes of paging had been developed by 1959.[p2] In 1961, the Burroughs Corporation independently released the first commercial computer with virtual memory, the B5000, with segmentation rather than paging.

Before virtual memory could be implemented in mainstream operating systems, many problems had to be addressed. Dynamic address translation required expensive and difficult to build specialized hardware; initial implementations slowed down access to memory slightly. There were worries that new system-wide algorithms utilizing secondary storage would be less effective than previously used application-specific algorithms. By 1969, the debate over virtual memory for commercial computers was over; an IBM research team led by David Sayre showed that their virtual memory overlay system consistently worked better than the best manually controlled systems. The first minicomputer to introduce virtual memory was the Norwegian NORD-1; during the 1970s, other minicomputers implemented virtual memory, notably VAX models running VMS.

Virtual memory was introduced to the x86 architecture with the protected mode of the Intel 80286 processor, but its segment swapping technique scaled poorly to larger segment sizes. The Intel

80386 introduced paging support underneath the existing segmentation layer, enabling the page fault exception to chain with other exceptions without double fault. However, loading segment descriptors was an expensive operation, causing operating system designers to rely strictly on paging rather than a combination of paging and segmentation.

Paged

Nearly all implementations of virtual memory divide a virtual address space into pages, blocks of contiguous virtual memory addresses. Pages on contemporary systems are usually at least 4 kilobytes in size; systems with large virtual address ranges or amounts of real memory generally use larger page sizes.

Page Tables

Page tables are used to translate the virtual addresses seen by the application into physical addresses used by the hardware to process instructions; such hardware that handles this specific translation is often known as the memory management unit. Each entry in the page table holds a flag indicating whether the corresponding page is in real memory or not. If it is in real memory, the page table entry will contain the real memory address at which the page is stored. When a reference is made to a page by the hardware, if the page table entry for the page indicates that it is not currently in real memory, the hardware raises a page fault exception, invoking the paging supervisor component of the operating system.

Systems can have one page table for the whole system, separate page tables for each application and segment, a tree of page tables for large segments or some combination of these. If there is only one page table, different applications running at the same time use different parts of a single range of virtual addresses. If there are multiple page or segment tables, there are multiple virtual address spaces and concurrent applications with separate page tables redirect to different real addresses.

Paging Supervisor

This part of the operating system creates and manages page tables. If the hardware raises a page fault exception, the paging supervisor accesses secondary storage, returns the page that has the virtual address that resulted in the page fault, updates the page tables to reflect the physical location of the virtual address and tells the translation mechanism to restart the request.

When all physical memory is already in use, the paging supervisor must free a page in primary storage to hold the swapped-in page. The supervisor uses one of a variety of page replacement algorithms such as least recently used to determine which page to free.

Pinned Pages

Operating systems have memory areas that are *pinned* (never swapped to secondary storage). Other terms used are *locked*, *fixed*, or *wired* pages. For example, interrupt mechanisms rely on an array of pointers to their handlers, such as I/O completion and page fault. If the pages containing these pointers or the code that they invoke were pageable, interrupt-handling would become far more complex and time-consuming, particularly in the case of page fault interruptions. Hence, some part of the page table structures is not pageable.

Some pages may be pinned for short periods of time, others may be pinned for long periods of time, and still others may need to be permanently pinned. For example:

- The paging supervisor code and drivers for secondary storage devices on which pages reside must be permanently pinned, as otherwise paging wouldn't even work because the necessary code wouldn't be available.

- Timing-dependent components may be pinned to avoid variable paging delays.

- Data buffers that are accessed directly by peripheral devices that use direct memory access or I/O channels must reside in pinned pages while the I/O operation is in progress because such devices and the buses to which they are attached expect to find data buffers located at physical memory addresses; regardless of whether the bus has a memory management unit for I/O, transfers cannot be stopped if a page fault occurs and then restarted when the page fault has been processed.

In IBM's operating systems for System/370 and successor systems, the term is "fixed", and such pages may be long-term fixed, or may be short-term fixed, or may be unfixed (i.e., pageable). System control structures are often long-term fixed (measured in wall-clock time, i.e., time measured in seconds, rather than time measured in fractions of one second) whereas I/O buffers are usually short-term fixed (usually measured in significantly less than wall-clock time, possibly for tens of milliseconds). Indeed, the OS has a special facility for "fast fixing" these short-term fixed data buffers (fixing which is performed without resorting to a time-consuming Supervisor Call instruction).

Multics used the term "wired". OpenVMS and Windows refer to pages temporarily made nonpageable (as for I/O buffers) as "locked", and simply "nonpageable" for those that are never pageable.

Virtual-real Operation

In OS/VS1 and similar OSes, some parts of systems memory are managed in "virtual-real" mode, called "V=R". In this mode every virtual address corresponds to the same real address. This mode is used for interrupt mechanisms, for the paging supervisor and page tables in older systems, and for application programs using non-standard I/O management. For example, IBM's z/OS has 3 modes (virtual-virtual, virtual-real and virtual-fixed).

Thrashing

When paging and page stealing are used, a problem called "thrashing" can occur, in which the computer spends an unsuitably large amount of time transferring pages to and from a backing store, hence slowing down useful work. A task's working set is the minimum set of pages that should be in memory in order for it to make useful progress. Thrashing occurs when there is insufficient memory available to store the working sets of all active programs. Adding real memory is the simplest response, but improving application design, scheduling, and memory usage can help. Another solution is to reduce the number of active tasks on the system. This reduces demand on real memory by swapping out the entire working set of one or more processes.

Segmented

Some systems, such as the Burroughs B5500, use segmentation instead of paging, dividing virtual address spaces into variable-length segments. A virtual address here consists of a segment number and an offset within the segment. The Intel 80286 supports a similar segmentation scheme as an option, but it is rarely used. Segmentation and paging can be used together by dividing each segment into pages; systems with this memory structure, such as Multics and IBM System/38, are usually paging-predominant, segmentation providing memory protection.

In the Intel 80386 and later IA-32 processors, the segments reside in a 32-bit linear, paged address space. Segments can be moved in and out of that space; pages there can "page" in and out of main memory, providing two levels of virtual memory; few if any operating systems do so, instead using only paging. Early non-hardware-assisted x86 virtualization solutions combined paging and segmentation because x86 paging offers only two protection domains whereas a VMM / guest OS / guest applications stack needs three. The difference between paging and segmentation systems is not only about memory division; segmentation is visible to user processes, as part of memory model semantics. Hence, instead of memory that looks like a single large space, it is structured into multiple spaces.

This difference has important consequences; a segment is not a page with variable length or a simple way to lengthen the address space. Segmentation that can provide a single-level memory model in which there is no differentiation between process memory and file system consists of only a list of segments (files) mapped into the process's potential address space.

This is not the same as the mechanisms provided by calls such as mmap and Win32's MapViewOf-File, because inter-file pointers do not work when mapping files into semi-arbitrary places. In Multics, a file (or a segment from a multi-segment file) is mapped into a segment in the address space, so files are always mapped at a segment boundary. A file's linkage section can contain pointers for which an attempt to load the pointer into a register or make an indirect reference through it causes a trap. The unresolved pointer contains an indication of the name of the segment to which the pointer refers and an offset within the segment; the handler for the trap maps the segment into the address space, puts the segment number into the pointer, changes the tag field in the pointer so that it no longer causes a trap, and returns to the code where the trap occurred, re-executing the instruction that caused the trap. This eliminates the need for a linker completely and works when different processes map the same file into different places in their private address spaces.

Address Space Swapping

Some operating systems provide for swapping entire address spaces, in addition to whatever facilities they have for paging and segmentation. When this occurs, the OS writes those pages and segments currently in real memory to swap files. In a swap-in, the OS reads back the data from the swap files but does not automatically read back pages that had been paged out at the time of the swap out operation.

IBM's MVS, from OS/VS2 Release 2 through z/OS, provides for marking an address space as unswappable; doing so does not pin any pages in the address space. This can be done for the duration of a job by entering the name of an eligible main program in the Program Properties Table with an unswappable flag. In addition, privileged code can temporarily make an address space unswappable With a SYSEVENT Supervisor Call instruction (SVC); certain changes in the address space properties require that the OS swap it out and then swap it back in, using SYSEVENT TRANSWAP.

Preemption

In computing, preemption is the act of temporarily interrupting a task being carried out by a computer system, without requiring its cooperation, and with the intention of resuming the task at a later time. Such changes of the executed task are known as context switches. It is normally carried out by a privileged task or part of the system known as a preemptive scheduler, which has the power to preempt, or interrupt, and later resume, other tasks in the system.

User Mode and Kernel Mode

In any given system design, some operations performed by the system may not be preemptible. This usually applies to kernel functions and service interrupts which, if not permitted to run to completion, would tend to produce race conditions resulting in deadlock. Barring the scheduler from preempting tasks while they are processing kernel functions simplifies the kernel design at the expense of system responsiveness. The distinction between user mode and kernel mode, which determines privilege level within the system, may also be used to distinguish whether a task is currently preemptible.

Most modern systems have preemptive kernels, designed to permit tasks to be preempted even when in kernel mode. Examples of such systems are Solaris 2.0/SunOS 5.0, Windows NT, Linux kernel (2.6.x and newer), AIX and some BSD systems (NetBSD, since version 5).

Preemptive Multitasking

The term preemptive multitasking is used to distinguish a multitasking operating system, which permits preemption of tasks, from a cooperative multitasking system wherein processes or tasks must be explicitly programmed to yield when they do not need system resources.

In simple terms: Preemptive multitasking involves the use of an interrupt mechanism which suspends the currently executing process and invokes a scheduler to determine which process should execute next. Therefore, all processes will get some amount of CPU time at any given time.

In preemptive multitasking, the operating system kernel can also initiate a context switch to satisfy the scheduling policy's priority constraint, thus preempting the active task. In general, preemption means "prior seizure of". When the high priority task at that instance seizes the currently running task, it is known as preemptive scheduling.

The term "preemptive multitasking" is sometimes mistakenly used when the intended meaning is more specific, referring instead to the class of scheduling policies known as *time-shared scheduling*, or *time-sharing*.

Preemptive multitasking allows the computer system to more reliably guarantee each process a regular "slice" of operating time. It also allows the system to rapidly deal with important external events like incoming data, which might require the immediate attention of one or another process.

At any specific time, processes can be grouped into two categories: those that are waiting for input or output (called "I/O bound"), and those that are fully utilizing the CPU ("CPU bound"). In early systems, processes would often "poll", or "busywait" while waiting for requested input (such as disk, keyboard or network input). During this time, the process was not performing useful work, but still maintained complete control of the CPU. With the advent of interrupts and preemptive multitasking, these I/O bound processes could be "blocked", or put on hold, pending the arrival of the necessary data, allowing other processes to utilize the CPU. As the arrival of the requested data would generate an interrupt, blocked processes could be guaranteed a timely return to execution.

Although multitasking techniques were originally developed to allow multiple users to share a single machine, it soon became apparent that multitasking was useful regardless of the number of users. Many operating systems, from mainframes down to single-user personal computers and no-user control systems (like those in robotic spacecraft), have recognized the usefulness of multitasking support for a variety of reasons. Multitasking makes it possible for a single user to run multiple applications at the same time, or to run "background" processes while retaining control of the computer.

Time Slice

The period of time for which a process is allowed to run in a preemptive multitasking system is generally called the *time slice* or *quantum*; this relates to the instruction cycle, which is the quantum of hardware execution. The scheduler is run once every time slice to choose the next process to run. The length of each time slice can be critical to balancing system performance vs process responsiveness - if the time slice is too short then the scheduler will consume too much processing time, but if the time slice is too long, processes will take longer to respond to input.

An interrupt is scheduled to allow the operating system kernel to switch between processes when their time slices expire, effectively allowing the processor's time to be shared between a number of tasks, giving the illusion that it is dealing with these tasks simultaneously, or concurrently. The operating system which controls such a design is called a multi-tasking system.

System Support

Today, nearly all operating systems support preemptive multitasking, including the current versions of Windows, macOS, Linux (including Android) and iOS.

Some of the earliest operating systems available to home users featuring preemptive multitasking were Sinclair QDOS (1984) and Amiga OS (1985). These both ran on Motorola 68000-family microprocessors without memory management. Amiga OS used dynamic loading of relocatable code blocks ("hunks" in Amiga jargon) to multitask preemptively all processes in the same flat address space.

Early PC operating systems such as MS-DOS and PC DOS, did not support multitasking at all, however alternative operating systems such as MP/M-86 (1981) and Concurrent CP/M-86 did support preemptive multitasking. Other Unix-like systems including MINIX and Coherent provided preemptive multitasking on 1980s-era personal computers.

Later DOS versions natively supporting preemptive multitasking/multithreading include Concurrent DOS, Multiuser DOS, Novell DOS (later called Caldera OpenDOS and DR-DOS 7.02 and higher). Since Concurrent DOS 386, they could also run multiple DOS programs concurrently in virtual DOS machines.

The earliest version of Windows to support a limited form of preemptive multitasking was Windows 2.1x, which used the Intel 80386's Virtual 8086 mode to run DOS applications in virtual 8086 machines, commonly known as "DOS boxes", which could be preempted. In Windows 95, 98 and Me, 32-bit applications were made preemptive by running each one in a separate address space, but 16-bit applications remained cooperative for backward compatibility. In Windows 3.1x (protected mode), the kernel and virtual device drivers ran preemptively, but all 16-bit applications were non-preemptive and shared the same address space.

Preemptive multitasking has always been supported by Windows NT (all versions), OS/2 (native applications), Unix and Unix-like systems (such as Linux, BSD and macOS), VMS, OS/360, and many other operating systems designed for use in the academic and medium-to-large business markets.

Although there were plans to upgrade the cooperative multitasking found in the classic Mac OS to a preemptive model (and a preemptive API did exist in Mac OS 9, although in a limited sense), these were abandoned in favor of macOS that, as a hybrid of the old Mac System style and NeXT-STEP, is an operating system based on the Mach kernel and derived in part from BSD, which had always provided Unix-like preemptive multitasking.

Device Driver

In computing, a device driver (commonly referred to simply as a *driver*) is a computer program that operates or controls a particular type of device that is attached to a computer. A driver provides a software interface to hardware devices, enabling operating systems and other computer programs to access hardware functions without needing to know precise details of the hardware being used.

A driver communicates with the device through the computer bus or communications subsystem to which the hardware connects. When a calling program invokes a routine in the driver, the driver issues commands to the device. Once the device sends data back to the driver, the driver may invoke routines in the original calling program. Drivers are hardware dependent and operating-system-specific. They usually provide the interrupt handling required for any necessary asynchronous time-dependent hardware interface.

Purpose

The main purpose of Device drivers is to provide abstraction by acting as translator between a hardware device and the applications or operating systems that use it. Programmers can write the higher-level application code independently of whatever specific hardware the end-user is using.

For example, a high-level application for interacting with a serial port may simply have two functions for "send data" and "receive data". At a lower level, a device driver implementing these functions would communicate to the particular serial port controller installed on a user's computer. The commands needed to control a 16550 UART are much different from the commands needed to control an FTDI serial port converter, but each hardware-specific device driver abstracts these details into the same (or similar) software interface.

Development

Writing a device driver requires an in-depth understanding of how the hardware and the software works for a given platform function. Because drivers require low-level access to hardware functions in order to operate, drivers typically operate in a highly privileged environment and can cause system operational issues if something goes wrong. In contrast, most user-level software on modern operating systems can be stopped without greatly affecting the rest of the system. Even drivers executing in user mode can crash a system if the device is erroneously programmed. These factors make it more difficult and dangerous to diagnose problems.

The task of writing drivers thus usually falls to software engineers or computer engineers who work for hardware-development companies. This is because they have better information than most outsiders about the design of their hardware. Moreover, it was traditionally considered in the hardware manufacturer's interest to guarantee that their clients can use their hardware in an optimum way. Typically, the Logical Device Driver (LDD) is written by the operating system vendor, while the Physical Device Driver (PDD) is implemented by the device vendor. But in recent years non-vendors have written numerous device drivers, mainly for use with free and open source operating systems. In such cases, it is important that the hardware manufacturer provides information on how the device communicates. Although this information can instead be learned by reverse engineering, this is much more difficult with hardware than it is with software.

Microsoft has attempted to reduce system instability due to poorly written device drivers by creating a new framework for driver development, called Windows Driver Foundation (WDF). This includes User-Mode Driver Framework (UMDF) that encourages development of certain types of drivers—primarily those that implement a message-based protocol for communicating with their devices—as user-mode drivers. If such drivers malfunction, they do not cause system instability. The Kernel-Mode Driver Framework (KMDF) model continues to allow development of kernel-mode device drivers, but attempts to provide standard implementations of functions that are known to cause problems, including cancellation of I/O operations, power management, and plug and play device support.

Apple has an open-source framework for developing drivers on Mac OS X called the I/O Kit.

In Linux environments, programmers can build device drivers as parts of the kernel, separately as loadable modules, or as user-mode drivers (for certain types of devices where kernel interfaces exist, such as for USB devices). Makedev includes a list of the devices in Linux: ttyS (terminal), lp (parallel port), hd (disk), loop, sound (these include mixer, sequencer, dsp, and audio).

The Microsoft Windows .sys files and Linux .ko modules contain loadable device drivers. The advantage of loadable device drivers is that they can be loaded only when necessary and then unloaded, thus saving kernel memory.

Kernel Mode vs. User Mode

Device drivers, particularly on modern Microsoft Windows platforms, can run in kernel-mode (Ring 0 on x86 CPUs) or in user-mode (Ring 3 on x86 CPUs). The primary benefit of running a driver in user mode is improved stability, since a poorly written user mode device driver cannot crash the system by overwriting kernel memory. On the other hand, user/kernel-mode transitions usually impose a considerable performance overhead, thereby prohibiting user-mode drivers for low latency and high throughput requirements.

Kernel space can be accessed by user module only through the use of system calls. End user programs like the UNIX shell or other GUI-based applications are part of the user space. These applications interact with hardware through kernel supported functions.

Applications

Because of the diversity of modern hardware and operating systems, drivers operate in many different environments. Drivers may interface with:

- Printers.
- Video adapters.
- Network cards.
- Sound cards.
- Local buses of various sorts—in particular, for bus mastering on modern systems.
- Low-bandwidth I/O buses of various sorts (for pointing devices such as mice, keyboards, USB, etc.).
- Computer storage devices such as hard disk, CD-ROM, and floppy disk buses (ATA, SATA, SCSI).
- Implementing support for different file systems.
- Image scanners.
- Digital cameras.

Common levels of abstraction for device drivers include:

- For hardware:
  - Interfacing directly.
  - Writing to or reading from a device control register.
  - Using some higher-level interface (e.g. Video BIOS).
  - Using another lower-level device driver (e.g. file system drivers using disk drivers).
  - Simulating work with hardware, while doing something entirely different.

- For software:
    - Allowing the operating system direct access to hardware resources.
    - Implementing only primitives.
    - Implementing an interface for non-driver software (e.g., TWAIN).
    - Implementing a language, sometimes quite high-level (e.g., PostScript).

So choosing and installing the correct device drivers for given hardware is often a key component of computer system configuration.

Virtual Device Drivers

Virtual device drivers represent a particular variant of device drivers. They are used to emulate a hardware device, particularly in virtualization environments, for example when a DOS program is run on a Microsoft Windows computer or when a guest operating system is run on, for example, a Xen host. Instead of enabling the guest operating system to dialog with hardware, virtual device drivers take the opposite role and emulate a piece of hardware, so that the guest operating system and its drivers running inside a virtual machine can have the illusion of accessing real hardware. Attempts by the guest operating system to access the hardware are routed to the virtual device driver in the host operating system as e.g., function calls. The virtual device driver can also send simulated processor-level events like interrupts into the virtual machine.

Virtual devices may also operate in a non-virtualized environment. For example, a virtual network adapter is used with a virtual private network, while a virtual disk device is used with iSCSI. A good example for virtual device drivers can be Daemon Tools.

There are several variants of virtual device drivers, such as VxDs, VLMs, VDDs.

Open Drivers

- Printers: CUPS.
- RAIDs: CCISS (Compaq Command Interface for SCSI-3 Support).
- Scanners: SANE.
- Video: Vidix, Direct Rendering Infrastructure.

Solaris descriptions of commonly used device drivers:

- fas: Fast/wide SCSI controller.
- hme: Fast (10/100 Mbit/s) Ethernet.
- isp: Differential SCSI controllers and the SunSwift card.
- glm: (Gigabaud Link Module) UltraSCSI controllers.
- scsi: Small Computer Serial Interface (SCSI) devices.

- sf: soc+ or social Fiber Channel Arbitrated Loop (FCAL).

- soc: SPARC Storage Array (SSA) controllers and the control device.

- social: Serial optical controllers for FCAL (soc+).

APIs

- Windows Display Driver Model (WDDM) – the graphic display driver architecture for Windows Vista, Windows 7, Windows 8, and Windows 10.

- Unified Audio Model(UAM).

- Windows Driver Foundation (WDF).

- Windows Driver Model (WDM).

- Network Driver Interface Specification (NDIS) – a standard network card driver API.

- Advanced Linux Sound Architecture (ALSA) – as of 2009 the standard Linux sound-driver interface.

- Scanner Access Now Easy (SANE) – a public-domain interface to raster-image scanner-hardware.

- I/O Kit – an open-source framework from Apple for developing Mac OS X device drivers.

- Installable File System (IFS) – a filesystem API for IBM OS/2 and Microsoft Windows NT.

- Open Data-Link Interface (ODI) – a network card API similar to NDIS.

- Uniform Driver Interface (UDI) – a cross-platform driver interface project.

- Dynax Driver Framework (dxd) – C++ open source cross-platform driver framework for KMDF and IOKit.

Identifiers

A device on the PCI bus or USB is identified by two IDs which consist of 4 hexadecimal numbers each. The vendor ID identifies the vendor of the device. The device ID identifies a specific device from that manufacturer/vendor.

A PCI device has often an ID pair for the main chip of the device, and also a subsystem ID pair which identifies the vendor, which may be different from the chip manufacturer.

Computer Security

Computer security, also known as cyber security or IT security, is the protection of computer systems from the theft or damage to the hardware, software or the information on them, as well as from disruption or misdirection of the services they provide.

It includes controlling physical access to the hardware, as well as protecting against harm that may come via network access, data and code injection, and due to malpractice by operators, whether intentional, accidental, or due to them being tricked into deviating from secure procedures.

The field is of growing importance due to the increasing reliance on computer systems and the Internet in most societies, wireless networks such as Bluetooth and Wi-Fi – and the growth of "smart" devices, including smartphones, televisions and tiny devices as part of the Internet of Things.

Vulnerabilities and Attacks

A vulnerability is a system susceptibility or flaw. Many vulnerabilities are documented in the Common Vulnerabilities and Exposures (CVE) database. An *exploitable* vulnerability is one for which at least one working attack or "exploit" exists.

To secure a computer system, it is important to understand the attacks that can be made against it, and these threats can typically be classified into one of the categories below:

Backdoors

A backdoor in a computer system, a cryptosystem or an algorithm, is any secret method of bypassing normal authentication or security controls. They may exist for a number of reasons, including by original design or from poor configuration. They may have been added by an authorized party to allow some legitimate access, or by an attacker for malicious reasons; but regardless of the motives for their existence, they create a vulnerability.

Denial of service Attack

Denial of service attacks (DoS) are designed to make a machine or network resource unavailable to its intended users. Attackers can deny service to individual victims, such as by deliberately entering a wrong password enough consecutive times to cause the victim account to be locked, or they may overload the capabilities of a machine or network and block all users at once. While a network attack from a single IP address can be blocked by adding a new firewall rule, many forms of Distributed denial of service (DDoS) attacks are possible, where the attack comes from a large number of points – and defending is much more difficult. Such attacks can originate from the zombie computers of a botnet, but a range of other techniques are possible including reflection and amplification attacks, where innocent systems are fooled into sending traffic to the victim.

Direct-access Attacks

An unauthorized user gaining physical access to a computer is most likely able to directly copy data from it. They may also compromise security by making operating system modifications, installing software worms, keyloggers, covert listening devices or using wireless mice. Even when the system is protected by standard security measures, these may be able to be by-passed by booting another operating system or tool from a CD-ROM or other bootable media. Disk encryption and Trusted Platform Module are designed to prevent these attacks.

Eavesdropping

Eavesdropping is the act of surreptitiously listening to a private conversation, typically between hosts on a network. For instance, programs such as Carnivore and NarusInsight have been used by the FBI and NSA to eavesdrop on the systems of internet service providers. Even machines that operate as a closed system (i.e., with no contact to the outside world) can be eavesdropped upon via monitoring the faint electro-magnetic transmissions generated by the hardware; TEMPEST is a specification by the NSA referring to these attacks.

Spoofing

Spoofing, in general, is a fraudulent or malicious practice in which communication is sent from an unknown source disguised as a source known to the receiver. Spoofing is most prevalent in communication mechanisms that lack a high level of security.

Tampering

Tampering describes a malicious modification of products. So-called "Evil Maid" attacks and security services planting of surveillance capability into routers are examples.

Privilege Escalation

Privilege escalation describes a situation where an attacker with some level of restricted access is able to, without authorization, elevate their privileges or access level. So for example a standard computer user may be able to fool the system into giving them access to restricted data; or even to "become root" and have full unrestricted access to a system.

Phishing

Phishing is the attempt to acquire sensitive information such as usernames, passwords, and credit card details directly from users. Phishing is typically carried out by email spoofing or instant messaging, and it often directs users to enter details at a fake website whose look and feel are almost identical to the legitimate one. Preying on a victim's trust, phishing can be classified as a form of social engineering.

Clickjacking

Clickjacking, also known as "UI redress attack" or "User Interface redress attack", is a malicious technique in which an attacker tricks a user into clicking on a button or link on another webpage while the user intended to click on the top level page. This is done using multiple transparent or opaque layers. The attacker is basically "hijacking" the clicks meant for the top level page and routing them to some other irrelevant page, most likely owned by someone else. A similar technique can be used to hijack keystrokes. Carefully drafting a combination of stylesheets, iframes, buttons and text boxes, a user can be led into believing that they are typing the password or other information on some authentic webpage while it is being channeled into an invisible frame controlled by the attacker.

Social Engineering

Social engineering aims to convince a user to disclose secrets such as passwords, card numbers, etc. by, for example, impersonating a bank, a contractor, or a customer.

A popular and profitable cyber scam involves fake CEO emails sent to accounting and finance departments. In early 2016, the FBI reported that the scam has cost US businesses more than $2bn in about two years.

In May 2016, the Milwaukee Bucks NBA team was the victim of this type of cyber scam with a perpetrator impersonating the team's president Peter Feigin, resulting in the handover of all the team's employees' 2015 W-2 tax forms.

Systems at Risk

Computer security is critical in almost any industry which uses computers. Currently, most electronic devices such as computers, laptops and cellphones come with built in firewall security software, but despite this, computers are not 100 percent accurate and dependable to protect our data (Smith, Grabosky & Urbas, 2004.) There are many different ways of hacking into computers. It can be done through a network system, clicking into unknown links, connecting to unfamiliar Wi-Fi, downloading software and files from unsafe sites, power consumption, electromagnetic radiation waves, and many more. However, computers can be protected through well built software and hardware. By having strong internal interactions of properties, software complexity can prevent software crash and security failure.

Financial Systems

Web sites and apps that accept or store credit card numbers, brokerage accounts, and bank account information are prominent hacking targets, because of the potential for immediate financial gain from transferring money, making purchases, or selling the information on the black market. In-store payment systems and ATMs have also been tampered with in order to gather customer account data and PINs.

Utilities and Industrial Equipment

Computers control functions at many utilities, including coordination of telecommunications, the power grid, nuclear power plants, and valve opening and closing in water and gas networks. The Internet is a potential attack vector for such machines if connected, but the Stuxnet worm demonstrated that even equipment controlled by computers not connected to the Internet can be vulnerable to physical damage caused by malicious commands sent to industrial equipment (in that case uranium enrichment centrifuges) which are infected via removable media. In 2014, the Computer Emergency Readiness Team, a division of the Department of Homeland Security, investigated 79 hacking incidents at energy companies. Vulnerabilities in smart meters (many of which use local radio or cellular communications) can cause problems with billing fraud.

Aviation

The aviation industry is very reliant on a series of complex system which could be attacked. A simple power outage at one airport can cause repercussions worldwide, much of the system relies on radio transmissions which could be disrupted, and controlling aircraft over oceans is especially dangerous because radar surveillance only extends 175 to 225 miles offshore. There is also potential for attack from within an aircraft.

In Europe, with the (Pan-European Network Service) and NewPENS, and in the US with the Next-Gen program, air navigation service providers are moving to create their own dedicated networks.

The consequences of a successful attack range from loss of confidentiality to loss of system integrity, which may lead to more serious concerns such as exfiltration of data, network and air traffic control outages, which in turn can lead to airport closures, loss of aircraft, loss of passenger life, damages on the ground and to transportation infrastructure. A successful attack on a military aviation system that controls munitions could have even more serious consequences.

Consumer Devices

Desktop computers and laptops are commonly infected with malware either to gather passwords or financial account information, or to construct a botnet to attack another target. Smart phones, tablet computers, smart watches, and other mobile devices such as Quantified Self devices like activity trackers have also become targets and many of these have sensors such as cameras, microphones, GPS receivers, compasses, and accelerometers which could be exploited, and may collect personal information, including sensitive health information. Wifi, Bluetooth, and cell phone networks on any of these devices could be used as attack vectors, and sensors might be remotely activated after a successful breach.

Home automation devices such as the Nest thermostat are also potential targets.

Large Corporations

Large corporations are common targets. In many cases this is aimed at financial gain through identity theft and involves data breaches such as the loss of millions of clients' credit card details by Home Depot, Staples, and Target Corporation. Medical records have been targeted for use in general identify theft, health insurance fraud, and impersonating patients to obtain prescription drugs for recreational purposes or resale.

Not all attacks are financially motivated however; for example security firm HBGary Federal suffered a serious series of attacks in 2011 from hacktivist group Anonymous in retaliation for the firm's CEO claiming to have infiltrated their group, and Sony Pictures was attacked in 2014 where the motive appears to have been to embarrass with data leaks, and cripple the company by wiping workstations and servers.

Automobiles

If access is gained to a car's internal controller area network, it is possible to disable the brakes and turn the steering wheel. Computerized engine timing, cruise control, anti-lock brakes, seat belt tensioners, door locks, airbags and advanced driver assistance systems make these disruptions possible, and self-driving cars go even further. Connected cars may use wifi and bluetooth to communicate with onboard consumer devices, and the cell phone network to contact concierge and emergency assistance services or get navigational or entertainment information; each of these networks is a potential entry point for malware or an attacker. Researchers in 2011 were even able to use a malicious compact disc in a car's stereo system as a successful attack vector, and cars with built-in voice recognition or remote assistance features have onboard microphones which could be used for eavesdropping.

A 2015 report by U.S. Senator Edward Markey criticized manufacturers' security measures as inadequate, and also highlighted privacy concerns about driving, location, and diagnostic data being collected, which is vulnerable to abuse by both manufacturers and hackers.

Government

Government and military computer systems are commonly attacked by activists and foreign powers. Local and regional government infrastructure such as traffic light controls, police and intelligence agency communications, personnel records, student records, and financial systems are also potential targets as they are now all largely computerized. Passports and government ID cards that control access to facilities which use RFID can be vulnerable to cloning.

Internet of Things and Physical Vulnerabilities

The Internet of Things (IoT) is the network of physical objects such as devices, vehicles, and buildings that are embedded with electronics, software, sensors, and network connectivity that enables them to collect and exchange data – and concerns have been raised that this is being developed without appropriate consideration of the security challenges involved.

While the IoT creates opportunities for more direct integration of the physical world into computer-based systems, it also provides opportunities for misuse. In particular, as the Internet of Things spreads widely, cyber attacks are likely to become an increasingly physical (rather than simply virtual) threat. If a front door's lock is connected to the Internet, and can be locked/unlocked from a phone, then a criminal could enter the home at the press of a button from a stolen or hacked phone. People could stand to lose much more than their credit card numbers in a world controlled by IoT-enabled devices. Thieves have also used electronic means to circumvent non-Internet-connected hotel door locks.

Medical devices have either been successfully attacked or had potentially deadly vulnerabilities demonstrated, including both in-hospital diagnostic equipment and implanted devices including pacemakers and insulin pumps.

Impact of Security Breaches

Serious financial damage has been caused by security breaches, but because there is no standard model for estimating the cost of an incident, the only data available is that which is made public by the organizations involved. "Several computer security consulting firms produce estimates of total worldwide losses attributable to virus and worm attacks and to hostile digital acts in general. The 2003 loss estimates by these firms range from $13 billion (worms and viruses only) to $226 billion (for all forms of covert attacks). The reliability of these estimates is often challenged; the underlying methodology is basically anecdotal."

However, reasonable estimates of the financial cost of security breaches can actually help organizations make rational investment decisions. According to the classic Gordon-Loeb Model analyzing the optimal investment level in information security, one can conclude that the amount a firm spends to protect information should generally be only a small fraction of the expected loss (i.e., the expected value of the loss resulting from a cyber/information security breach).

Attacker Motivation

As with physical security, the motivations for breaches of computer security vary between attackers. Some are thrill-seekers or vandals, others are activists or criminals looking for financial gain. State-sponsored attackers are now common and well resourced, but started with amateurs such as Markus Hess who hacked for the KGB, as recounted by Clifford Stoll, in *The Cuckoo's Egg*.

A standard part of threat modelling for any particular system is to identify what might motivate an attack on that system, and who might be motivated to breach it. The level and detail of precautions will vary depending on the system to be secured. A home personal computer, bank, and classified military network face very different threats, even when the underlying technologies in use are similar.

Computer Protection (Countermeasures)

In computer security a countermeasure is an action, device, procedure, or technique that reduces a threat, a vulnerability, or an attack by eliminating or preventing it, by minimizing the harm it can cause, or by discovering and reporting it so that corrective action can be taken.

Some common countermeasures are listed in the following sections:

Security by Design

Security by design, or alternately secure by design, means that the software has been designed from the ground up to be secure. In this case, security is considered as a main feature.

Some of the techniques in this approach include:

- The principle of least privilege, where each part of the system has only the privileges that are needed for its function. That way even if an attacker gains access to that part, they have only limited access to the whole system.

- Automated theorem proving to prove the correctness of crucial software subsystems.

- Code reviews and unit testing, approaches to make modules more secure where formal correctness proofs are not possible.

- Defense in depth, where the design is such that more than one subsystem needs to be violated to compromise the integrity of the system and the information it holds.

- Default secure settings, and design to "fail secure" rather than "fail insecure". Ideally, a secure system should require a deliberate, conscious, knowledgeable and free decision on the part of legitimate authorities in order to make it insecure.

- Audit trails tracking system activity, so that when a security breach occurs, the mechanism and extent of the breach can be determined. Storing audit trails remotely, where they can only be appended to, can keep intruders from covering their tracks.

- Full disclosure of all vulnerabilities, to ensure that the "window of vulnerability" is kept as short as possible when bugs are discovered.

Security Architecture

The Open Security Architecture organization defines IT security architecture as "the design artifacts that describe how the security controls (security countermeasures) are positioned, and how they relate to the overall information technology architecture. These controls serve the purpose to maintain the system's quality attributes: confidentiality, integrity, availability, accountability and assurance services".

Techopedia defines security architecture as "a unified security design that addresses the necessities and potential risks involved in a certain scenario or environment. It also specifies when and where to apply security controls. The design process is generally reproducible." The key attributes of security architecture are:

- the relationship of different components and how they depend on each other.

- the determination of controls based on risk assessment, good practice, finances, and legal matters.

- the standardization of controls.

Security Measures

A state of computer "security" is the conceptual ideal, attained by the use of the three processes: threat prevention, detection, and response. These processes are based on various policies and system components, which include the following:

- User account access controls and cryptography can protect systems files and data, respectively.

- Firewalls are by far the most common prevention systems from a network security perspective as they can (if properly configured) shield access to internal network services, and block certain kinds of attacks through packet filtering. Firewalls can be both hardware- or software-based.

- Intrusion Detection System (IDS) products are designed to detect network attacks in-progress and assist in post-attack forensics, while audit trails and logs serve a similar function for individual systems.

- "Response" is necessarily defined by the assessed security requirements of an individual system and may cover the range from simple upgrade of protections to notification of legal authorities, counter-attacks, and the like. In some special cases, a complete destruction of the compromised system is favored, as it may happen that not all the compromised resources are detected.

Today, computer security comprises mainly "preventive" measures, like firewalls or an exit procedure. A firewall can be defined as a way of filtering network data between a host or a network and another network, such as the Internet, and can be implemented as software running on the machine, hooking into the network stack (or, in the case of most UNIX-based operating systems such as Linux, built into the operating system kernel) to provide real time filtering and blocking. Another implementation is a so-called "physical firewall", which consists of a separate machine filtering network traffic. Firewalls are common amongst machines that are permanently connected to the Internet.

Some organizations are turning to big data platforms, such as Apache Hadoop, to extend data accessibility and machine learning to detect advanced persistent threats.

However, relatively few organisations maintain computer systems with effective detection systems, and fewer still have organised response mechanisms in place. As result, as Reuters points out: "Companies for the first time report they are losing more through electronic theft of data than physical stealing of assets". The primary obstacle to effective eradication of cyber crime could be traced to excessive reliance on firewalls and other automated "detection" systems. Yet it is basic evidence gathering by using packet capture appliances that puts criminals behind bars.

Vulnerability Management

Vulnerability management is the cycle of identifying, and remediating or mitigating vulnerabilities", especially in software and firmware. Vulnerability management is integral to computer security and network security.

Vulnerabilities can be discovered with a vulnerability scanner, which analyzes a computer system in search of known vulnerabilities, such as open ports, insecure software configuration, and susceptibility to malware.

Beyond vulnerability scanning, many organisations contract outside security auditors to run regular penetration tests against their systems to identify vulnerabilities. In some sectors this is a contractual requirement.

Reducing Vulnerabilities

While formal verification of the correctness of computer systems is possible, it is not yet common. Operating systems formally verified include seL4, and SYSGO's PikeOS – but these make up a very small percentage of the market.

Cryptography properly implemented is now virtually impossible to directly break. Breaking them requires some non-cryptographic input, such as a stolen key, stolen plaintext (at either end of the transmission), or some other extra cryptanalytic information.

Two factor authentication is a method for mitigating unauthorized access to a system or sensitive information. It requires "something you know"; a password or PIN, and "something you have"; a card, dongle, cellphone, or other piece of hardware. This increases security as an unauthorized person needs both of these to gain access.

Social engineering and direct computer access (physical) attacks can only be prevented by non-computer means, which can be difficult to enforce, relative to the sensitivity of the information. Training is often involved to help mitigate this risk, but even in a highly disciplined environments (e.g. military organizations), social engineering attacks can still be difficult to foresee and prevent.

It is possible to reduce an attacker's chances by keeping systems up to date with security patches and updates, using a security scanner or/and hiring competent people responsible for security. The effects of data loss/damage can be reduced by careful backing up and insurance.

Hardware Protection Mechanisms

While hardware may be a source of insecurity, such as with microchip vulnerabilities maliciously introduced during the manufacturing process, hardware-based or assisted computer security also offers an alternative to software-only computer security. Using devices and methods such as dongles, trusted platform modules, intrusion-aware cases, drive locks, disabling USB ports, and mobile-enabled access may be considered more secure due to the physical access (or sophisticated backdoor access) required in order to be compromised. Each of these is covered in more detail below.

- USB dongles are typically used in software licensing schemes to unlock software capabilities, but they can also be seen as a way to prevent unauthorized access to a computer or other device's software. The dongle, or key, essentially creates a secure encrypted tunnel between the software application and the key. The principle is that an encryption scheme on the dongle, such as Advanced Encryption Standard (AES) provides a stronger measure of security, since it is harder to hack and replicate the dongle than to simply copy the native software to another machine and use it. Another security application for dongles is to use them for accessing web-based content such as cloud software or Virtual Private Networks (VPNs). In addition, a USB dongle can be configured to lock or unlock a computer.

- Trusted platform modules (TPMs) secure devices by integrating cryptographic capabilities onto access devices, through the use of microprocessors, or so-called computers-on-a-chip. TPMs used in conjunction with server-side software offer a way to detect and authenticate hardware devices, preventing unauthorized network and data access.

- Computer case intrusion detection refers to a push-button switch which is triggered when a computer case is opened. The firmware or BIOS is programmed to show an alert to the operator when the computer is booted up the next time.

- Drive locks are essentially software tools to encrypt hard drives, making them inaccessible to thieves. Tools exist specifically for encrypting external drives as well.

- Disabling USB ports is a security option for preventing unauthorized and malicious access to an otherwise secure computer. Infected USB dongles connected to a network from a computer inside the firewall are considered by the magazine Network World as the most common hardware threat facing computer networks.

- Mobile-enabled access devices are growing in popularity due to the ubiquitous nature of cell phones. Built-in capabilities such as Bluetooth, the newer Bluetooth low energy (LE), Near field communication (NFC) on non-iOS devices and biometric validation such as thumb print readers, as well as QR code reader software designed for mobile devices, offer new, secure ways for mobile phones to connect to access control systems. These control systems provide computer security and can also be used for controlling access to secure buildings.

Secure Operating Systems

One use of the term "computer security" refers to technology that is used to implement secure operating systems. In the 1980s the United States Department of Defense (DoD) used the "Orange Book" standards, but the current international standard ISO/IEC 15408, "Common Criteria" defines a number of progressively more stringent Evaluation Assurance Levels. Many common operating systems meet the EAL4 standard of being "Methodically Designed, Tested and Reviewed", but the formal verification required for the highest levels means that they are uncommon. An example of an EAL6 ("Semiformally Verified Design and Tested") system is Integrity-178B, which is used in the Airbus A380 and several military jets.

Secure Coding

In software engineering, secure coding aims to guard against the accidental introduction of security vulnerabilities. It is also possible to create software designed from the ground up to be secure. Such systems are "secure by design". Beyond this, formal verification aims to prove the correctness of the algorithms underlying a system; important for cryptographic protocols for example.

Capabilities and Access Control Lists

Within computer systems, two of many security models capable of enforcing privilege separation are access control lists (ACLs) and capability-based security. Using ACLs to confine programs has been proven to be insecure in many situations, such as if the host computer can be tricked into indirectly allowing restricted file access, an issue known as the confused deputy problem. It has also been shown that the promise of ACLs of giving access to an object to only one person can never be guaranteed in practice. Both of these problems are resolved by capabilities. This does not mean practical flaws exist in all ACL-based systems, but only that the designers of certain utilities must take responsibility to ensure that they do not introduce flaws.

Capabilities have been mostly restricted to research operating systems, while commercial OSs still use ACLs. Capabilities can, however, also be implemented at the language level, leading to a style of programming that is essentially a refinement of standard object-oriented design. An open source project in the area is the E language.

The most secure computers are those not connected to the Internet and shielded from any interference. In the real world, the most secure systems are operating systems where security is not an add-on.

Response to Breaches

Responding forcefully to attempted security breaches (in the manner that one would for attempted physical security breaches) is often very difficult for a variety of reasons:

- Identifying attackers is difficult, as they are often in a different jurisdiction to the systems they attempt to breach, and operate through proxies, temporary anonymous dial-up accounts, wireless connections, and other anonymising procedures which make backtracing difficult and are often located in yet another jurisdiction. If they successfully breach security, they are often able to delete logs to cover their tracks.

- The sheer number of attempted attacks is so large that organisations cannot spend time pursuing each attacker (a typical home user with a permanent (e.g., cable modem) connection will be attacked at least several times per day, so more attractive targets could be presumed to see many more). Note however, that most of the sheer bulk of these attacks are made by automated vulnerability scanners and computer worms.

- Law enforcement officers are often unfamiliar with information technology, and so lack the skills and interest in pursuing attackers. There are also budgetary constraints. It has been argued that the high cost of technology, such as DNA testing, and improved forensics mean less money for other kinds of law enforcement, so the overall rate of criminals not getting dealt with goes up as the cost of the technology increases. In addition, the identification of attackers across a network may require logs from various points in the network and in many countries, the release of these records to law enforcement (with the exception of being voluntarily surrendered by a network administrator or a system administrator) requires a search warrant and, depending on the circumstances, the legal proceedings required can be drawn out to the point where the records are either regularly destroyed, or the information is no longer relevant.

Notable Attacks and Breaches

Some illustrative examples of different types of computer security breaches are given below.

Robert Morris and the First Computer Worm

In 1988, only 60,000 computers were connected to the Internet, and most were mainframes, minicomputers and professional workstations. On November 2, 1988, many started to slow down, because they were running a malicious code that demanded processor time and that spread itself to other computers – the first internet "computer worm". The software was traced back to 23-year-old Cornell University graduate student Robert Tappan Morris, Jr. who said 'he wanted to count how many machines were connected to the Internet'.

Rome Laboratory

In 1994, over a hundred intrusions were made by unidentified crackers into the Rome Laboratory, the US Air Force's main command and research facility. Using trojan horses, hackers were able to obtain unrestricted access to Rome's networking systems and remove traces of their activities. The intruders were able to obtain classified files, such as air tasking order systems data and furthermore able to penetrate connected networks of National Aeronautics and Space Administration's Goddard Space Flight Center, Wright-Patterson Air Force Base, some Defense contractors, and other private sector organizations, by posing as a trusted Rome center user.

TJX Customer Credit Card Details

In early 2007, American apparel and home goods company TJX announced that it was the victim of an unauthorized computer systems intrusion and that the hackers had accessed a system that stored data on credit card, debit card, check, and merchandise return transactions.

Stuxnet Attack

The computer worm known as Stuxnet reportedly ruined almost one-fifth of Iran's nuclear centrifuges by disrupting industrial programmable logic controllers (PLCs) in a targeted attack generally believed to have been launched by Israel and the United States although neither has publicly acknowledged this.

Global Surveillance Disclosures

In early 2013, massive breaches of computer security by the NSA were revealed, including deliberately inserting a backdoor in a NIST standard for encryption and tapping the links between Google's data centres. These were disclosed by NSA contractor Edward Snowden.

Target and Home Depot Breaches

In 2013 and 2014, a Russian/Ukrainian hacking ring known as "Rescator" broke into Target Corporation computers in 2013, stealing roughly 40 million credit cards, and then Home Depot computers in 2014, stealing between 53 and 56 million credit card numbers. Warnings were delivered at both corporations, but ignored; physical security breaches using self checkout machines are believed to have played a large role. "The malware utilized is absolutely unsophisticated and uninteresting," says Jim Walter, director of threat intelligence operations at security technology company McAfee – meaning that the heists could have easily been stopped by existing antivirus software had administrators responded to the warnings. The size of the thefts has resulted in major attention from state and Federal United States authorities and the investigation is ongoing.

Ashley Madison Breach

In July 2015, a hacker group known as "The Impact Team" successfully breached the extramarital relationship website Ashley Madison. The group claimed that they had taken not only company data but user data as well. After the breach, The Impact Team dumped emails from the company's CEO, to prove their point, and threatened to dump customer data unless the website was taken down permanently. With this initial data release, the group stated "Avid Life Media has been instructed to take Ashley Madison and Established Men offline permanently in all forms, or we will release all customer records, including profiles with all the customers' secret sexual fantasies and matching credit card transactions, real names and addresses, and employee documents and emails. The other websites may stay online." When Avid Life Media, the parent company that created the Ashley Madison website, did not take the site offline, The Impact Group released two more compressed files, one 9.7GB and the second 20GB. After the second data dump, Avid Life Media CEO Noel Biderman resigned, but the website remained functional.

Legal Issues and Global Regulation

Conflict of laws in cyberspace has become a major cause of concern for computer security community. Some of the main challenges and complaints about the antivirus industry are the lack of global web regulations, a global base of common rules to judge, and eventually punish, cyber crimes and cyber criminals. There is no global cyber law and cybersecurity treaty that can be invoked for enforcing global cybersecurity issues.

International legal issues of cyber attacks are complicated in nature. Even if an antivirus firm locates the cyber criminal behind the creation of a particular virus or piece of malware or form of cyber attack, often the local authorities cannot take action due to lack of laws under which to prosecute. Authorship attribution for cyber crimes and cyber attacks is a major problem for all law enforcement agencies.

"[Computer viruses] switch from one country to another, from one jurisdiction to another – moving around the world, using the fact that we don't have the capability to globally police operations like this. So the Internet is as if someone [had] given free plane tickets to all the online criminals of the world." Use of dynamic DNS, fast flux and bullet proof servers have added own complexities to this situation.

Government

The role of the government is to make regulations to force companies and organizations to protect their systems, infrastructure and information from any cyber-attacks, but also to protect its own national infrastructure such as the national power-grid.

The question of whether the government should intervene or not in the regulation of the cyberspace is a very polemical one. Indeed, for as long as it has existed and by definition, the cyberspace is a virtual space free of any government intervention. Where everyone agree that an improvement on cybersecurity is more than vital, is the government the best actor to solve this issue? Many government officials and experts think that the government should step in and that there is a crucial need for regulation, mainly due to the failure of the private sector to solve efficiently the cybersecurity problem. R. Clarke said during a panel discussion at the RSA Security Conference in San Francisco, he believes that the "industry only responds when you threaten regulation. If industry doesn't respond (to the threat), you have to follow through." On the other hand, executives from the private sector agree that improvements are necessary, but think that the government intervention would affect their ability to innovate efficiently.

Actions and Teams in the US

Legislation

The 1986 18 U.S.C. § 1030, more commonly known as the Computer Fraud and Abuse Act is the key legislation. It prohibits unauthorized access or damage of "protected computers" as defined in 18 U.S.C. § 1030(e)(2).

Although various other measures have been proposed, such as the "Cybersecurity Act of 2010 – S. 773" in 2009, the "International Cybercrime Reporting and Cooperation Act – H.R.4962" and

"Protecting Cyberspace as a National Asset Act of 2010 – S.3480" in 2010 – none of these has succeeded.

Executive order 13636 *Improving Critical Infrastructure Cybersecurity* was signed February 12, 2013.

Agencies

The Department of Homeland Security has a dedicated division responsible for the response system, risk management program and requirements for cybersecurity in the United States called the National Cyber Security Division. The division is home to US-CERT operations and the National Cyber Alert System. The National Cybersecurity and Communications Integration Center brings together government organizations responsible for protecting computer networks and networked infrastructure.

The third priority of the Federal Bureau of Investigation (FBI) is to: *"Protect the United States against cyber-based attacks and high-technology crimes"*, and they, along with the National White Collar Crime Center (NW3C), and the Bureau of Justice Assistance (BJA) are part of the multi-agency task force, The Internet Crime Complaint Center, also known as IC3.

In addition to its own specific duties, the FBI participates alongside non-profit organizations such as InfraGard.

In the criminal division of the United States Department of Justice operates a section called the Computer Crime and Intellectual Property Section. The CCIPS is in charge of investigating computer crime and intellectual property crime and is specialized in the search and seizure of digital evidence in computers and networks.

The United States Cyber Command, also known as USCYBERCOM, is tasked with the defense of specified Department of Defense information networks and *"ensure US/Allied freedom of action in cyberspace and deny the same to our adversaries."* It has no role in the protection of civilian networks.

The U.S. Federal Communications Commission's role in cybersecurity is to strengthen the protection of critical communications infrastructure, to assist in maintaining the reliability of networks during disasters, to aid in swift recovery after, and to ensure that first responders have access to effective communications services.

The Food and Drug Administration has issued guidance for medical devices, and the National Highway Traffic Safety Administration is concerned with automotive cybersecurity. After being criticized by the Government Accountability Office, and following successful attacks on airports and claimed attacks on airplanes, the Federal Aviation Administration has devoted funding to securing systems on board the planes of private manufacturers, and the Aircraft Communications Addressing and Reporting System. Concerns have also been raised about the future Next Generation Air Transportation System.

Computer Emergency Readiness Team

"Computer emergency response team" is a name given to expert groups that handle computer security incidents. In the US, two distinct organization exist, although they do work closely together.

- US-CERT: part of the National Cyber Security Division of the United States Department of Homeland Security.

- CERT/CC: created by the Defense Advanced Research Projects Agency (DARPA) and run by the Software Engineering Institute (SEI).

International Actions

Many different teams and organisations exist, including:

- The Forum of Incident Response and Security Teams (FIRST) is the global association of CSIRTs. The US-CERT, AT&T, Apple, Cisco, McAfee, Microsoft are all members of this international team.

- The Council of Europe helps protect societies worldwide from the threat of cybercrime through the Convention on Cybercrime.

- The purpose of the Messaging Anti-Abuse Working Group (MAAWG) is to bring the messaging industry together to work collaboratively and to successfully address the various forms of messaging abuse, such as spam, viruses, denial-of-service attacks and other messaging exploitations. France Telecom, Facebook, AT&T, Apple, Cisco, Sprint are some of the members of the MAAWG.

- ENISA : The European Network and Information Security Agency (ENISA) is an agency of the European Union with the objective to improve network and information security in the European Union.

Europe

CSIRTs in Europe collaborate in the TERENA task force TF-CSIRT. TERENA's Trusted Introducer service provides an accreditation and certification scheme for CSIRTs in Europe. A full list of known CSIRTs in Europe is available from the Trusted Introducer website.

National Teams

Here are the main computer emergency response teams around the world. Most countries have their own team to protect network security.

Canada

On October 3, 2010, Public Safety Canada unveiled Canada's Cyber Security Strategy, following a Speech from the Throne commitment to boost the security of Canadian cyberspace. The aim of the strategy is to strengthen Canada's "cyber systems and critical infrastructure sectors, support economic growth and protect Canadians as they connect to each other and to the world." Three main pillars define the strategy: securing government systems, partnering to secure vital cyber systems outside the federal government, and helping Canadians to be secure online. The strategy involves multiple departments and agencies across the Government of Canada. The Cyber Incident Management Framework for Canada outlines these responsibilities, and provides a plan for coordinated response between government and other partners in the event of a cyber incident. The Action Plan 2010–2015 for Canada's Cyber Security Strategy outlines the ongoing implementation of the strategy.

Public Safety Canada's Canadian Cyber Incident Response Centre (CCIRC) is responsible for mitigating and responding to threats to Canada's critical infrastructure and cyber systems. The CCIRC provides support to mitigate cyber threats, technical support to respond and recover from targeted cyber attacks, and provides online tools for members of Canada's critical infrastructure sectors. The CCIRC posts regular cyber security bulletins on the Public Safety Canada website. The CCIRC also operates an online reporting tool where individuals and organizations can report a cyber incident. Canada's Cyber Security Strategy is part of a larger, integrated approach to critical infrastructure protection, and functions as a counterpart document to the National Strategy and Action Plan for Critical Infrastructure.

On September 27, 2010, Public Safety Canada partnered with STOP.THINK.CONNECT, a coalition of non-profit, private sector, and government organizations dedicated to informing the general public on how to protect themselves online. On February 4, 2014, the Government of Canada launched the Cyber Security Cooperation Program. The program is a $1.5 million five-year initiative aimed at improving Canada's cyber systems through grants and contributions to projects in support of this objective. Public Safety Canada aims to begin an evaluation of Canada's Cyber Security Strategy in early 2015. Public Safety Canada administers and routinely updates the GetCyberSafe portal for Canadian citizens, and carries out Cyber Security Awareness Month during October.

China

China's network security and information technology leadership team was established February 27, 2014. The leadership team is tasked with national security and long-term development and co-ordination of major issues related to network security and information technology. Economic, political, cultural, social and military fields as related to network security and information technology strategy, planning and major macroeconomic policy are being researched. The promotion of national network security and information technology law are constantly under study for enhanced national security capabilities.

Germany

Berlin starts National Cyber Defense Initiative: On June 16, 2011, the German Minister for Home Affairs, officially opened the new German NCAZ (National Center for Cyber Defense) Nationales Cyber-Abwehrzentrum located in Bonn. The NCAZ closely cooperates with BSI (Federal Office for Information Security) Bundesamt für Sicherheit in der Informationstechnik, BKA (Federal Police Organisation) Bundeskriminalamt (Deutschland), BND (Federal Intelligence Service) Bundesnachrichtendienst, MAD (Military Intelligence Service) Amt für den Militärischen Abschirmdienst and other national organisations in Germany taking care of national security aspects. According to the Minister the primary task of the new organisation founded on February 23, 2011, is to detect and prevent attacks against the national infrastructure and mentioned incidents like Stuxnet.

India

Some provisions for cybersecurity have been incorporated into rules framed under the Information Technology Act 2000.

The National Cyber Security Policy 2013 is a policy framework by Department of Electronics and Information Technology (DeitY) which aims to protect the public and private infrastructure from cyber attacks, and safeguard "information, such as personal information (of web users), financial and banking information and sovereign data".

The Indian Companies Act 2013 has also introduced cyber law and cyber security obligations on the part of Indian directors.

Pakistan

Cyber-crime has risen rapidly in Pakistan. There are about 34 million Internet users with 133.4 million mobile subscribers in Pakistan. According to Cyber Crime Unit (CCU), a branch of Federal Investigation Agency, only 62 cases were reported to the unit in 2007, 287 cases in 2008, ratio dropped in 2009 but in 2010, more than 312 cases were registered. However, there are many unreported incidents of cyber-crime.

"Pakistan's Cyber Crime Bill 2007", the first pertinent law, focuses on electronic crimes, for example cyber-terrorism, criminal access, electronic system fraud, electronic forgery, and misuse of encryption.

National Response Centre for Cyber Crime (NR3C) – FIA is a law enforcement agency dedicated to fight cybercrime. Inception of this Hi-Tech crime fighting unit transpired in 2007 to identify and curb the phenomenon of technological abuse in society. However, certain private firms are also working in cohesion with the government to improve cyber security and curb cyberattacks.

South Korea

Following cyberattacks in the first half of 2013, when government, news-media, television station, and bank websites were compromised, the national government committed to the training of 5,000 new cybersecurity experts by 2017. The South Korean government blamed its northern counterpart for these attacks, as well as incidents that occurred in 2009, 2011, and 2012, but Pyongyang denies the accusations.

Other Countries

- CERT Brazil, member of FIRST (Forum for Incident Response and Security Teams).
- CARNet CERT, Croatia, member of FIRST.
- AE CERT, United Arab Emirates.
- SingCERT, Singapore.
- CERT-LEXSI, France, Canada, Singapore.

- INCIBE, Spain.

- ID-CERT, Indonesia.

Modern Warfare

Cybersecurity is becoming increasingly important as more information and technology is being made available on cyberspace. There is growing concern among governments that cyberspace will become the next theatre of warfare.

In the future, wars will not just be fought by soldiers with guns or with planes that drop bombs. They will also be fought with the click of a mouse a half a world away that unleashes carefully weaponized computer programs that disrupt or destroy critical industries like utilities, transportation, communications, and energy. Such attacks could also disable military networks that control the movement of troops, the path of jet fighters, the command and control of warships.

This has led to new terms such as *cyberwarfare* and *cyberterrorism*. More and more critical infrastructure is being controlled via computer programs that, while increasing efficiency, exposes new vulnerabilities. The test will be to see if governments and corporations that control critical systems such as energy, communications and other information will be able to prevent attacks before they occur. As Jay Cross, the chief scientist of the Internet Time Group, remarked, "Connectedness begets vulnerability."

Job Market

Cybersecurity is a fast-growing field of IT concerned with reducing organizations' risk of hack or data breach. According to research from the Enterprise Strategy Group, 46% of organizations say that they have a "problematic shortage" of cybersecurity skills in 2016, up from 28% in 2015. Commercial, government and non-governmental organizations all employ cybersecurity professionals. The fastest increases in demand for cybersecurity workers are in industries managing increasing volumes of consumer data such as finance, health care, and retail. However, the use of the term "cybersecurity" is more prevalent in government job descriptions.

Typical cybersecurity job titles and descriptions include:

Security analyst:

> Analyzes and assesses vulnerabilities in the infrastructure (software, hardware, networks), investigates using available tools and countermeasures to remedy the detected vulnerabilities, and recommends solutions and best practices. Analyzes and assesses damage to the data/infrastructure as a result of security incidents, examines available recovery tools and processes, and recommends solutions. Tests for compliance with security policies and procedures. May assist in the creation, implementation, and/or management of security solutions.

Security engineer:

> Performs security monitoring, security and data/logs analysis, and forensic analysis, to detect security incidents, and mounts incident response. Investigates and utilizes new

technologies and processes to enhance security capabilities and implement improvements. May also review code or perform other security engineering methodologies.

Security architect:

Designs a security system or major components of a security system, and may head a security design team building a new security system.

Security administrator:

Installs and manages organization-wide security systems. May also take on some of the tasks of a security analyst in smaller organizations.

Chief Information Security Officer (CISO):

A high-level management position responsible for the entire information security division/ staff. The position may include hands-on technical work.

Chief Security Officer (CSO):

A high-level management position responsible for the entire security division/staff. A newer position now deemed needed as security risks grow.

Security Consultant/Specialist/Intelligence:

Broad titles that encompass any one or all of the other roles/titles, tasked with protecting computers, networks, software, data, and/or information systems against viruses, worms, spyware, malware, intrusion detection, unauthorized access, denial-of-service attacks, and an ever increasing list of attacks by hackers acting as individuals or as part of organized crime or foreign governments.

Student programs are also available to people interested in beginning a career in cybersecurity. Meanwhile, a flexible and effective option for information security professionals of all experience levels to keep studying is online security training, including webcasts.

Terminology

The following terms used with regards to engineering secure systems are explained below.

- Access authorization restricts access to a computer to group of users through the use of authentication systems. These systems can protect either the whole computer – such as through an interactive login screen – or individual services, such as an FTP server. There are many methods for identifying and authenticating users, such as passwords, identification cards, and, more recently, smart cards and biometric systems.

- Anti-virus software consists of computer programs that attempt to identify, thwart and eliminate computer viruses and other malicious software (malware).

- Applications with known security flaws should not be run. Either leave it turned off until it can be patched or otherwise fixed, or delete it and replace it with some other application.

Publicly known flaws are the main entry used by worms to automatically break into a system and then spread to other systems connected to it. The security website Secunia provides a search tool for unpatched known flaws in popular products.

- Authentication techniques can be used to ensure that communication end-points are who they say they are.

- Automated theorem proving and other verification tools can enable critical algorithms and code used in secure systems to be mathematically proven to meet their specifications.

- Backups are a way of securing information; they are another copy of all the important computer files kept in another location. These files are kept on hard disks, CD-Rs, CD-RWs, tapes and more recently on the cloud. Suggested locations for backups are a fireproof, waterproof, and heat proof safe, or in a separate, offsite location than that in which the original files are contained. Some individuals and companies also keep their backups in safe deposit boxes inside bank vaults. There is also a fourth option, which involves using one of the file hosting services that backs up files over the Internet for both business and individuals, known as the cloud.

    o Backups are also important for reasons other than security. Natural disasters, such as earthquakes, hurricanes, or tornadoes, may strike the building where the computer is located. The building can be on fire, or an explosion may occur. There needs to be a recent backup at an alternate secure location, in case of such kind of disaster. Further, it is recommended that the alternate location be placed where the same disaster would not affect both locations. Examples of alternate disaster recovery sites being compromised by the same disaster that affected the primary site include having had a primary site in World Trade Center I and the recovery site in 7 World Trade Center, both of which were destroyed in the 9/11 attack, and having one's primary site and recovery site in the same coastal region, which leads to both being vulnerable to hurricane damage (for example, primary site in New Orleans and recovery site in Jefferson Parish, both of which were hit by Hurricane Katrina in 2005). The backup media should be moved between the geographic sites in a secure manner, in order to prevent them from being stolen.

- Capability and access control list techniques can be used to ensure privilege separation and mandatory access control. This section discusses their use.

- Chain of trust techniques can be used to attempt to ensure that all software loaded has been certified as authentic by the system's designers.

- Confidentiality is the nondisclosure of information except to another authorized person.

- Cryptographic techniques can be used to defend data in transit between systems, reducing the probability that data exchanged between systems can be intercepted or modified.

- Cyberwarfare is an internet-based conflict that involves politically motivated attacks on information and information systems. Such attacks can, for example, disable official websites and networks, disrupt or disable essential services, steal or alter classified data, and cripple financial systems.

- Data integrity is the accuracy and consistency of stored data, indicated by an absence of any alteration in data between two updates of a data record.

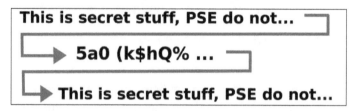

Cryptographic techniques involve transforming information, scrambling it so it becomes unreadable during transmission. The intended recipient can unscramble the message; ideally, eavesdroppers cannot.

- Encryption is used to protect the message from the eyes of others. Cryptographically secure ciphers are designed to make any practical attempt of breaking infeasible. Symmetric-key ciphers are suitable for bulk encryption using shared keys, and public-key encryption using digital certificates can provide a practical solution for the problem of securely communicating when no key is shared in advance.

- Endpoint security software helps networks to prevent exfiltration (data theft) and virus infection at network entry points made vulnerable by the prevalence of potentially infected portable computing devices, such as laptops and mobile devices, and external storage devices, such as USB drives.

- Firewalls are an important method for control and security on the Internet and other networks. A network firewall can be a communications processor, typically a router, or a dedicated server, along with firewall software. A firewall serves as a gatekeeper system that protects a company's intranets and other computer networks from intrusion by providing a filter and safe transfer point for access to and from the Internet and other networks. It screens all network traffic for proper passwords or other security codes and only allows authorized transmission in and out of the network. Firewalls can deter, but not completely prevent, unauthorized access (hacking) into computer networks; they can also provide some protection from online intrusion.

- Honey pots are computers that are either intentionally or unintentionally left vulnerable to attack by crackers. They can be used to catch crackers or fix vulnerabilities.

- Intrusion-detection systems can scan a network for people that are on the network but who should not be there or are doing things that they should not be doing, for example trying a lot of passwords to gain access to the network.

- A microkernel is the near-minimum amount of software that can provide the mechanisms to implement an operating system. It is used solely to provide very low-level, very precisely defined machine code upon which an operating system can be developed. A simple example is the early '90s GEMSOS (Gemini Computers), which provided extremely low-level machine code, such as "segment" management, atop which an operating system could be built. The theory (in the case of "segments") was that—rather than have the operating system itself worry about mandatory access separation by means of military-style labeling—it is safer if a low-level, independently scrutinized module can be charged solely with the management of individually labeled segments, be they memory "segments" or file system "segments" or executable text "segments." If software below the visibility of the operating system is (as in this case) charged with labeling, there is no theoretically viable means for a clever hacker to subvert the labeling scheme, since the operating system *per se* does not provide mechanisms for interfering with labeling: the operating system is, essentially, a client (an "application," arguably) atop the microkernel and, as such, subject to its restrictions.

- Pinging The ping application can be used by potential crackers to find if an IP address is reachable. If a cracker finds a computer, they can try a port scan to detect and attack services on that computer.

- Social engineering awareness keeps employees aware of the dangers of social engineering and/or having a policy in place to prevent social engineering can reduce successful breaches of the network and servers.

Shell

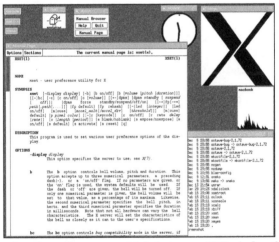

A graphical interface from the 1990s, which features a TUI window for a main page.
Another text window for a Unix shell is partially visible.

In computing, a shell is a user interface for access to an operating system's services. In general, operating system shells use either a command-line interface (CLI) or graphical user interface (GUI), depending on a computer's role and particular operation. It is named a shell because it is a layer around the operating system kernel.

The design of a shell is guided by cognitive ergonomics and the goal is to achieve the best workflow possible for the intended tasks; the design can be constricted by the available computing power (for example, of the CPU) or the available amount of graphics memory. The design of a shell is also dictated by the employed computer periphery, such as computer keyboard, pointing device (a mouse with one button, or one with five buttons, or a 3D mouse) or touchscreen, which is the direct human–machine interface.

CLI shells allow some operations to be performed faster, especially when a proper GUI has not been or cannot be created, however they require the user to memorize commands and their calling syntax, and to learn the shell-specific scripting language (for example bash script). CLIs are also easier to be operated via refreshable braille display and provide certain advantages to screen readers.

Graphical shells place a low burden on beginning computer users, and they are characterized as being simple and easy to use. With the widespread adoption of programs with GUIs, the use of graphical shells has gained greater adoption. Since graphical shells come with certain disadvantages (for example, lack of support for easy automation of operation sequences), most GUI-enabled operating systems also provide additional CLI shells.

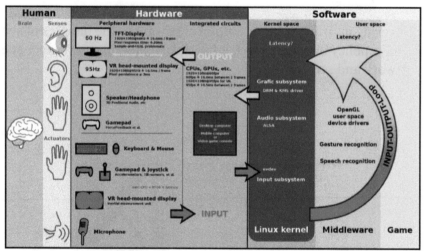

A particular view on the interaction between the end user, hardware and software.

Operating systems provide various services to their users, including file management, process management (running and terminating applications), batch processing, and operating system monitoring and configuration.

Most operating system shells are not *direct* interfaces to the underlying kernel, even if a shell communicates with the user via peripheral devices attached to the computer directly. Shells are actually special applications that use the kernel API in just the same way as it is used by other application programs. A shell manages the user–system interaction by prompting users for input, interpreting their input, and then handling an output from the underlying operating system (much like a read–eval–print loop, REPL). Since the operating system shell is actually an application, it may easily be replaced with another similar application, for most operating systems.

In addition to shells running on local systems, there are different ways to make remote systems available to local users; such approaches are usually referred to as remote access or remote administration. Initially available on multi-user mainframes, which provided text-based UIs for each active user *simultaneously* by means of a text terminal connected to the mainframe via serial line or modem, remote access has extended to Unix-like systems and Microsoft Windows. On Unix-like systems, Secure Shell protocol is usually used for text-based shells, while SSH tunneling can be used for X Window System–based graphical user interfaces (GUIs). On Microsoft Windows, Remote Desktop Protocol can be used to provide GUI remote access.

Most operating system shells fall into one of two categories – command-line and graphical. Command line shells provide a command-line interface (CLI) to the operating system, while graphical shells provide a graphical user interface (GUI). Other possibilities, although not so common, include voice user interface and various implementations of a text-based user interface (TUI) that are not CLI. The relative merits of CLI- and GUI-based shells are often debated.

Text (CLI) Shells

Command Prompt, a CLI shell in Windows.

Bash, a widely adopted Unix shell.

A command-line interface (CLI) is an operating system shell that uses alphanumeric characters typed on a keyboard to provide instructions and data to the operating system, interactively. For example, a teletypewriter can send codes representing keystrokes to a command interpreter program running on the computer; the command interpreter parses the sequence of keystrokes and responds with an error message if it cannot recognize the sequence of characters, or it may carry out some other program action such as loading an application program, listing files, logging in a user and many others. Operating systems such as UNIX have a large variety of shell programs with different commands, syntax and capabilities. Some operating systems had only a single style of command interface; commodity operating systems such as MS-DOS came with a standard command interface but third-party interfaces were also often available, providing additional features or functions such as menuing or remote program execution.

Application programs may also implement a command-line interface. For example, in Unix-like systems, the telnet program has a number of commands for controlling a link to a remote computer system. Since the commands to the program are made of the same keystrokes as the data being sent to a remote computer, some means of distinguishing the two are required. An escape sequence can be defined, using either a special local keystroke that is never passed on but always interpreted by the local system. The program becomes modal, switching between interpreting commands from the keyboard or passing keystrokes on as data to be processed.

A feature of many command-line shells is the ability to save sequences of commands for re-use. A data file can contain sequences of commands which the CLI can be made to follow as if typed in by a user. Special features in the CLI may apply when it is carrying out these stored instructions. Such batch files (script files) can be used repeatedly to automate routine operations such as initializing a set of programs when a system is restarted. Batch mode use of shells usually involves structures, conditionals, variables, and other elements of programming languages; some have the bare essentials needed for such a purpose, others are very sophisticated programming languages in and of themselves. Conversely, some programming languages can be used interactively from an operating system shell or in a purpose-built program.

The command-line shell may offer features such as command-line completion, where the interpreter expands commands based on a few characters input by the user. A command-line interpreter may offer a history function, so that the user can recall earlier commands issued to the system and repeat them, possibly with some editing. Since all commands to the operating system had to be typed by the user, short command names and compact systems for representing program options were common. Short names were sometimes hard for a user to recall, and early systems lacked the storage resources to provide a detailed on-line user instruction guide.

Various Unix shells and their derivatives including the DOS shell exist.

Graphical Shells

Graphical shells provide means for manipulating programs based on graphical user interface (GUI), by allowing for operations such as opening, closing, moving and resizing windows, as well as switching focus between windows. Graphical shells may be included with desktop environments or come separately, even as a set of loosely coupled utilities.

Most graphical user interfaces develop the metaphor of an "electronic desktop", where data files are represented as if they were paper documents on a desk, and application programs similarly have graphical representations instead of being invoked by command names.

Microsoft Windows

Modern versions of the Microsoft Windows operating system use the Windows shell as their shell. Windows Shell provides the familiar desktop environment, start menu, and task bar, as well as a graphical user interface for accessing the file management functions of the operating system. Older versions also include Program Manager, which was the shell for the 3.x series of Microsoft Windows, and which in fact ships with later versions of Windows of both the 95 and NT types at least through Windows XP. The interfaces of Windows versions 1 and 2 were markedly different.

Desktop applications are also considered shells, as long as they use a third-party engine. Likewise, many individuals and developers dissatisfied with the interface of Windows Explorer have developed software that either alters the functioning and appearance of the shell or replaces it entirely. WindowBlinds by StarDock is a good example of the former sort of application. LiteStep and Emerge Desktop are good examples of the latter.

Interoperability programmes and purpose-designed software lets Windows users use equivalents of many of the various Unix-based GUIs discussed below, as well as Macintosh. An equivalent of the OS/2 Presentation Manager for version 3.0 can run some OS/2 programmes under some conditions using the OS/2 environmental subsystem in versions of Windows NT.

Unix-like Systems

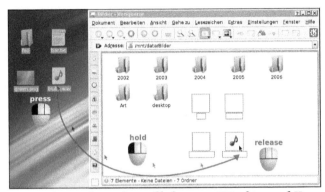

Drag and drop operation performed on a file between KDesktop and Konqueror in KDE.

Graphical shells typically build on top of a windowing system. In the case of X Window System or Wayland, the shell consists of an X window manager or a Wayland compositor, respectively, as well as of one or multiple programs providing the functionality to start installed applications, to manage open windows and virtual desktops, and often to support a widget engine.

In the case of OS X, Quartz could be thought of as the windowing system, and the shell consists of the Finder, the Dock, SystemUIServer, and Mission Control.

Other Uses

"Shell" is also used loosely to describe application software that is "built around" a particular component, such as web browsers and email clients, in analogy to the shells found in nature.

In expert systems, a shell is a piece of software that is an "empty" expert system without the knowledge base for any particular application.

References

- Ball, Stuart R. (2002) [2002]. Embedded Microprocessor Systems: Real World Designs (first ed.). Elsevier Science. ISBN 0-7506-7534-9

- Silberschatz, Abraham; James L. Peterson; Peter B. Galvin (1991). Operating system concepts. Boston, Massachusetts: Addison-Wesley. p. 696. ISBN 0-201-51379-X

- Baiardi, F.; A. Tomasi, M. Vanneschi (1988). Architettura dei Sistemi di Elaborazione, volume 1 (in Italian). Franco Angeli. ISBN 88-204-2746-X. Cite uses deprecated parameter

- Vahalia, Uresh (1996). "Chapter 2. The Process and the Kernel". UNIX Internals: The New Frontiers. Prentice-Hall Inc. ISBN 0-13-101908-2

- Hyde, Randall (November 2004). "12.10. Protected Mode Operation and Device Drivers". Write Great Code. O'Reilly. ISBN 1-59327-003-8

- Silberschatz, Abraham; Cagne, Greg; Galvin, Peter Baer (2004). "Chapter 4. Processes". Operating system concepts with Java (Sixth ed.). John Wiley & Sons. ISBN 0-471-48905-0

Permissions

Index

9 781639 874095